Sports Management

Sports Management

A guide to professional practice

Aaron Smith and Bob Stewart

ALLEN & UNWIN

First published in 1999 by
Allen & Unwin Pty Ltd
83 Alexander Street, Crows Nest NSW 2065 Australia
Phone: (61 2) 8425 0100
Fax: (61 2) 9906 2218
E-mail: info@allen-unwin.com
Web: www.allenandunwin.com

National Library of Australia
Cataloguing-in-Publication entry:

Smith, Aaron, 1972– .
    Sports management: a guide to professional practice.

    Includes index.
    ISBN 1 86448 751 8.

    1. Sports—Australia—Management. 2. Sports administration—
Australia. I. Stewart, Bob, 1946– . II. Title.

796.069

Set in 10/12 pt Garamond by DOCUPRO, Sydney
Printed by McPherson's Printing Group, Maryborough, Vic.

10 9 8 7 6 5 4 3

▌Contents

Introduction

Alan McGilvray, arguably the world's most famous cricket commentator during the 1960s and 1970s, was chronically anxious about the direction the game was taking during the 1980s, and lamented its commercialisation and professionalisation.[1] That the game was 'not the same' was, for him and many other cricket followers, a damning indictment on its so-called progress. If Alan were alive today he would be positively overwhelmed by cricket's commercial development. Cricket is a prime example of the transformation of elite sport during the last 10–15 years. But there are literally scores of similar cases where sport has outgrown its traditions and historical structures.

Sport has become a complex set of business enterprises which are competing for scarce consumer dollars and continually looking for those opportunities that will best carry them forward into the new millennium.

The commercial complexity of sport is exemplified in the leadup to the Sydney 2000 Olympics. The Games, which by any measure will be massive, will cost nearly $2300 million to run and will attract more than 10 000 athletes from more than 200 countries. The international TV rights alone will provide $950 million, while global corporate sponsors will pay a total of $830 million for the privilege of using the Olympic logos and mascots. Indeed, the Olympic rings have become the most recognised and valued cultural symbol in the world. However, the success of the Sydney Olympics will depend not just upon the quality of the athletic performances but also upon the quality of Games management.

The 1998 Soccer World Cup in France also demonstrated just how complex it is to mount a successful international sports event, and what a logistical nightmare it can be to ensure a smooth-running and fan-friendly event. While it provided a memorable cultural experience, captured the public imagination and showcased the world game, it was also a huge commercial enterprise. The event was in many respects a giant commodity supported by a team of experts in facility design, event planning, financial management, marketing, merchandising, human resource development and many other areas. A cumulative audience of 40 billion watched the 64 matches.

The development of the new $420 million Docklands stadium in Melbourne is another clear example of the direction that sport is taking. This is no kitchen table idea dreamed up by an enthusiastic football official, but instead combines the political and commercial 'muscle' of the Victorian State Government, the Australian Football League and the Channel 7 television network.

Each of these major sports projects clearly shows just how much sport has changed over the last fifteen years, and why it is now essential to have highly trained staff in order to ensure a successful outcome. But it is not just elite national and international sporting organisations that are experiencing this need. State bodies and their affiliated clubs now find that hundreds of other sports and leisure activities are competing for the scarce time and money of potential members and players. As a result, even low profile sports like canoeing and badminton are forced to design development plans, undertake market research and pursue ongoing promotional campaigns in order to maintain their membership and participation levels. Moreover, the emergence of national leagues in Australian football, baseball, basketball, cricket, netball, rugby league, soccer, softball and water polo has created a demand for qualified and competent staff. They will be expected to manage a variety of facilities and events, and to meet the disparate needs of fans, members, players, casual staff, volunteers and corporate stakeholders.

This transformation of sport is not peculiar to Australia and its surrounding regions. The explosive growth in commercial sport around the world can also be seen in the increase of serious journalistic coverage and analysis. *Sport Business* has paved the way in this respect, by becoming the first genuinely global sports magazine that analyses the business of sport. It commenced publication in 1996, comes out every month, and provides a detailed review of various sports' commercial progress in every region of the world. While its lead stories usually focus on international bodies like the IOC, FINA and FIFA, it also examines significant regional and local developments.

PROFESSIONAL BEST PRACTICE MANAGEMENT: STRUCTURE OF THE BOOK

This book is a response to the need for professional management at all levels of sport. We have established a model of professional best practice management, or PBPM, which aims to set a sports management benchmark. We present it in an accessible form that provides the theory behind management concepts as well as dealing with their practical application. Our PBPM model is not just a compilation of traditional principles or a list of useful skills taken from a training manual. It is, instead, a synthesis of contemporary theory with practice; one that covers every aspect of the sports management process.

Our PBPM model is divided into three parts (see Figure 1).

The central part comprises three core 'principles' that drive the sports management process. These principles are:

Figure 1 Professional Best Practice Management—a model

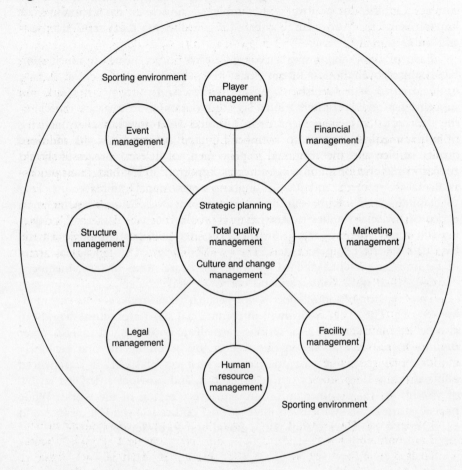

- strategic planning
- total quality management
- organisational culture and change management

Strategic planning is fundamental to successful sport management. As we show in Chapter 3, designing a strategic direction and setting strategic plans is a time-consuming activity, but if done properly will deliver massive benefits.

Total quality management, which we address in Chapter 4, is also fundamental to PBPM. It highlights the need to continually improve service delivery and not to rest on the laurels of previous successes.

The final core principle is organisational culture and change management, which is considered in Chapter 5. An understanding of a sporting organisation's culture is essential, since it influences the behaviour and work output of staff, members and players alike. But, as we demonstrate, many cultures can be dysfunctional and impede future success. It is therefore important to create a culture that places high value on quality service delivery and on continual improvement in the way things get done.

Core principles need to be integrated with every facet of a sporting organisation's functions and activities. Event management and marketing operations, for example, should be set within the strategic framework and support the vision that will drive the organisation's performance. Similarly, the 'culture' that management desires should filter through every activity, from paramedical support to membership and subscriptions. In addition, quality service and the continual improvement of delivery processes should appear in all functions, and will be just as important in the budgeting process as they will be in the recruitment, selection and training of staff.

The next part of our model comprises eight 'functions'. These areas of management encompass administrative systems and service delivery. All sporting organisations must engage in these systems in order to provide a basic level of service to fans, members, clients and players. The eight areas are:

■ player management
■ financial management
■ marketing management
■ facility management
■ human resource management
■ legal management
■ structure management
■ event management

To emphasise the point, if sports administrators are serious about achieving good outcomes for their customers, they must ensure that each function is managed in accordance with the core principles. That is, each function should be placed within a strategic framework, be continually evaluated and improved, and be guided by a cultural frame of reference based on innovation and customer service.

The eight functional areas are explored in Chapters 6–13 respectively.

The outer part of the model is the sporting environment, or context, in which the above functions and core principle activities occur. It is with this outer part that we begin our discussion of sports management.

Chapter 1 looks at the issue of professionalism in sport—what it is, its foundations, and how it links in with the process of management.

Chapter 2 examines the special nature of sport. We identify a number of features that make sport different from straightforward commercial activities like computer manufacturing, banking or book selling. We highlight the role that passion and tradition play in the administration of sport, but we also warn that attempts to separate sports practice from its commercial context are fraught with danger. That is, sport should be treated as something different from, but also increasingly connected with, the world of business and commerce.

Professional best practice management in sport therefore requires a holistic approach. It is more than making sure that job descriptions have been designed for all permanent and casual staff. It is more than taking out professional indemnity insurance to protect coaches and medical staff from claims of negligence. It is certainly more than deciding to outsource the management of a special event previously run 'in house'. PBPM involves setting up structures and systems to support and deliver quality service to the community. But this is only the beginning. It also involves understanding the special features of sport and managing it accordingly. The most important element of PBPM lies in a management philosophy that adapts and embraces principles and practices that have been a catalyst for success in almost every field of commercial endeavour to date.

Plan of attack

We recommend that you begin by familiarising yourself with Chapters 1 and 2: first, in order to become further acquainted with the notions of professionalism and best practice management; and second, to acquire a deeper understanding of the special features of sport and how the passion and traditions of sport can be shaped to good effect by sound management.

After this, you should spend time on Chapters 3, 4 and 5, because strategic planning, quality management and the issue of organisational culture lie at the heart of effective sports administration.

Finally, the eight chapters dealing with the functional areas of management may be read in any order, depending on your interests and priorities. These chapters are followed by a brief conclusion to the book.

1 Professionalism and the management of sport

After reading this chapter you should have a basic understanding of the notion of professionalism and how it applies in the sporting world.

More specifically, you should be able to:

- outline the approaches to the issue of professionalism
- explain in broad terms what is meant by best practice management, and identify its implications for sports administration

PROFESSIONALISM IN A CHANGING WORLD

We are living in turbulent times. The computer revolution has completely changed the way people run their lives and do their work. At the same time, massive increases in manufacturing productivity have created a broad-based leisure industry in which customer service and product innovation are used to gain a competitive advantage over rival suppliers. These changes have been interwoven with a general globalisation of trade, telecommunications, social policy and cultural development, where the market is sovereign over most aspects of human endeavour. In short, both the commercial and the cultural worlds have been transformed. We have entered a new epoch, in which the most valuable currency is knowledge.[1]

Many businesses have responded to these pressures by overhauling their structures and procedures and often by embracing a clutter of management theories, administrative processes and employee development programs.[2] At the heart of all this is a compulsive need to do things better and smarter; that is, to become more 'professional'—and there is no shortage of advice on how to do this.[3] Above all, in today's world of the flexible business enterprise, where the focus is on decentralised decision making and the so-called 'learning organisation', professionalism is regarded as a prerequisite for success.[4] While traditionally 'professionalism' has referred to behaviour like that of a professional—a person belonging to a profession—the contemporary understanding of the term is wider. Today it simply means expert

1

competence.[5] Professionalism refers not only to occupations that emphasise training, service and ethical standards, but also to the best, smartest, most efficient and effective management practices that can be employed in any given situation. The management literature suggests that to describe a person as professional is to pay them the highest compliment about their work.[6]

The sports industry has not been immune to the need for professionalism, particularly as it becomes increasingly commercialised. Clubs and associations must perform financially (or at the very least remain viable) if they want to survive in the highly competitive world of 'hypercommercialised' leisure. With this increasing emphasis on commerce, commodification, merchandising, sponsorship, contracting and entertainment, many sports followers concede that sport has developed into a business.[7] Sport and leisure practices in Asia, Australasia and Europe are increasingly constrained by the same commercial pressures and legal framework that govern private sector business firms.[8] A more systematic and serious approach to the management of sport has emerged, which has caused many sports administrators to strive to increase the level of professionalism by emulating the private sector. In other words, an increasingly commercialised sports world has induced a need for professional sports management practices. However, while sports administrators use the term 'professional' in referring to the need to copy the competitive business world, the specific components of 'professional' best practice management in sport are rarely identified, other than by an occasional reference to the need for more staff training in planning, finance and promotion.

APPROACHES TO THE ISSUE OF PROFESSIONALISM

It is one thing to say that someone is a manager, but it is another thing to conclude that he or she is a *professional* manager. The word 'professional' is often misused and misunderstood, and can be thrown around with so much abandon that it ends up describing anyone who wears a designer suit, carries a leather briefcase and uses a mobile phone. We must therefore discover what it means to be professional.

There are two approaches to the issue of professionalism: the *conduct* approach and the *competence* approach. The conduct approach has 'appropriate' interpersonal and social behaviour as its central theme, while the competence approach holds that abilities and skills are the pivotal factors.

The conduct approach

This approach to professionalism is concerned with individual and organisational conduct.[9] There are four closely allied but discernible dimensions:

■ ethical behaviour
■ image

- service
- effort

Ethical behaviour

Professionalism must include a moral philosophy that governs behaviour in a formal and systematic way, leaving no room for ambiguity or confusion, and that focuses on fairness, honesty, integrity, safety and authenticity as well as moral and legal propriety.

Image

Image and perception also characterise professional conduct. Image refers to the symbols or perceptions that are associated with representatives of organisations, and are judged by others as positive or negative. At an individual level, image revolves around etiquette, style, personality and attire. Thus physical cleanliness, neatness, confidence, a strong physical presence and smart dress sense contribute to image.

Organisations must present a positive image to enhance their customers' perceptions of their professionalism. This includes control of office decorum, as well as the wider perceptions that clients may hold about efficiency and effectiveness. It's easy to confuse this element of professionalism with the competence approach. However, there is a considerable difference between the perception of competence and actual competence. Naturally, organisations want to present themselves as efficient and well managed, whether or not it mirrors reality. The power of image should not be underestimated since it can affect customer satisfaction and organisational culture. Culture is a potent determinant of an organisation's performance. In other words, if an organisation puts enormous value on presenting a positive image, then employees are under strong pressure to meet that cultural expectation.

Service

The provision of a quality service is intrinsic to professionalism, and could probably be included in either the conduct approach or the competence approach. However, it has been included here because service emphasises the social sensitivity aspect of professionalism rather than the specific abilities required. It includes the provision of what an organisation's customers want, delivered in a manner appropriate to their needs and values.

Customers will often be impressed with the 'little things', since the larger, more fundamental services are often taken for granted. Accordingly, what separates capable service from professional service is attention to detail and the incorporation of the other components of appropriate conduct (ethical behaviour, image and effort). As a result, service includes a focus on such courtesies as genuinely listening to customer problems and anxieties, returning phone calls, ensuring reliable letter quality, and responding to requests for information promptly.

Effort

The final element of the conduct approach involves the application of effort. Whenever conduct is appropriate it invariably requires considerable effort. In other words, professionalism does not come easily; it must be earned. Under the banner of 'effort' comes enthusiasm, dedication and passion. Effort is so intrinsic to professionalism that it may also find a place in the competence approach.

The competence approach

This approach also has four interrelated dimensions:

- abilities
- insight and vision
- qualifications and experience
- excellence

Abilities

Competence cannot be achieved without the possession of specific abilities. Abilities refer to anything that helps get the job done. In this case, there are two forms of abilities allied with professionalism: the first relates to practices; the second to skills. Practices, which cover techniques and processes, are dealt with in later chapters of this book, particularly where we examine the core of PBPM. Skills are also important professional attributes, since they form part of the foundation of an individual's work output, and directly contribute to quality work practice.

The skills that contribute to professionalism can be summarised in four generic skill processes. The first set of skills involves data acquisition, which includes any expertise related to finding information, such as networking, interviewing, reading and researching, and all forms of communication. The second set of skills involves the interpretation and analysis of the information gathered during the first process. They include skills such as clear, independent thinking, the ability to comprehend the data, the capacity to apply knowledge of the subject (in this case the structure of the sports industry), the ability to see things holistically and the ability to reduce complex information into a simple form. The third process is based on the first two, and entails the skills of decision making. Included are the ability to deal with pressure, the ability to 'think on one's feet' and the ability to make 'courageous' decisions. The last set of skills is concerned with the consequences of *taking* courageous decisions. They include critical, reflective and objective thinking, listening to employees, the preparedness to learn from mistakes, and the insight to make appropriate adjustments to the way things are done.

Insight and vision

While insight and vision might be placed among the above skill processes, they are so critical that they warrant a place of their own. Insight combines information gathering with information analysis and interpretation, and is a special kind of ability that results in an accurate understanding of the environment and its associated pitfalls and opportunities. It includes able time management, an awareness of the politics of the industry, an affinity with the needs of stakeholders and customers, an understanding of what is important and what isn't, a knowledge of the capacities and skills of employees and volunteers, and a degree of acumen and intelligence. In other words, you have to be astute to be a professional.

Vision is the application of insight into the future. It involves efficient planning, setting directions, and anticipating the needs of the organisation, its customers and employees. We look at 'the vision thing' in detail in Chapter 3.

Qualifications and experience

The competence approach holds that sound practice can never be obtained without appropriate training and experience, although it may be formal or informal. Australian and New Zealand sport is at the moment in transition concerning the relative importance of qualifications. More and more qualified sports administrators are emerging from tertiary institutions and entering the sports industry. There is a growing belief that 'professional' sports administrators will not only have a broad range of sports experiences but also possess a university degree in the field of management. Moreover, these 'professionally' qualified administrators will be able to work in any type of sporting organisation, irrespective of their personal sports background or preference.

Excellence

Professionalism has also become a surrogate for excellence, or working to the very best of your abilities. Professionalism is directly related to the pursuit of excellence, which is in turn a function of commitment, enthusiasm and continuing career development. Thus excellence is not just a dimension of professionalism, and professionalism is not just the pursuit of excellence. Excellence is an outcome of professionalism.

Synthesis

Having examined the dimensions of professionalism under the conduct and competence approaches, a definition can now be provided from a synthesis of the two. Professionalism can be defined as follows:

> Professionalism is a commitment to appropriate conduct and competence, where ethics, image, service and effort are paramount and where the combination of ability, insight, vision, qualifications and experience culminate in excellence.

PROFESSIONALISM IN SPORT

The emergence of professionalism in sports administration reflects the view that sport is becoming a serious business. As Murray Massey[10] highlighted in his examination of Australian business and sport, sport has transcended its amateur foundations to become a complex and highly competitive activity. Massey noted that, 'as professionalism engulfs sport in Australia, sports managers increasingly face the same commercial pressures and benchmarks as their counterparts in mainstream business'. However, this new era of professionalism is just over a decade old, and sport still has, according to Massey, a disproportionate share of 'amateurs' with poor skills and question-able ethical practices. He also noted that the trend toward full-time paid staff and the professionalisation of sports management is irreversible, and that 'today sports managers are challenged to upgrade their knowledge and skills to ensure that organisations within the sport industry remain competitive and financially viable'.

While the connection between business and sport in Australia is strength-ening, the linkage has existed for some time in Europe and North America. Aris[11] and Wilson,[12] for example, view sport as a professional business— as reflected by the titles of their respective books: *Sportsbiz: Inside the Sports Business* and *The Sports Business*. Canadian academic Trevor Slack,[13] the author of *Understanding Sporting Organisations*, has frequently commented that sport is *big* business, and that 'big business is involved in sport'. In other words, sport is part of a much larger competitive leisure industry in which partici-pants pay for the experience, players are paid for performing, and sportswear suppliers will do almost anything to obtain a player endorsement.[14]

The concept of professionalism sketched in the preceding pages is a move in the right direction, but it does not provide a very precise picture of how professional sports administrators should conduct themselves. For this, we need to turn to the insights and disciplines of best practice management.

BEST PRACTICE MANAGEMENT

Before we move on to the issue of best practice, though, let's take a brief look at the notion of management itself. This has scarcely changed in contrast with the dramatic progress that has occurred in organisational life. For example, back in 1947 Kimball and Kimball[15] put the view that the man-agement process incorporates all duties and functions that relate to the initiation of an enterprise: its financing, the establishment of policies, the provision of equipment, the design of the general form of the organisation, and the selection of the organisation's principal officers. In 1960, Terry[16] compressed the functions of management into four categories:

- *planning*, or what is to be done, and where, when and how
- *organising*, or who is to do what
- *actuating (leading)*, or obtaining employee willingness and co-operation
- *controlling*, or checking that the planned work is being properly carried out, and remedying any difficulties

Contemporary definitions of management are still based on these four fundamental categories, and encapsulate the view that the essence of management is co-ordination. The principles underlying sports management are no different. We therefore view it as:

> The system of planning, organising, actuating and controlling the co-ordination of resources for the efficient and effective delivery and exchange of sporting products and services.

Despite the plethora of pedantic distinctions and definitions, the term 'administration' is, as far we are concerned, synonymous with 'management'. Mason and Paul,[17] in an early book on sports management, concluded that administration means 'providing the constructive leadership that plans and maintains the program, and which enables the program to function effectively in accomplishing the established and worthwhile goals'.[18] In addition, it is a 'system of people working together in a pattern of co-operative activity in which the specialised talents of various individuals are brought together to achieve a common purpose'. Mason and Paul noted that sports administration is concerned with guiding and managing human behaviour, via a focus on achievement, 'getting things done' and dealing with progress and change.[19] Similarly, Hogg[20] defined (sports) administration in terms of the management, forward planning and development of sport as well as the routine operation of sporting organisations.

Best practice

According to Arthur Andersen Consulting,[21] best practice techniques are those proven management methods that contribute to the most efficient and effective functioning of organisations. In short, they are the best ways to perform an administrative process. By contrast, Alan Reder[22] defines best management practices as those innovative and successful practices that can be integrated into the workplace to ensure that the organisation produces socially responsible outcomes. When these two approaches are combined, the research reveals a number of best practice strands:

- effective and open communications
- quality management and continuous improvement

- culture consciousness
- interdependence between sections of the organisation
- preparedness to take risks
- strategy and commitment
- focus on value

Best practice management in sport

There have been a number of attempts to link the professionalisation of sport with 'best practice', and in doing so to establish a profile of the 'professional' sports administrator.

Lawrence Watt,[23] for example, in his examination of the professionalism of sports management in New Zealand, maintained that 'good' sports managers rate personal and people skills at the top of their list of required professional attributes, followed by quality management procedures. Ramish Patel, executive director of the New Zealand Hockey Federation, believes that the high rating for people skills is due to the prevalence of volunteers in sporting organisations, and the fact that volunteers must be managed intelligently if they are to perform effectively. Furthermore, according to Peter McDermott, Chair of New Zealand Cricket Inc., professional management in sport is not very different from professional management in running a commercial company. McDermott pointed to five key management areas besides dealing with people:

- marketing
- financial planning
- merchandising
- retail selling and ticketing
- marketing and television rights

Taking a similar 'checklist' approach to professional management, Matene Love[24] examined the skills and competencies of modern sports managers. She noted that specific sports knowledge rates poorly, compared with other technical disciplines, as a prerequisite to gaining employment in the sports management industry. According to Love, eight competencies are essential for sports management executives. They are, in order of importance:

- marketing skills
- business planning skills
- accounting and financial management abilities
- general management abilities
- economic experience
- sports science knowledge
- human resource management skills
- leisure and recreation theory

Love hypothesised that the emphasis on marketing skills is a consequence of commercialisation and professionalisation of sport, and the need to sell sport as an entertainment package to both sponsors and the public. Modern professional management requires a 'hardnosed' approach in order to successfully deal with marketing, sponsorship and media issues in sport; while the human aspects of management, and meeting the needs of voluntary officials and coaches, are not as important as service delivery skills. In other words, the need to satisfy customers has demanded a focus on rigorous management techniques.

Maloy,[25] an American sports researcher, also concluded that the commercialisation and professionalisation of sports management have pressured administrators to broaden their management competencies. In reference to collegiate sport in the United States, Maloy advocated a greater emphasis on long-term planning, a renewed focus on values and quality, and the need to address situational variables. Furthermore, he argued that charisma and bluff are not enough and that, instead, sports managers require tangible abilities and skills. Maloy predicted that future successful sporting organisations will typically concentrate on performance and productivity, set in an ethical framework and surrounded by strong leadership.

A similar viewpoint was offered by Dene Moore,[26] former executive director of the Confederation of Australian Sport, in his examination of the development of professional management in the sports industry. He concluded that, despite an early reluctance to embrace change, better management expertise and planning by sporting organisations has led to the acknowledgement that full-time paid administrators are essential to the development of an efficient and effective sports structure. Moreover, Moore argued that those sports in Australia that are progressing are generally the best managed.

However, Moore cautioned that the successful sports administrator needs to be skilled in a number of areas—public relations, marketing, media relations, legal expertise, insurance knowledge, personnel qualifications, facility and technical knowhow, financial skills and public speaking. This wide array 'requires the modern sports administrator to be more qualified than ever before'.[27] The future will see an increase in the number of specialists employed in sporting organisations, and the fields of marketing and finance will expand in line with the growing emphasis on strategic planning and a corporate approach to sport.

The Australian government's Standing Committee on Recreation and Sport (SCORS) has echoed Moore's call for greater sports management, proposing that a national program of 'management improvement' be introduced by the year 2000. SCORS research revealed that national sporting bodies were often resistant to change and frequently failed to document the roles and responsibilities of board and committee members. SCORS recommended that national governing bodies should streamline their structure, develop shared visions, more effectively co-ordinate State bodies, become more flexible, create a customer focus and encourage a culture of ongoing management training.

SUMMARY

This chapter discussed the notion of professionalism and why it is so important to the effective administration of sport in the 1990s. We explained that professionalism has two components. First it requires a certain level of conduct—ethical behaviour, a presentable public image, a sensitivity to customer needs and a passionate commitment to the job. Second, it requires the display of continuing competence—a combination of intelligence and ability, education, technical skill and 'worldliness'. These qualities and practices are explained in terms of best practice management and core practices such as strategic thinking, risk taking, quality service, continuous improvement and open communication.

We demonstrated that the qualities and practices associated with professionalism are essential for professional sports administration, even though historically many proven commercial business practices have been under-utilised in sports management. More than ever before, the sports area needs skilled staff, who can do more than cite the grand traditions of a game. Sports administrators must also be able to design a coherent strategic plan, establish a culture of quality, prepare detailed financial forecasts, anticipate the legal constraints on their operations, and manage a marketing effort in which both the corporate and community interests are met.

FURTHER READING

Kiernan, M.J. (1996) *The Eleven Commandments of 21st Century Management*, Prentice-Hall, Englewood Cliffs, NJ.

Peters, T. (1993) *Liberation Management*, Pan Books, London.

Scholtes, P. (1998) *The Leader's Handbook: Making Things Happen, Getting Things Done*, McGraw-Hill, New York.

Slack, T. (1997) *Understanding Sport Organizations: The Application of Organization Theory*, Human Kinetics, Champaign, Ill.

2 The special features of sport

After reading this chapter you should be able to describe the special features of sport, showing the ways in which it is structurally and functionally different from purely commercial industries and enterprises.

More specifically, you should be able to:

- outline the competing perspectives held in relation to the nature of sport, in particular the 'sport as a unique enterprise' model versus the 'sport as a generic business' model
- appreciate the implications of taking a one-sided view of the nature of sport and its administration

COMPETING PERSPECTIVES ON SPORT

Sport means different things to different people. On the one hand, it can be all about fun, healthy competition and character building, where the game is everything, and where the instrumental values of commerce and work are to be resisted because they contaminate the real purpose of sport. On the other hand, it can be just another leisure industry—in which customer satisfaction is the measure of its success.

The perspective adopted will obviously have a significant impact on the way the individual administrator thinks his or her sport should be managed. Our investigations show that opinion is largely divided into two camps: those who believe sport is unique, and should therefore be managed differently from business; and those who believe that sport is part of a generic business system, and should be managed like any other type of business. In addition, there are some administrators who have a bet each way, and believe in a 'situational' approach. That is, professional sports clubs and bodies can be managed as generic businesses, while volunteer-based sporting organisations need to be managed as a unique form of enterprise. These different perspectives are illustrated in Figure 2.1

There are several contrasting features that distinguish these approaches

Figure 2.1 Perspectives on the nature of sport

GENERIC	SITUATIONAL	UNIQUE
Sport is just like any other business	Some sporting organisations are like businesses, others need to be managed as sports	Sport is essentially a community-based social activity, requiring a unique management approach

to the administration of sport. 'Sport as a unique enterprise' adherents tend to believe that sport's association with leisure and recreation, and its mythological separation from 'commerce', make the management of sport both special and difficult. In addition, they believe that the emotion inherent in sport forces managers to avoid making rational decisions that might destroy old traditions, cause member dissatisfaction and reduce volunteer participation. These practitioners believe that they have to manage objectives that are frequently divergent and that they need to rely heavily on externally generated income, which is often insufficient to satisfy the demands. Then there is the difficulty of managing volunteers, who are essential for the conduct of fundraising programs, tournaments and special events. In summary, the 'sport is unique' school believe that many management practices are not transferable between sport and business, since sport and recreation are essentially community-based social activities, and not commercial enterprises.

In contrast, proponents of the 'sport as a generic business' approach view the leisure orientation of sport, the emotion, the ambiguous objectives and the limited resources as irrelevant to the best management practices used in operating a sporting organisation. Furthermore, they often take a corporate view of volunteers, insisting that they are just another organisational 'human resource' who must be inducted, rewarded, trained and counselled like any other valuable member of staff. Instead of viewing sport as a unique enterprise, they insist that sport is a client-based service business, operating within a specific but not necessarily unique marketplace—with management practices being transferable between any business and any marketplace.

IS SPORT UNIQUE OR JUST ANOTHER BUSINESS?

The recent commercial development of sport has been criticised by journalists and commentators who argue that increasing levels of professionalisation,[1] bureaucratisation and specialisation[2] have undermined the community and recreational focus of sport. The ensuing debate about future directions has challenged many views about the nature and place of sport in society, but in the end has mainly highlighted the commercial complexity of the sports industry and crucial importance of having it well managed. Sport, even at the local or community level, can no longer operate effectively in a cultural frame that focuses exclusively on amateurism and volunteerism, and which seeks to divorce sport from work and commerce. It has not taken long for many sporting organisations to adopt some of the processes and practices of private sector business enterprises referred to in Chapter 1.[3] This business-like approach to the management of sporting organisations and clubs has escalated over the last few years. In many cases, players and administrators are often paid employees,[4] visionary plans are designed, changes in the sport product are made, member and customer needs are monitored, and alliances with corporate supporters are developed.[5] Sporting organisations, whatever their size or spread, can no longer be managed as fun and games, or be divorced from the wider commercial world.

Whereas, in the past, sporting club goals were bound up with winning, many organisations now seek to achieve profits as much as premierships. A 'not for profit' club, for example, must *perform* financially if it wants to survive in the highly competitive world of commercialised sport,[6] with its increasing emphasis on commodification and entertainment. The subsequent focus on rationalisation and productivity has forced sports administrators to translate their human and material resources (particularly players) into economic equations in which division of labour, efficiency, regulation, rational work practices and management control become crucial management issues.[7]

Sport is therefore not so unique that it cannot be put in a commercial framework. But neither is it just another form of private enterprise. Sport is business, but it is a special form of business. In the remainder of this chapter we explore those features of organised sport that give it its special quality. We examine the idiosyncratic nature of the sports market, and why it remains troublesome for managers who wish to place it neatly within a conventional business paradigm.

SPECIAL FEATURES

What exactly are the special features of the sports business that every professional sports manager needs to understand?

Irrational passions

Clearly, sport and commerce are inextricably linked in many people's minds. We need look no further than the metaphors used to describe specific business situations. For example, to 'drop the ball' or 'let the team down' commonly describes corporate failure, whereas to 'kick a goal', 'put one through the middle' or 'get runs on the board' describes a business success. Sporting analogies are used in business to demonstrate the value of loyalty, commitment and teamwork. However, sport has a symbolic significance and emotional intensity that is rarely found in an insurance company, bank or even a betting shop. David James[8] succinctly captured the powerful symbolic and metaphorical significance of sport when he noted:

> Sport exposes one of the greater ironies of human nature: although work determines a person's standard of living and social position, many people are more concerned about a piece of inflated leather passing between white sticks. Most managers can only dream of getting the passion and commitment from their workforce that sport arouses.

Sport and business therefore often operate within different behavioural parameters. While profit-centred businesses need to obtain strong emotional support from their employees, their overriding concern is efficiency, productivity and responding quickly to changing market conditions. Sport, on the other hand, is consumed by strong emotional attachments that are linked to the past through nostalgia and tradition.[9] A proposal to change club colours in order to project a more attractive image may be defeated because it breaks a link with tradition. Similarly, a coach can be appointed on the basis of his or her previous loyalty to the club rather than because of a capacity to manage players better than the other applicants. The behaviour of sports supporters, and their response to both club and league structures, can also be irrational. For example, fans are more attracted to a game where the result is problematic than to one where the winner is virtually known in advance.

Predictability and certainty, which are goals to be aimed for in the commercial world, particularly with respect to product quality, are not always valued in the sporting world. This is the paradoxical nature of sport. Sports administrators must understand these ambiguities, and adopt a perspective that fits the sporting world's social, cultural and commercial context, where romantic visions, emotion and passion can override commercial logic and economic rationality. On the other hand, sports administrators should not allow tradition and history to dictate a sport's future. Being a slave to the old ways of doing things will impede its capacity to adapt to changing cultural and commercial circumstances. This problem is addressed in chapters 5 and 8. Chapter 5 discusses the problem of organisational inertia, and how a process of change management can produce creative outcomes without sacrificing traditional strengths. Chapter 8 looks at how repositioning a sport, club or team can attract more fans, participants and members.

Profits or premierships?

The most significant difference between professional competitive sporting organisations and private business is the way in which they measure performance. While business firms have many goals, their underlying purpose is to optimise profits. For example, Coles Myer and Woolworths are fierce retail competitors, but may both produce a profit and claim a successful year. However, large profits will do little to convince sporting clubs of their success if they finish the season at the bottom of the ladder. While the Coles Myer or Woolworths shareholders find the achievement of profits pleasing, sports club members and fans judge performance on the basis of trophies, championships, premierships and pennants. For example, in the Australian National Basketball League during the middle of the 1990s the Sydney Kings basketball club succeeded famously in financial terms, but failed dismally on the court. At the other extreme, the North Melbourne Giants had bankrupted themselves, but were successful in the championship race, where it 'mattered most'.

This visionary dilemma facing sports clubs has its roots in two prevailing models of organisational behaviour in sports markets. The first is the profit maximisation model, which assumes that a club is simply a firm in a competitive product market and that profit is the single driving motivational force. The second is the utility maximisation model, which emphasises the relationship between clubs playing in the same league, and their desire to win as many matches as possible.[10] The utility view assumes that sporting organisations are by nature highly competitive and status conscious, and that the single most important performance yardstick is competitive success.[11]

However, as our earlier analysis indicates, changes in the sporting context and changing management practices in sporting organisations have complicated this issue. The growth of a broad-based leisure industry, with blurred market boundaries, increasing competition for the discretionary consumer dollar and increasing professionalisation of players and officials, has forced many clubs previously solely concerned with winning to focus more strongly on profits and cash flow. The processes involved in setting up a quality financial management system are examined in Chapter 9. The structures for ensuring optimal player management and competitive success are reviewed in Chapter 6.

Designing a level playing field

While many sporting organisations acknowledge the need for financial viability, they sometimes operate as if on-field domination is the only thing necessary for long-term financial success. However, the drive to dominate a league or competition may, if too successful, be self-defeating.[12] Studies show that consistent winning by a few elite teams does not maximise profits either for themselves or for the competition as a whole. In particular, when a team dominates a fixture so much that the results become a foregone conclusion, the interests of fans will wane.[13] Therefore, what is in the best interests of individual clubs is not in the best interests of the league or competition as a whole. Highly predictable outcomes will fail to attract large attendances,[14] and if regularly repeated will diminish the gate, media and sponsorship revenue. The ongoing viability of the competition, and the financial health of constituent clubs, will be sustained only if rules are introduced which distribute playing talent equally between teams.[15] It is no surprise that the two most successful professional sports leagues in Australia, the Australian Football League and Australian Rugby League, have implemented a package of salary caps, player-draft rules and ceilings on lists of contracted players. Morely and Wilson[16] and Quirk and Fort[17] concluded that 'outcome uncertainty' and competitive balance are the keys to the commercial success of team sport competitions. However, as it also happens, this contrived uncertainty comes at the cost of a competitive market. The problems associated with regulating the movement of professional athletes are discussed in Chapter 11.

Variable quality

As we have already indicated, sport is one of the few products or services that depend upon unpredictability for their success. Dabscheck[18] suggested that sports league profits will be maximised where the results cannot be easily predicted. Similarly, Cairns, Jennert and Sloan[19] and Vamplew[20] found that attendances at sporting contests were higher where the outcome of an event was uncertain, in contrast to games where results were predictable. However, this lack of predictability also has its problems, since it brings with it enormous variability in the quality of sporting performances. Many factors contribute to this variability, including weather, player injuries, the venue, the quality of the opponents, the closeness of the scores, and even the size of the crowd. The tactics employed by the opposing teams can also influence the level of customer satisfaction—as exemplified in cricket. Captains can either make the contest dull and defensive by slowing down play and designing ultra-defensive field placements, or make it exciting and adventurous by the use of attacking bowling and batting. A day at the cricket may be exhilarating or boring, but the admission price remains the same.

However, in business markets most products and services have only minor variability in their quality; consistency and reliability are highly valued traits. The current interest in quality management and quality assurance aims to guarantee a consistent level of excellence in product performance and service delivery. In Chapter 4 we examine ways of improving the reliability of sporting services, and in Chapter 8 we look at ways the sports product can be extended to guarantee a minimum level of quality.

Collaboration and cartels

The differences between the sports market and the 'business' market are highlighted by the differing impact of structural forces on each activity. Unlike the competitive benefits that may come from something like the Coles–Myer amalgamation, team sports clubs in particular depend upon the continued commercial viability of their opponents. At the most basic level clubs must co-operate with their rivals in order to deliver an attractive sporting experience to their fans or customers.[21] As Morely and Wilson[22] pointed out, clubs are mutually interdependent, and the chronic division of clubs into wealthy and high performing, and poor and low performing, will ultimately damage all clubs involved in the competition.

This interdependency can produce arrangements that constrain the activities of the powerful, dominant member clubs by cross-subsidising the less powerful clubs.[23] This strategy is not uncommon in Australian sporting competitions, which in the case of the Australian Football League involves sharing of television revenue between the sixteen member clubs. The Fitzroy Lions was the worst performing AFL club of the 1990s and recently amalgamated with Brisbane. However, even through its darkest years it received the same return from television as the grossly successful West Coast, one of the most televised and profitable clubs. Such revenue sharing in the retail industry would be unthinkable, unless, of course, it was organised as a cartel. On the other hand, cartel arrangements are common in sport, where clubs can share revenue, prevent other clubs from entering the market, collectively fix prices, and generally limit the amount of competition.[24] However, as we suggest in Chapter 11, these essentially anti-competitive practices now risk being challenged under the provisions of the *Trade Practices Act*. In Chapters 8 and 13 we discuss the benefits that arise from collaborative arrangements with other sporting organisations.

Product and brand loyalty

For the most part, sport engenders a high degree of loyalty at both the product (or sporting competition) level and the brand (or team) level. First, the sports industry has a low cross-elasticity of demand. That is, there is a low degree of substitutability between competing sports leagues and competitions. Match day fixtures provide a clutch of entertainment benefits that attract spectators and television viewers, but these benefits are usually sport specific, and the satisfactions that come from watching one sport will not easily transfer to another. Most sporting competitions have an inelastic demand and a high degree of product loyalty. Even where fans are unhappy about the result of a particular game, the winning margin or the standard of umpiring, it is unlikely that they would change their sporting preferences. If, for instance, a supporter's soccer team is playing interstate and the match isn't televised, she or he would be unlikely to attend a hockey or bocce game instead, even if it was played nearby at an attractive venue and admission was free. In contrast, if consumers purchased computing equipment or a paramedical service, and were dissatisfied with the quality, they would readily consider changing providers or products, even if prices were higher. In sport, no such easy substitutability occurs.

While a low degree of product substitution can be advantageous to a sporting competition, there are concealed drawbacks. For example, low levels of substitutability can limit a sport's ability to achieve immediate market penetration. The customs, habits and traditions of sports fans make it difficult to attract them from one sport to another in large numbers by using incentives or price discounts. Neither price reductions nor an increase in fans' income levels will have a significant impact on the watching and viewing preferences of sports consumers.[25] Other material inducements may therefore be necessary to convert fans; these issues are canvassed in Chapter 8.

Second, club or brand affiliation, and the emotional attachment consumers hold for teams and their symbolic representations, are also very strong. This is not the case for many consumer goods. It can range from very low for takeaway foods to moderately high for sports footwear. A good indicator of product loyalty is a preparedness to 'repeat purchase', even where the price of competing products falls. Few Queenslanders would choose to watch the Auckland Warriors rugby league team play against the Adelaide Rams—in preference to viewing their own club play—even if the admission price was severely discounted. Parochial supporters have strong emotional attachments to their local team and little interest in interstate fixtures. Despite the fact that an 'interstate match' might provide higher quality performance, their affiliation to 'their' club is of paramount importance. Fans invest an enormous amount of personal energy in their favourite team, and this can create lifetime attachments. Fans often see their team as an extension of themselves.[26] It is this emotional attachment and personal identification inherent in sports that retailers and service organisations would kill for. Popular advertising subsequently attempts to link emotions and identifying symbols with brand features. The importance of brand marks, symbols and images in attracting fans, and strategies for creating product identification, are discussed in Chapter 8.

Vicarious identification

The identification that fans have with sports and teams can also spin off into their relationships with family, friends, sporting heroes and their heroes' behaviour. It is not unusual to see primary school children at sports matches wearing the uniform of their parents' favourite team. Supporters also follow a hierarchy of loyalty, which begins with the sport and moves down to the club and finally to their sporting heroes. Supporters who enjoy playing or watching basketball may vehemently support the Melbourne Tigers, and also emulate the feats of Andrew Gaze. If Gaze wears Puma basketball shoes, so will many supporters. Many businesses recognise the power of sporting identification, and have attempted to market their products via sporting heroes. By so doing, they aim to capture some of the loyalty and charisma associated with the sport, team or player, rather than working through price, convenience or quality. This 'symbiotic relationship' between sporting hero, player identification and product promotion has a powerful influence on the spending patterns of consumers.[27] Again, it all comes back to the deep emotional attachments that fans form with their favourite sporting pastimes—addressed in detail in Chapter 8.

Blind optimism

The sporting world is full of contradictions. We have already pointed out that many sports administrators and fans will sometimes go to any lengths to preserve a traditional practice, symbol or motif. On the one hand, there are situations where fans have a surprisingly high tolerance for changes in personnel and product quality. The emotional glue that joins members and fans to their clubs means that they will accept countless changes to the personnel of their club if it offers a greater chance of success. If a star player moves from one club to another club, the supporters' allegiances will in the main remain fixed. Consider the case of Mark Bradtke, the star centre for the Adelaide Thirtysixers, who transferred to the Melbourne Tigers basketball team in the mid-1990s. Adelaide fans continued to support their home team even though its 'product quality' fell, while Melbourne supporters embraced Bradtke as if he was 'a long lost son'. On the other hand, a consumer seeking a new car or a tennis racquet will seriously want to change products if the product has lost its major attribute, or somehow changed its image. In Chapter 3 we discuss the importance of quality in sports product delivery, and in Chapter 8 we highlight the need for image making through the promotion of the star player.

Technology

Sporting organisations rarely pass up the opportunity to trade players or sack staff where it might lead to more success. This keen interest in human resource development does not always extend to technology. There are many examples where commercial business seeks to gain a competitive edge by achieving a technological breakthrough. In cars, for example, the introduction of airbags and anti-lock braking systems have revolutionised automobile safety, while in the computer industry the rate of change is so dramatic that a product is likely to become obsolete soon after its purchase. In contrast, sports science affords slow, progressive improvements to sports performance. At the extreme, sports administrators will resist change that threatens traditions, which can range from diet and player counselling to the role of massage and heavy resistance training. In Chapter 6 we consider the ways that a good performance management system can assist the delivery of a continually improving sports science and player support program. In Chapter 5 we describe how to create a culture that emphasises innovation and quality service delivery.

Fixed supply schedules

Fixed short-run supply is often another hindrance for sporting clubs. Whereas most private sector businesses can fairly quickly increase their production to meet demand, sporting clubs have fixed, or highly inelastic, production curves for their products. (This point excludes the sale of memberships and memorabilia). Clubs can only play a certain number of times during their business cycle, or season. In the event that the spectator demand for a club or a particular game is high, the governing body may change the venue to allow a larger crowd to attend, but cannot decide, say, to play the match twice. When fans and members are unable to gain admission, revenue is lost.

In the *long run*, however, the problem of unmet demand can be resolved. The supply of a sports product can be increased by providing more seats or playing more games. For example, the steady increase in demand for cricket over the past thirty years has resulted in more matches being played, thereby increasing both productivity and supply.[28] The success of sports ventures is in part based on the extent to which they can deliver the right games, under the right conditions, at the right time, and in the right venue to large numbers of people who are willing to pay for quality and 'delightful' experiences.[29] This means that sports administrators must be prepared to do extensive research to establish not just the level of demand for their services but also when fans and members want the services delivered. The market research issue is examined in Chapter 8.

IMPLICATIONS

The special features of the sports market must be appreciated. Without an understanding of these features sports administrators will fail to maximise their organisation's successes, both on the field and off. The special nature of sport was succinctly summarised by Gorman and Calhoun[30] when they commented: 'Sport. It is at once a business and an emotional experience, money and heart. Neither side can be dismissed by the fan, or by the people in charge.'

Viewing sport in mechanistic and narrowly commercial terms fails to provide a full understanding of its special features and frequently paradoxical behaviours. Also, sport is an inherently conservative institution and radical change cannot be pursued without significant and sometimes massive resistance from supporters. Volunteers, fans and members must be handled gently, since they often invest an enormous amount of emotional energy and financial resources in their favourite sporting interests. But they should not be expected to set the planning or managerial agenda.

At the same time, it is precisely sport's special features that *demand* the application of sophisticated and 'professional' business principles. One of the real weaknesses of so much sports administration, particularly at the community level, is its failure to grasp recent developments in management theory and best practice models, and its reluctance to use these powerful tools to improve the overall performance of the sports system. Thus anyone who intends to manage sport as if it is somehow culturally privileged and immune from business influences is also destined to fail.

The way to go is to recognise that, while its special features must be considered, sport is not so unique that it cannot be improved by a system of professional best practice management.

SUMMARY

This chapter discussed the ways in which sport is both similar to and different from the world of commerce and business. While there are many people who argue that sport is far removed from business, we demonstrated that sport and business are linked closely. However, one should not be seduced into thinking that sport is like any other business.

We provided four reasons why sport is a special form of business. First, there is a passionate/emotional connection with its members, players and fans. This passion is demonstrated by the serious ways in which thousands of people identify with their favourite teams, clubs and players. This identification creates a strong sense of loyalty and sense of ownership, but can also mean that change is resisted, even where there are substantial commercial benefits to be gained. Second, the quality of the sporting event or experience can vary from one situation to another. This can disappoint the customer, as good money is sometimes spent on a bad experience. Third, the provision of quality sports products is dependent upon the relationship between competing clubs and teams. This means that sports leagues must ensure close competitions or competitive balance in order to delight customers and retain their loyalty over the long term. Finally, the conservative ethos of many sporting organisations can lead to the slow adoption of new developments in information technology and exercise sciences.

FURTHER READING

Adair, D. and Vamplew, W. (1997) *Sport in Australian History*, Oxford University Press, Melbourne.

Gorman, J. and Calhoun, K. (1994) *The Name of the Game: The Business of Sport*, John Wiley, New York.

Slack, T. (1997) *Understanding Sport Organizations: The Application of Organization Theory*, Human Kinetics, Champaign, Ill.

Stewart, R. (1989). 'The nature of sport under capitalism and its relation to the capitalist labour process', *Sporting Traditions*, 6(1), pp. 50–62.

3 Strategic planning

After reading this chapter you should be able to understand and engage in the process of strategic planning for a sporting organisation.
  More specifically, you should be able to:

- determine a strategic direction incorporating a mission statement and a vision statement, together with a set of organisational objectives
- carry out a strategic analysis, using the tools of competitor analysis and strength/weakness/opportunity/threat (SWOT) analysis
- determine strategic options, applying the tools of gap analysis and bench-marking
- design and implement a plan including strategies, tactics and activities
- complete a strategic evaluation by examining key performance indicators

THE STRATEGIC PLAN

Nearly every successful sporting organisation has some form of strategic plan. The terminology may range from development plan to corporate plan to business plan, but the principles are the same. A strategic plan is a document that presents a strategic direction, lists its objectives, and records the actions that will be taken to meet the objectives. Simply put, a strategic plan describes where you want to go and how you want to get there.

There is no substitute for good planning. It creates a sense of collective direction, mobilises the energies of people and reveals a variety of opportunities and possibilities. It produces intelligent action. It is the starting point for professional best practice management, and is applicable to large and small sporting organisations alike.

Ideally, a strategic plan will contain components from every management function that we cover in this book. Many sporting organisations, however, struggle to find the time to document even rudimentary financial plans, and feel pleased if they get so far as creating a budget. Some do not dare contemplate the nuances of setting up detailed marketing, facility or human

22

resource strategies. The problem may not only result from a lack of knowledge and guidance, but may also reflect a lack of time and resources. Even the most qualified and experienced sports administrator cannot hope to complete the prodigious task of designing a full-scale strategic plan singlehandedly. As a result, there is a need for a strategic planning approach that serves both the well-resourced and the resource-challenged sporting organisation.

COMMON STRATEGIC PLANNING TERMINOLOGY

Corporate/business/strategic plan
A one to ten year document covering the intended future of the entire organisational entity. It may have a 'glossy' version (10–20 pages) for shareholders/members and an operational version (30–200 pages) for management.

Mission statement
Statement of an organisation's purpose and reason for existence.

Vision statement
Broad, high level statement of intended strategic direction. An organisation's intended position for the future. May be set one to twenty years in the future.

Objectives
Objectives translate the vision into action statements that express what is to be achieved and when. May be expressed as goals or aims.

Key performance indicators/performance measures/performance indicators/success measures/performance targets/key outcomes/benchmarks
Internal measures of an organisation's success. Measurable and time-related outcomes that provide evidence for success or failure in meeting objectives or goals.

Strategies/tactics/activities/actions/plans/execution stages
Steps that turn objectives into more detailed action. Usually structured on a tiered basis of increasing detail.

Shareholders/members
Those with a stake in the business/enterprise/organisation, usually as a result of financial contribution.

Values/core values
Statements that formally indicate a moral or ethical stance. Usually used to help mould an organisation's culture.

> **SWOT analysis/environmental analysis/operating environment/
> competitor analysis/environmental scan/position audit**
> Methods of evaluating an organisation's relative position in the market-
> place.

What follows is a generic approach to strategic planning. The process can be applied across the entire organisation, or to a specific management function like finance or performance. Strategic planning is just as important for a local community club or a small State governing body as it is for a professional sports team and a high profile national sporting body.

DEVELOPING THE STRATEGY

Every action taken by an organisation should have a strategic focus.[1] In other words, if an action, policy, procedure or process is not contributing to the progressive realisation of the organisation's objectives, then it has no strategic value.

The term 'strategy' can be traced back to military origins. It effectively means to engage the enemy on your own favoured terms. Implicit in this view is the notion of the enemy, or competition, which is pivotal to success in the world of hypercommercialised sport. Strategy consists of the pattern of actions that collectively move an organisation toward realising its aims, by matching its internal capabilities with the external environment. In a military sense, it means that an organisation must choose its battles and battleground carefully. The planning process is a systematic method of designing and implementing strategies in order to defeat the corporate or sporting enemy.

While there are scores of complex and fashionable techniques that may be used in strategic planning, the basic steps do not change. The five steps are set out in Figure 3.1.

The starting point for any organisation is determining a *strategic direction*. The purpose is to specify identity and ambition. This is achieved by creating:

- a mission statement, which describes the purpose of an organisation
- a vision statement, which identifies the ultimate aim of the organisation
- objectives, which are manageable steps on the way to the ultimate aim
- performance indicators, which help to establish whether the objectives have been met.

The second step requires a *strategic analysis*. It ensures that organisations monitor the environment in which they operate, and it fully recognises their

Figure 3.1 Strategic planning framework

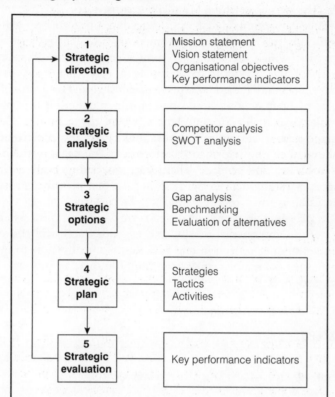

own capabilities and deficiencies as well as those of their competitors. Tools employed for the purpose include a competitor analysis, which examines the impact of other similarly placed organisations, and a SWOT analysis, which considers an organisation's strengths and weaknesses, as well as opportunities and threats. The analysis stage reveals the possibilities and opportunities that can be exploited. It also identifies the problems and challenges presented by new products, rival suppliers and new technologies. Where the time and resources are available, the competitor and SWOT analyses may be supported by an industry analysis. The industry analysis will provide greater detail on the demographics of the sports industry and expand the research base for development of market opportunities.

The consideration of *strategic options* is the third step in the strategic planning process, and evolves naturally from the analysis stage. At this point, tools such as benchmarking and gap analysis highlight the gap between current and desired performance. They also show how we may proceed from where we are at the moment to where we would like to be. This stage stimulates the development of potential options, and ranks the strategic possibilities.

Options are converted into tangible and achievable strategies in the fourth step, the actual *strategic plan*. This constitutes the implementation phase of strategic planning. Here tactics are developed to help achieve each strategy, and activities for each tactic, in a cascading system of increasing detail. Activities, which are the bottom-most level of the plan, are precise statements specifying action to be taken at a particular time, incurring a particular cost, and undertaken by a particular individual or group. This stage involves a lot of documentation and precise statements, but it is essential to ensure that things actually happen. This is where the action is.

The final step requires a *strategic evaluation*. Here the effectiveness of the plan is assessed with the use of key performance indicators, which are used to identify successes and failures. These performance measures are attached to the objectives established in the first step of our planning process. They provide the catalyst for a repeat of the five steps listed above.[2]

Strategic planning is therefore never merely a linear process that has a beginning, various intermediate steps, and an end. Successful strategic planning demands ongoing reflection and revision, from direction to evaluation. This never-ending contemplation is commonly known as strategic thinking, and is discussed later.

THE FIVE STEPS

We now look at each of the steps in greater detail.

1 Determining strategic direction

At the outset of the strategic planning process, any sporting organisation has to ask itself two fundamental questions: why do we exist?; and what do we want? This is achieved by developing a mission statement and a vision statement. Having defined a purpose and what success means in the long term, a sporting organisation must create landmarks on the way to ultimate success, in the form of measurable and time-related objectives that incorporate key performance indicators (KPIs). Therefore, setting a *strategic direction* involves three principal phases. They are the mission phase, the vision phase and the objective-setting phase, all of which are interconnected.

A. Defining the mission

The first step in strategy formation is to define a mission. An organisation's mission reveals its purpose and reason for existence, and is a statement that clearly defines what the organisation was set up to achieve, what general services or products it provides, and for whom it provides them. The mission is expressed in an official and documented form. This 'mission statement' is a *concise* proclamation declaring an organisation's vocation and can range in size from one sentence to a full paragraph or more.[3]

Mission statements should not contain details of measurable targets or outcomes, but they should set an organisation apart from others in identifying the scope of its operation in both service and customer terms.

The New Zealand Hillary Commission was established through legislation to develop sport and promote physical activity. Its mission statement is a suitably concise example:

> The Hillary Commission is dedicated to improving quality of life by enabling all New Zealanders to participate and achieve in sport, fitness and leisure.

At first glance, mission statements appear easy to construct, but in reality they are quite difficult to get 'just right'. Consider the role of national or State sporting organisations. Is their mission to co-ordinate, to promote, to increase participation, or to win at the elite level? Do they exist to provide health and recreational opportunities for a specific group of the community, or potentially for everyone in the community? Mission statements can become complex when organisations have difficulty prioritising their purposes. Even a professional team competing in a national sporting competition must grapple with the relative importance of on-field performance against service to its shareholder equivalent, the members. The mission for an organisation at the other end of the spectrum, like a local club, is just as difficult to define, as it faces the dilemma of whether it should focus on members, players or the sport's development. Nonetheless, as the renowned management writer Peter Drucker[4] pointed out, mission statements have to be operational. In other words, they must revolve around what actually happens or should happen, or else they end up being little more than statements of good intentions. Remember that organisations cannot do everything—priorities must be established.

There are three components in an effective mission statement. The first is the general purpose or nature of the 'business' in which the organisation operates. By business we do not mean a list of transactions but rather a broad description of the field, industry or market in which an organisation functions. In indicating a purpose for existence, a good mission statement establishes a consistent and unified expectation within the organisation, where every employee can look at the statement and instantly see how they are contributing to the effective functioning of the organisation.

Second, and allied to this notion, are the services and products that are being created and offered. It is important to look at the marketplace in which the organisation operates with the intention of finding the right niche, or what Drucker calls opportunities. In this sense, the mission is a response to the needs of the marketplace or community. This is where a sports-based organisation must ask itself what it can offer that no other sporting organisation can.

The third component refers to the parties to whom these products and services are offered. A mission statement should contain information concerning what specific types of services are provided to which specific customers or beneficiaries. Indoor Cricket Victoria may point out, for example, that while it plays a pivotal role in co-ordinating, promoting, officiating and playing indoor cricket, the sport is driven by commercial facility operators who must, for the sake of their livelihood, seek profits. In response, Indoor Cricket Victoria has astutely developed a mission statement that reflects the needs of a diverse marketplace (see box).

The power of a good mission statement is well documented. Jones and Kahaner,[5] Handy[6] and Argenti[7] provide valuable information on the subject.

EXAMPLES OF MISSION STATEMENTS

Australian Football League
The Australian Football League exists to develop and manage the AFL competition, ensuring it is Australia's most successful national sports competition in the entertainment industry. It also seeks to maximise the economic, cultural and social benefits of Australian football to its member clubs, the players, the football fraternity and the community at large. Thirdly the AFL promotes and develops participation and support for Australian football throughout Australia and overseas.

Indoor Cricket Victoria
Indoor Cricket Victoria, Inc. is the governing body for the sport of Indoor Cricket in the state of Victoria. Its role is to act as a neutral body answerable to its members that will provide them with:

■ a resource centre to implement improvements in coaching, playing and officiating standards;

■ an equal opportunity to participate in competently and fairly run representative level tournaments open to all sections of the community;

■ representation and liaison with the media, government bodies and the Australian Indoor Cricket Federation; and

■ a forum to exchange information, which will improve operating procedures and playing standards and consequently enhance the image of the sport as being desirable to play at all levels.

Vertical Leap Rock Climbing Centre
Our mission is to provide safe and competent rock climbing services within a unique and friendly atmosphere to our members and customers in order to achieve a fair and reasonable profit.

Bennetswood Rugby League Club
Our mission is to provide a safe and efficient structure and friendly social environment in which to play and enjoy the sport of rugby league, in which individual and team ambitions and skills may be pursued and developed.

Mission statement checklist

The following checklist has been collated in order to simplify the design of a mission statement, and to ensure that the key items are included. The following questions should be addressed:

- Have you indicated the broad nature of your organisation's business? (e.g. entertainment; recreation; competitive sport)
- Have you included the type of services offered? (e.g. officiating; running programs; conducting workshops)
- Have you included who your customers are? (e.g. members; general public; senior citizens)
- Have you included what the broad purpose of your organisation is? (e.g. coordination; promotion; participation; elite success/performance)
- Can any employee look at the mission statement and instantly pinpoint where they fit into the organisation's operations?
- Have you included the values and beliefs that are intrinsic to your organisation? (e.g. customer orientation; ethical behaviour; safety; loyalty)
- If your statement was the one and only advertisement your organisation employed, would it accurately reflect the way you wish to be seen? (e.g. competent; safe; unified; innovative)
- Have you indicated in your statement what your organisation can provide that no other organisation can?

You should now be able to write a full mission statement.

B. *Defining the vision*

The next stage in establishing a *strategic direction* is to define the vision, which is documented in the form of a vision statement. Whereas the mission statement identifies an organisation's *purpose*, the vision statement specifies an organisation's *long-term aims*. In short, the mission is about the reason for being, here and now, while the vision is concerned with future achievements.

Vision has become a central theme running through much management literature, and is typically identified as the foundation of effective planning and the starting point for outstanding achievement.[8] For example, Jim

Clemmer described vision as the critical focal point of an organisation and the catalyst for high performance,[9] while Lew Haskell noted that the first step to exceptional organisational performance is to create a compelling vision of the future.[10] Although sometimes misunderstood as a mystical and elusive concept, developing a vision is a critical element in making any organisation highly effective and quality oriented.[11]

Vision is often defined as:

- an act or power of imagination[12]
- a mode of seeing or conceiving with unusual discernment or foresight[13]
- a realistic, credible and attractive future[14]
- a method of creating meaning, direction, purpose and a guiding philosophy[15]

Using vision as the primary organisational compass is commonly associated with several beneficial outcomes including: the provision of an overarching 'big picture',[16] the creation of energy, inspiration and enthusiasm for change and improvement,[17] and increased competitiveness, effectiveness and focus.[18] Vision is also closely connected to organisational culture and change and can act as a management beacon, which signals the direction that an organisation aims to take.[19]

The vision statement aims are usually set for achievement in five to seven years, although this may depend on the organisational context. For example, most Olympic sporting associations find it convenient to plan around the four-year Olympic cycle, although their planning sometimes stalls immediately after the Games, particularly when a crisis of confidence occurs as a result of poor medal tallies. Other related organisations, such as sports clothing and footwear manufacturers, often set a vision approximately two or three years in the future, in response to rapid environmental changes. In general, we recommend a minimum of about four years.

If this strategic approach were to be conceptualised as a skeleton, the vision would be the spine. The vision holds an organisation in place at all times; it is there to ensure that the organisation never just exists and functions, but actively moves towards its aims. Every operation, function and activity serves to move the organisation toward its vision, and if it does not, then either the operations need reworking or the vision does. This raises an important point: the vision, and for that matter the mission, are never set in stone. They may require periodic refinement and readjustment. If and when this is done, it is essential to ensure that the two statements remain compatible.

Vision statements can range substantially in length but, like the mission statement, they should be concise. Many organisations employ a short, pithy sentence as their vision, which can be tremendously effective. We recommend a single sentence—preferably containing enough 'oomph' to jolt the reader (what Collins and Porras[20] call 'big, hairy, and audacious')—followed by a more detailed explanation of several sentences, if necessary.

EXAMPLES OF VISION STATEMENTS

Nike (1960s):
Crush Adidas.

Northern Territory Underwater Hockey Association
To become the premier sporting organisation, and most popular sporting activity, in northern Australia by the new millennium.

Adelaide Crows (Australian Football League Club)
Become a respected playing force, competing consistently in finals. Win the AFL premiership and further improve the off-field achievement of the club.

Bennetswood Rugby League Club
To become the most successful and prominent rugby league team in the competition by winning another two premierships, and increasing membership to 1000 by the end of season 2003.

Vision statement checklist

The following checklist should help you design a succinct vision statement:

■ Does your statement reflect a future image? In other words, does it immediately create a picture in your mind? (e.g. excellence; equity; largest; dynamic)
■ Does it represent a long-term goal or goals?
■ Is it short and powerful?
■ Is it set at least four years in the future?
■ Is it achievable in the time set?
■ Is it consistent with the mission statement?
■ Does it reflect the vision of your primary customers?

Try writing a vision statement for your own organisation.

C. Creating organisational objectives

Organisational objectives are *manageable* steps on the way to achieving a vision. The easiest and fastest way of determining such objectives is to derive them directly from the vision. For example, if a professional club has a five year vision of winning its competition, and is presently positioned last out of ten in that competition, then a suitable objective may be to finish the next season in sixth or seventh position. Similarly, if the vision of an aerobics studio states that, in three years, profit will be 150 per cent of the current figure, then a reasonable Year One objective may be 115 per cent.

Probably the biggest difficulty facing sporting organisations is a tendency to confuse strategies with objectives. Strategies are the 'driving' initiatives through which objectives may be reached, whereas objectives are core statements of intent, which are derived directly from the vision. A clear hierarchy exists: vision at the top as the ultimate goal, then objectives as steps on the way to that vision, followed by strategies designed to fulfil objectives. The trick is to understand that strategies are 'means to an end', while objectives are 'ends in themselves'. Consider the professional club we mentioned in the previous paragraph. It wants to reach the top of its competition, and may set an objective to improve its final placing in the competition ladder. Strategies to achieve that performance objective may revolve around recruiting systems, the quality of coaching, player support, or conditioning facilities. In the case of the aerobics studio, possible strategies for a profit increase may include the introduction of new classes catering for a new customer demographic, or increasing the awareness of potential customers about the services offered, via a selective advertising campaign. However, these are strategies not objectives. They are means rather than ends. So, what are the ends?

There are only four categories or generic types of objectives that a sports-based organisation can pursue, although there is an infinite number of ways in which objectives can be stated. We can label the categories as follows, each beginning with the letter P:

■ Participation
■ Performance
■ Promotion
■ Profit

It does not matter what sort of sporting organisation it is, and where it pretends to position itself, all its objectives statements must fall into one of the above categories.

Participation concerns the number of people or clubs involved in a sport or who utilise a service offered by an organisation. This may take the form of membership or spectator levels for a professional sports team, or the numbers of people and associated clubs playing the sport under a governing body. Members, players, clubs and volunteer officials are all participants. Developing a core objective of membership has propelled the Singapore Netball Association into the largest female team sport in that country.

Performance encompasses all elite success, and is often the first priority for professional clubs in the form of championship victories. It is also important for governing associations in State, national and international competition. It can even be a priority objective for local, community-based sporting clubs. Through a singleminded focus on performance, Malaysian football club Sabah has emerged as a consistent top four finisher.

Any organisation that believes in the social value of its sport or activity and wishes to 'spread the word' or 'share the fun', holds the *Promotion* objective highly. This objective is usually common to governing bodies. In these cases they primarily aim to promote the health, well-being, character development and personal growth virtues of the sport and its related activities. The Hong Kong Sport Climbing Association was assembled with the public-spirited objective of promoting the sport as a community service.

Finally, *Profit* involves the objective of making sure that income exceeds expenditure over the playing season. It is suited to professional, privately owned clubs like the Brisbane Broncos rugby league team and the Sydney Kings basketball team. The profit objective also applies to the majority of privately owned facilities such as gyms, swimming pools, indoor rock-climbing centres, squash and racquetball courts and leisure centres. The Yokohama Flugels J-League soccer club was established by a consortium of five Japanese companies as a financial investment, and therefore pursues profits as its primary objective.

The Profit objective is an area of some confusion to sports managers and fans alike. While some clubs and associations may downplay the need to earn profits, many other sporting organisations actively pursue financial goals, which is not only perfectly valid but also a desperate necessity in many sports marketplaces. Clubs like the recently departed Fitzroy Australian Rules football club, and many financially fragile local sports clubs, were or are continually aiming to improve their cash flow position. However, this need for financial solvency should not hide the primary purpose for their existence. Sporting clubs that are member-based should not set profit as the primary objective. If they do, they not only violate their Articles of Association as non-profit entities, but they muddy their strategic waters. Instead, they should focus on the objectives of Participation and Performance. Profits are better seen as the means by which these objectives can be achieved. Thus financial expansion, which in the short term translates into an operating surplus, becomes a prime strategy to achieve a greater participation base or more on-field success.

Sporting organisations vary in the primacy they give to the four categories of objectives. Many, such as privately owned gymnasiums, will focus on the profit objective. Others, like professional sports clubs, may focus on both performance and participation. National and State bodies and some local community-based clubs may have up to three major objectives, spreading their energies over performance, participation and promotion. However, one of the keys to harnessing the power of the strategic framework is to narrow objectives to as few as possible, and then to rank them. Narrowing them down should not be too difficult; in fact, it should be straightforward, especially if the mission and vision have been correctly documented. Ranking them, however, is harder, and requires considerable discussion and sometimes controversy. In the end, though, it is worth it, keeping in mind they can always be modified at a later stage. By formally prioritising organisational objectives it becomes clearer how resources should be utilised. Objectives setting can run into trouble, of course, when the objectives are vague and open to a variety of interpretations. They must be measurable, since if they cannot be measured in some impartial way then they cannot be managed. This is where key performance indicators fit in.

D. Establishing key performance indicators (KPIs)

Objectives such as 'winning matches' or 'making a profit' are in themselves too vaguely stated to pursue. Objectives require in-built measures of success, otherwise it is not clear whether they have been achieved or not. In order to make objectives measurable, standards of performance need to be established in the form of KPIs, which then become part of the objective itself. KPIs provide the quantifiable and time-related component of an objective. For example, if a rugby league team identifies on-field success (performance) as an objective, then the key performance indicator spells out the precise outcome desired, such as 'finishing in the top four in the league', as well as the timing nominated for success, such as 'next season'.

The examples given in the box should help you in designing objectives that incorporate key performance indicators.

EXAMPLES OF ORGANISATIONAL OBJECTIVES WITH IN-BUILT KPIS

Alice Springs Surf Lifesaving Club
- To increase membership to 10 by 1 February 1999.
- To send a minimum of five competitors to compete in the Australian Surf Lifesaving Championships in January 2000.

Green Lake Health Retreat
- To increase profit to $120 000, calculated at the end of the 1999 financial year.

New South Wales Underwater Weightlifting Association
- To increase the number of people who have heard of the sport in the suburb of Manly to 1000 by 1 March 1999, measured by phone survey.
- To increase the number of clubs participating in the competition to four, by summer season 1999.

Bennetswood Rugby League Club
- To win the premiership in season 1999.
- To increase membership by 20% to 600 by the end of season 1999.

Organisational objectives checklist

A checklist for adequately setting out your objectives is:

- Which of the four Ps are contained in your vision statement?

- Performance
- Participation
- Promotion
- Profit

■ Are your objectives suitable 'chunks' taken from the vision?

■ Are your objectives time-related?

■ Are your objectives measurable in a standard and consistent way?

2 Making a strategic analysis

Once your organisation's strategic direction has been clarified, it is time to undertake a *strategic analysis* in order to clarify any internal organisational features or external environmental characteristics that might affect the selection of appropriate strategies to meet the organisational objectives. Strategic analysis is the information gathering and interpretation stage of the strategic planning process (see Figure 3.1 above), and serves to ensure that all relevant information has been considered before decisions are made and actions are taken. The best place to begin is with an analysis of any competing organisations, followed by an examination of your own strengths and weaknesses and any opportunities or threats that may exist elsewhere in the marketplace.

A. The competitor analysis

A competitor analysis is completed in order to assess the impact of other organisations that are fighting for the same group of customers. The traditional approach in sport was to *ignore* competing organisations. However, this approach is no longer practical in the cutthroat sport and leisure industry, where competing products and services now exist in every nook and cranny of the marketplace. For example, competitors to a suburban soccer club include not only neighbouring soccer clubs but also any local sporting clubs that offer a substitutable activity; for example, basketball, netball, indoor cricket or volleyball. While in many instances serious competition may also come from television, computer games and the Internet, they are better included as threats in the SWOT analysis that follows. You should limit the competitor analysis to other sports-related organisations.

A competitor analysis should begin by identifying the names of the competitors and their geographical locations. It follows with a listing of their typical range of products and services, with an emphasis on things that your organisation does not deliver. You can then describe their general strategic approach, and whether they may be considered an opportunity or threat. Keep in mind that weak opposition can be exploited and represent an opportunity, while imposing competitors present a threat to be neutralised. As we mentioned earlier, this strategic approach can be applied to all management areas in order to generate action plans.

Table 3.1 Competitor analysis

Competitor	Geographic location (immediate area)	Range of products/services	Unique products/services	General strategic approach	Opportunity/threat/neutral
(a) Bennetswood Rugby League Club					
East Bennetswood Touch Rugby Club	Bennetswood	Playing Training Social club Gaming	Social club and gaming facilities	Focus on attracting families Safe sport for everyone	Threat
Bennetswood Rugby Union Club	Bennetswood	Playing Training	Unique sport activity	None	Opportunity
Bennetswood Australian Football Club	Bennetswood	Playing Training	Unique sport activity	None	Opportunity
Bennetswood Basketball Club	Bennetswood	Playing Training	Unique sport activity	Emphasis on junior development	Neutral
(b) FILA sporting apparel company					
Nike	Sold through major and minor sporting outlets	75% athletic footwear: basketball, football, running, cross-training, tennis 25% clothing	Variations on common themes but nothing unique Air Jordan	Medium quality, high price Strong reliance on image and high profile athlete sponsorship	Threat
Adidas	Sold through major and minor sporting outlets	60% athletic footwear: basketball, football, running, cross-training, tennis 40% clothing	Nothing unique	Medium quality, high price Focus on experience in industry and quality	Threat

In Table 3.1 we provide two examples of competitor analysis. The first, Bennetswood Rugby League Club, is an example of how a small, poorly resourced sporting club may approach strategic analysis. By contrast, the second example, FILA sporting apparel, occurs specifically within a marketing framework—that is, within a particular management support area.

B. The strengths/weaknesses/opportunities/threats (SWOT) analysis

The SWOT technique is a method of analysing organisations by revealing:

■ *internally:* their own competencies in the form of strengths and weaknesses
■ *externally:* factors beyond their direct control such as opportunities and threats

According to planning expert John Argenti,[21] the SWOT analysis is the point in the planning process where the organisation attempts to identify what it does outstandingly well or badly, what its special abilities and disabilities are, and where its advantages and disadvantages lie compared with its competitors, and its expectations. Thus a feature of the SWOT analysis is that it implicitly considers an organisation's *strategic* position, in relation to its market and to its competition. Of course, before this can be done adequately, a competitor analysis must be performed to gather background information on potential opportunities and threats. We are looking for major factors that will condition the organisation's destiny for many years into the future, which means that any unique features that distinguish it from other organisations or mark it out from the norm should be highlighted. So it is unlikely that an organisation will have more than about ten strengths or weaknesses, regardless of its size and resources. The International Olympic Committee will have approximately the same number of SWOT factors as the Western Region Sports Assembly in Victoria. Both possess strengths and weaknesses, can capitalise on opportunities and face threats.

A strength can be defined as a resource or capability that an organisation can use to achieve an objective, while a weakness is a limitation or inadequacy that will prevent or hinder an objective from being met. An opportunity is any favourable situation or occurrence provided by others or a circumstance that can be exploited by the organisation to meet objective. A threat is any unfavourable situation that will make it impossible or difficult for an organisation to achieve an objective.

In order to properly assess strengths and weaknesses it is necessary to address all management functions; however, it is sometimes difficult to establish the impact of certain external opportunities and threats on specific management areas. To combat this problem it is useful to consider a number of generic external circumstances which Argenti highlighted, including political, economic, social, technological and industrial changes. Some external changes are easy to identify, such as the political shift in Victoria allowing

Sunday trading. The fact that consumers may choose to shop on Sundays may pose a threat to some leisure and sporting organisations. On the other hand, unless a sporting organisation has a considerable investment in the commodities market, which few do, then it is difficult to see how an economic factor such as a fall in the price of gold might affect them. A comprehensive SWOT checklist appears at the end of this section.

There are two common mistakes associated with the use of a SWOT analysis. The first and biggest mistake is getting caught up in needless detail. Day-to-day operational concerns are irrelevant. The purpose is to construct a general picture of an organisation's position. For example, a weakness in a national body could be its financial position if it runs at a consistent loss, but a weakness would never include the fact that the photocopier continually breaks down. The broken photocopier may be indicative of a wider structural or operational weakness.

The other typical mistake made by organisations is to focus only on sport-related factors and to ignore important organisational factors. For example, Basketball Australia may assert that basketball is 'strong' because it is a non-contact, gender-neutral sport that can be accessed by disabled and able-bodied competitors alike. This is a sport-related factor. The group should also identify its comparatively wealthy financial situation as an organisational strength. Similarly, if netball is on the brink of being declared an Olympic sport, then All Australia Netball Association suddenly has a sport-related opportunity that it can potentially turn into a dazzling strength, just as the threatened withdrawal of a government grant is a disastrous organisational threat. The SWOT analysis examples given in Table 3.2 may help you to generate your own factors. Note that the nominated opportunities and threats have been carried forward from the competitor analysis in Table 3.1 and that, for FILA, two aggressive competitors can present a marketing opportunity.

SWOT checklist

As with missions, visions and objectives, a checklist of items to address can help you work through the SWOT process:

- In completing the *internal* analysis—strengths and weaknesses—have you considered all management areas?
- In completing the *external* analysis—opportunities and threats—have you considered Argenti's five major factors? . . .

    - Political and legal changes (e.g. government policy on sport; employment legislation; legal liability; tax; immigration policy)
    - Economic changes (e.g. economic growth; inflation; unemployment; interest rates; availability of capital)
    - Social changes (e.g. population trends; education; lifestyle and leisure time)

Table 3.2 SWOT analysis

SWOT components	SWOT results
(a) Bennetswood Rugby League Club	
Strengths	■ Successful senior squad ■ Positive and friendly environment ■ Strong community involvement ■ Former first-grade coach ■ Inexpensive membership
Weaknesses	■ Lack of a junior team to feed into seniors ■ Lack of financial resources ■ No full-time administrators (overworked volunteers) ■ Shared council-owned facilities ■ Image as male-dominated, aggressive and dangerous sport
Opportunities	■ Bennetswood Rugby Union/Bennetswood Australian Rules clubs: potential to lure customers away ■ Increasing number of residents in Bennetswood ■ Possible sponsorship deal with local newsagency owned by a member ■ Interest in the development of a women's team ■ New facility being constructed by council
Threats	■ East Bennetswood Touch Rugby Club: social and gaming facilities, image of safe family sport ■ Computer games, television and Internet for junior team ■ Decreasing interest in elite rugby league ■ Dangerous sport—potential lawsuits ■ Seasonal income
(b) FILA sporting apparel	
Strengths	■ High quality and well-tested products ■ Credibility and reputation in Europe ■ Lean management structure ■ Well-recognised logo ■ Well-exposed and influential sponsored athletes
Weaknesses	■ Underexposed and limited brand awareness in Australasia ■ Small market share compared with major competitors ■ Lack of female consumers ■ Limited budget for advertising ■ Expense of products eliminates part of potential market
Opportunities	■ Nike and Adidas are preoccupied with battling each other ■ Upcoming Sydney Olympics may provide marketing opportunities ■ Options for sponsorship of Australasian athletes/teams ■ Possibility of opening retail outlets in Australasia ■ Introduction of quality management program to improve quality of products and decrease costs
Threats	■ Major competitors: Nike and Adidas ■ Economic recession: lack of disposable income to spend on leisurewear ■ Booming surf apparel industry ■ Inexpensive generic copies of FILA products on market ■ Major companies' stranglehold on distribution wholesalers

- Technological changes (e.g. sports science innovation; computer developments; new products; cost of technological sophistication)
- Industry changes (e.g. increase or decrease in competition; cost of entry into the market; market segmentation; market share)

3 Generating strategic options

Once your strategic analysis has been completed, the information should be converted into some possibilities for action. The key to generating *strategic options* is to build on the data acquired thus far. The strength of this strategic planning model is that every step is cumulative. The first step in the *options* process is to list all SWOT factors, with the clear intention of deciding how they might best be tackled. In order to achieve your objectives, strengths must be maximised, weaknesses minimised, opportunities capitalised upon, and threats neutralised. For each SWOT factor, a desired situation should be documented. This is followed by creating options for bridging the 'gap' between the current situation, revealed by the SWOT analysis, and the desired situation. This process is known as a gap analysis and may be helped with the use of a technique called benchmarking. The final steps are to link each option with an objective and then to bring all options for the same objectives together. They can then be evaluated on the basis of their perceived effectiveness. The outcome should be a ranked list of options for each objective.

A: Gap analysis

As implied above, the gap analysis is an examination of the difference between an organisation's present position and some future position expressed in an objective. The gap analysis is a formal way of asking the simple question: 'What options are there in moving from A to B?'

B: Benchmarking

Volumes have been written about benchmarking, a technique that assists in establishing and implementing strategic options. Benchmarking is a systematic and continuous system of improving organisational processes and functions by comparing, studying and measuring other processes and functions that are of a higher quality. Thus to 'benchmark' is to use another level of performance as a direct goal to aim for. In practical terms, this means that one group identifies something specific that another group does particularly well, and sets that level of performance as a benchmark or standard. This benchmark can then be used by the first group to rate its own performance. The methods employed by the other group to attain that benchmark performance should then be studied in the hope that they can be duplicated. Benchmarking is therefore little more than a fancy way of copying someone else's successes.

For example, assume that team A is seeking to improve its recruiting process, as the players it has 'discovered' over the past few years have been of poor quality. Also assume that team B is renowned for its ability to acquire young talented players through its recruiting system. On average it 'discovers' five players per year that ultimately play at the highest level. Because team A wants to emulate this recruiting success, it sets five players as its recruiting benchmark. Upon examination of team B's recruiting process, team A discovers that B uses former players as talent scouts. Team A is then provided with an option to accompany its benchmarked goal, which represents its desired future.

According to benchmarking expert Anne Evans,[22] there are four main types of benchmarking:

- *internal:* using other parts of the same organisation as a standard
- *competitive:* using business competitors as a standard
- *industry:* using general industry levels and systems as a standard
- *process:* using specific processes as a standard, irrespective of their location or industry relevance

Benchmarking can and should be undertaken in any management area, and can be industry specific, or externally generated, with an organisation comparable but superior in the area in question. For example, an opera company may have a highly efficient ticketing system, a carpet cleaning franchise may have a particularly effective customer complaints procedure and a gymnasium may have a successful marketing strategy that are all worth benchmarking. One point to consider is the importance of benchmarking against *comparable* organisations, rather than against the 'best' or substantially superior ones. Research has demonstrated that benchmarking against the 'next best', and subsequently duplicating some of their methods, is a powerful and effective strategic practice, while benchmarking against the world's best is actually counterproductive.[23]

C: Evaluation of alternatives

Evaluating the optional methods of bridging the gap between the existing situation and the benchmarked or desired situation is the next step, although it is often not formalised. Traditionally, this step, which is the strategy selection, has been largely intuitive in the sporting world. Competitor analysis, SWOT, gap analysis and benchmarking make it more systematic. It generates choices that depend upon strengths, weaknesses, opportunities, threats, available resources, risk and feasibility.

The evaluation process is based on the question: 'What are the visionary implications of potential strategies?' For example, if an organisation's objective is to increase profits from $100 000 to $110 000 in one year, it may require one strategy concentrating on decreasing operating expenses, and another strategy that focuses on increasing membership. Similarly, if winning the premiership is the objective, the strategy of recruiting the league's best player may have serious financial implications, as the acquisition may 'blow

Table 3.3 Strategic options

(a) Bennetswood Rugby League Club

SWOT components	Gap analysis			Related objective (performance, participation)
	Current situation (SWOT results)	Desired situation to achieve objective	Options for bridging gap to achieve objective	
Strengths	Successful senior squad	Best team in competition	Become more professional in training	Performance
	Positive and friendly environment	Reputation as the friendly club	Organise social events where friends of members are invited	Participation
	Strong community involvement	Complete community support	Club involvement in community activities	Participation
	Former first-grade coach	Players to capitalise on expertise of coach	Coach given full support by management and members	Performance
	Inexpensive membership	More value for membership	Offer additional services within membership	Participation
Weaknesses	Lack of a junior team to feed into seniors	Plenty of junior players to feed into senior ranks	Introduce a junior development program	Performance
	Lack of financial resources	Adequate income to support training needs	Increase revenue to upgrade training facilities and equipment	Performance
	No full-time administrators (overworked volunteers)	Manageable work load for volunteer committee	Introduce sub-committees to undertake additional work	Participation
	Shared council-owned facilities	Privately owned facilities	Investigate possibility of moving home ground elsewhere	Performance
	Image as male-dominated, aggressive and dangerous sport	Image as gender-neutral and safe sport	Discourage dangerous on-field behaviour by introducing playing standards	Participation
Opportunities	Bennetswood Rugby Union/ Bennetswood Australian Rules clubs: potential to lure customers away	Other clubs' members join Bennetswood	Advertise unique features of club	Participation
	Increasing number of residents in Bennetswood	Membership increased by new residents	Advertise generally in community	Participation

Table 3.3 (cont.)

SWOT components	Gap analysis			Related objective (performance, participation)
	Current situation (SWOT results)	Desired situation to achieve objective	Options for bridging gap to achieve objective	
Opportunities (cont.)	Possible sponsorship deal with local newsagency owned by a member	Obtain sponsorship	Deliver a sponsorship proposal to member.	Performance
	Interest in the development of a women's team	Women's team part of club	Introduce a women's team on a trial basis	Participation
	New facility being constructed by council	Use new facility	Send proposal for use of new facility to council	Performance
Threats	East Bennetswood Touch Rugby Club: social and gaming facilities, image of safe family sport	Bennetswood has gaming and social facilities	Investigate possibility of a gaming licence and licence to sell alcohol	Participation
			Introduce summer touch rugby competition	
	Computer games, television and Internet for junior team	Young members of the community prefer to participate in rugby league	Emphasise heroes and the possibility of playing representative rugby league	Performance
	Decreasing interest in elite rugby league	Strong interest in elite rugby league	Contact closest professional rugby league club to establish more formalised relationship	Participation
	Dangerous sport—potential lawsuits	The potential of lawsuits minimised	Introduce legal policies and procedures	Participation
	Seasonal income	Income generated all year round	Investigate alternative methods of income generation such as merchandise	Performance

Table 3.3 (cont.)

(b) FILA sporting apparel

SWOT components	Gap analysis			Related marketing objective: increase . . .
	Current situation (SWOT results)	Desired situation to achieve objective	Options for bridging gap to achieve objective	
Strengths	High quality and well-tested products	Even higher quality of products	Introduce quality management program	market share
	Credibility and reputation in Europe	Credibility and reputation throughout world	Focus on European reputation and develop an image of cosmopolitan sophistication	market share
	Lean management structure	Even more efficient management structure	Review internal staffing	market share
	Well-recognised logo	Universally recognised logo	Develop an aggressive advertising campaign focusing on logo	market share
	Well-exposed and influential sponsored athletes	Increase share of youth market	Promote sponsored athletes to schools	market share
Weaknesses	Underexposed and limited brand awareness in Australasia	Well-exposed and strong brand awareness in Australasia	Focus on aggressive advertising campaign	market share
	Small market share compared with major competitors	Comparable market share with two major competitors	Win an increased market share with several new product lines	market share
	Lack of female consumers	Significant proportion of female consumers	Introduce more specific lines of products for females	market share
	Limited budget for marketing	Value for money in marketing	Only run high-priced advertising prior to Christmas	market share
	Expense of products eliminates part of potential market	Expense not a factor in eliminating potential customers	Introduce budget-priced product line	market share

Table 3.3 (cont.)

SWOT components	Current situation (SWOT results)	Gap analysis		Related marketing objective: increase . . .
		Desired situation to achieve objective	Options for bridging gap to achieve objective	
Opportunities	Nike and Adidas are preoccupied battling each other	Consumers seek an alternative brand, not fighting	Focus on being above the fight; spend resources promoting, not fighting	market share
	Upcoming Sydney Olympics may provide marketing opportunities	FILA linked with Olympics	Sponsor athletes likely to perform successfully in the Olympics	market share
	Options for sponsorship of Australasian athletes/teams	FILA associated with prominent Australasian athletes/teams	Sponsor high profile Australasian athletes	market share
	Possibility of opening retail outlets in Australasia	Retail outlets distribute FILA products throughout Australasia	Make specific plans to open retail stores	market share
	Introduction of quality management program to improve quality of products and decrease costs	Manufacturing defects reduced, costs reduced	Implement total quality management program	market share
Threats	Major competitors: Nike and Adidas	Major competitors lose ground and have less impact on market	Use a marketing approach which differentiates FILA products from the major competition	market share
	Economic recession: lack of disposable income to spend on leisurewear	Consumers spend disposable income on FILA despite adverse economic climate	Decrease prices during periods of economic depression	market share
	Booming surf apparel industry	Consumers wear FILA products instead of other surf industry products	Introduce FILA line of surfwear	market share
	Inexpensive generic copies of FILA products on market	Copies disappear from market	Take legal action to enforce copyright on imitations	market share
	Major companies' stranglehold on distribution wholesalers	Distribution wholesalers have supplier arrangements with FILA	Approach wholesale distributors to strike deals	market share

the budget'. Thus alternative strategies must be considered with respect to their intra-organisational impact.

The whole process of generating strategic options is summarised in Table 3.3. Note how the process is cumulative and is based on the results of the strategic analysis. For FILA, all options are linked to the marketing objective of increasing market share, which in turn supports the broader organisational objective of profit. For the Bennetswood Rugby League Club, the options support two organisational objectives. You can include as many options for each SWOT result entry as you wish.

The final stage of alternatives evaluation is the construction of a *ranked list of strategic options*. Ranking options is never easy, but you should notice a number of recurring themes, highlighted by a number of options that effectively have the same meaning. Concentrate on these themes and rank highest the options you feel will have the greatest impact upon successful achievement of the objective in question. For the moment, don't waste time ranking beyond the top five (see Table 3.4). Practical limitations such as cost, work involved and likelihood of success are also considerations. Note that because the FILA example focuses specifically on marketing strategies, non-marketing options (while noted for use in other management support area plans) are put aside for the moment.

4 Documenting the strategic plan

A: The cascading plan: strategies, tactics and activities

The hard work has been done. We now have a ranked list of options for achieving each objective, ready to be converted into action. This is achieved through a three-tiered system of strategies, tactics and activities. The system works in the same conceptual fashion as a tree diagram. First, consider each option a potential strategy. For each option a number of tactics will be formulated, and for each tactic, activities will be developed. In this way the implementation process takes care of itself, becoming progressively more detailed as the method evolves, until at the activity level the task to be undertaken is expressed in a simple and action-oriented form. In the case of a large organisation such as FILA, an additional level may be added in the form of a management support area objective. In our FILA example, this is a marketing objective. The relationship between objectives, strategies, tactics and activities is illustrated in Figure 3.2.

Figure 3.2 shows how objectives can be translated into simple menial tasks, which can and should be easily measurable. Therefore, it is important to set a performance measure, a time scale for implementation, a responsible individual or party and an expected cost of the activity. Table 3.5 illustrates a practical method of recording these details.

In contrast to FILA, it would be naive to expect Bennetswood Rugby League Club to produce a detailed plan for every management area. Resources

Table 3.4 Ranking strategic options

(a) Bennetswood Rugby League Club

Objective	Rank	Options summary
Performance (on-field success)	4	**Performance management** Introduce a junior development program
Win competition in season 1999	5 2	Coach given full support by management and members Become more professional in training **Facility management**
	3 2	Investigate possibility of moving home ground elsewhere Send proposal for use of new facility to council **Financial management**
	1	Increase revenue to upgrade training facilities and equipment
Participation (increase membership)	4	**Marketing management** Deliver a sponsorship proposal to member
Increase membership to 500 by end of 1999	1	Offer additional services within membership Advertise unique features of club Advertise generally in community Emphasise heroes and the possibility of playing representative rugby league Investigate alternative methods of income generation such as merchandise
	5	Introduce a women's team on a trial basis Introduce summer touch rugby competition Contact closest professional rugby league club to establish more formalised relationship **Legal management**
	2	Investigate possibility of a gaming licence and a licence to sell alcohol **Human resource management/structure management** Introduce sub-committees to undertake additional work **Event management**
	3	Organise social events where friends of members are invited Club involvement in community activities **Legal management** Introduce legal policies and procedures

Table 3.4 (cont.)

(b) FILA sporting apparel

Objective	Rank	Options summary
Increase market share by 5% by the end of financial year 2000		**Marketing strategies**
	5	Develop an aggressive advertising campaign focusing on logo
		Promote sponsored athletes to schools
	1	Win an increased market share with several new product lines
		Introduce more specific lines of products for females
		Only run high-priced advertising prior to Christmas
		Focus on being above the fight; spend resources promoting not fighting
		Sponsor high profile Australasian athletes
	4	Sponsor athletes likely to perform successfully in the Olympics
		Focus on European reputation and develop an image of cosmopolitan sophistication
	3	Make specific plans to open retail stores
		Develop a marketing approach which differentiates FILA products from the competition
		Decrease prices during periods of economic depression
		Introduce FILA line of surfwear
	2	Approach wholesale distributors to strike deals
		Quality strategies
		Implement total quality management program
		Human resource strategies
		Review internal staffing
		Legal strategies
		Take legal action to enforce copyright on imitations

Figure 3.2 Strategy implementation

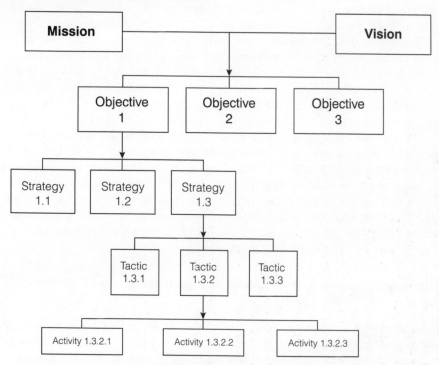

are precious to all sporting clubs and rare in most, and Bennetswood would be no exception. The remedy for these circumstances lies in the ranking of options. Bennetswood should concentrate on creating tactics and activities for only the two highest ranking options. However, just because only one option is translated into a strategy does not mean that all the other options have no use. Several of the other options may perform admirably as tactics or activities.

Table 3.5 Objective A, record of details

Objective A

Strategy	Tactic	Activity	Measure	Time	Responsibility	Cost
A1	A1.1	A1.11	W number	X time	Y responsible	$Z
		A1.12				
		A1.13				
	A1.2	A1.21				
		A1.22				
		A1.23				
	A1.3	A1.31				
		A1.32				
		A1.33				

The concept works exactly the same for FILA. For example, FILA's highest ranked strategy is to introduce new product lines. Other options indicate that opportunities exist in the development of products specifically for females and in surfwear. These two options make excellent tactics to support the introduction of new product lines. Nothing is wasted from the strategic analysis. Incidentally, if you find yourself wondering how to implement a 'technical' management tactic or activity, such as writing a sponsorship proposal, you will find the answer in the relevant chapter of this book. In *this* case it can be found in Chapter 8 on marketing management.

Tactics and activities are unlimited in their potential, confined only by an organisation's capacity for innovation and imagination, a theme central to Gareth Morgan's[24] seminal book *Imaginization*. However, they need not be original to be effective. As Henry Mintzberg[25] pointed out, strategies, tactics and activities are plans for the future as well as patterns from the past. Don't be afraid to reintroduce or bolster old or existing programs just because they are already a strength. Table 3.6 demonstrates how strategic options may be converted into tactics and activities.

B: Strategic responsiveness: matching strategy to the environment and resources

The concept of strategic responsiveness was developed in order to combat two common objections to the employment of detailed and documented planning practices by sporting organisations. The first relates to the paucity of time and resources that can be allocated to planning organisational strategy, while the second concerns the dynamic circumstances that surround the sports marketplace. We will deal briefly with the second objection first: that the sports industry environment is inherently too dynamic to plan around.

It is true that some industries are more susceptible to change than others, and it is true that these turbulent conditions make strategic decision making difficult. The computer industry is perhaps the best example. This book was written on computers that could be outperformed before they were even purchased and, despite the fact that they work adequately, the authors are contemplating upgrading their respective systems for no other reason than to have the 'latest' software games and technological gadgets. However, although the computer industry moves at an alarmingly rapid pace, it remains clear that the companies that prosper within this manic environment are the ones that successfully innovate and envision the needs of consumers in the future. In other words, the faster, more variable and unpredictable the environment, the more comprehensive and more innovative the strategy required. A failure to grasp this basic principle causes the undoing of more sporting organisations than any other single misconception.

In general, the chief reason sporting organisations fail to plan adequately (other than through ignorance and indolence) is because they fear that doing so will lock them into strategies that may become obsolete, irrelevant or

Table 3.6 Strategic (business) plan

(a) Bennetswood Rugby League Club
Objective A: Win competition in season 1999

Strategy	Tactic	Activity	Measure	Time	Cost	Responsibility
Strategy A1: Increase net income						
Option number 1: increase revenue to upgrade training facilities and equipment	Tactic A1.1 Submit sponsorship proposal to owner of newsagency and follow up	*Activity A1.1.1* Proposal written and sent	completed or not	completed by deadline or not	$20 stationery	President
		Activity A1.1.2 Follow up with a phone call	letter sent or not sent/call made or not made	monthly and weekly check	$40	President/ Secretary
	Tactic A1.2	*Activity A1.2.1* *Activity A1.2.2*				
	Tactic A1.3	*Activity A1.3.1* *Activity A1.3.2*				

Table 3.6 (cont.)

(b) FILA sporting apparel
Marketing objective A: Increase market share by 5 per cent over current figure by the end of financial year 2000

Strategy	Tactic	Activity	Measure	Time	Cost	Responsibility
Strategy A1: Introduce new product lines						
Option number 1: Introduce new product lines converts to	*Tactic A1.1* Introduce product line exclusively for females	*Activity A1.1.1* Conduct market research to determine appropriate product styles, price ranges, promotional methods and retail outlets, and consumer segments	By results	Completed by early 1999	$100 000	Outsourced to research company
		Activity A1.1.2 Determine positioning approach for each female market segment and construct marketing mix	Not applicable	Completed by late 1999	No additional costs	Marketing department
	Tactic A1.2	*Activity A1.2.1* *Activity A1.2.2*				
	Tactic A1.3	*Activity A1.3.1* *Activity A1.3.2*				

more difficult to achieve due to sudden environmental changes. For example, the operators of a gymnasium who have embraced the strategy of implementing a quality 'pump' aerobics class may be discouraged to discover that a new fad is sweeping through neighbouring gyms, and that 'pump' is aerobics history. If their response is to abandon the process of strategic planning, lamenting that it is just luck or the whimsical preference of consumers, and to adopt a so called 'flexible' approach, they will inevitably set their own feet in concrete, sentencing themselves to perpetual and expensive re-activity. However, if they instead commit themselves to genuine strategic pro-activity, including sound strategic analysis which will assist in predicting the needs of their marketplace, they will improve their performance significantly. After all, some gymnasiums do successfully and consistently predict fitness 'fads'. Are they lucky—or would benchmarking their processes show they have realised that fitness fads are often imported from the United States and so have adopted strategies to adapt those fads to their domestic market? Irrespective of the specific reason for their superior performance, the point is that success necessitates sound strategy, and sound strategy requires anticipating customer needs, which are highlighted by sensible strategic planning.

Change and flexibility are intrinsic components of the strategic process; they are normal and should be expected. Do not expect to ever write the final draft of a plan, put it on the shelf, and still expect it to work. Plans are working documents, requiring incessant modification and constant re-visioning. They should never be rigid and stuffy, but instead should rely on imagination and innovation.

To be strategically responsive, it is also necessary to adopt a planning framework that matches the resources committed to the plan's implementation. Dealing with the first objection referred to above is easier if we think in terms of models for strategic responsiveness.

As noted earlier, in a perfect world all sporting organisations would develop strategic plans that contained details of intended actions in all management support areas. They would establish objectives, strategies, tactics and activities in each of these areas that supported their broader organisational objectives. Assuming that, say, six management areas were identified, then for each of them three strategies developed, then likewise three tactics, and in turn three activities, the strategic plan would contain 162 activities. Unfortunately, such a comprehensive approach, while commendable, is impracticable in most cases, given the time and resources available. The following models may help overcome this problem.

The 4 × 3 (3 × 3 × 3 × 3) model

Medium-sized organisations with up to three primary organisational objectives should consider a relatively detailed approach, which we have termed the '4 × 3' model. Here, for each of the three objectives, three strategies are

Figure 3.3 The 4 × 3 (3 × 3 × 3 × 3) model

developed; for each strategy, three tactics are formed; and for each tactic, three activities are designed. The plan thus contains 81 activities that are measurable and time-related, with cost and responsibility identified. (See Figure 3.3.)

This pattern is only a general guideline, as organisations can change the specific numbers to suit their own needs. However, it is suggested that, except for the largest organisations, no more than approximately 80–100 activities should be attempted at any one time. Instead, as an activity is completed, it should be replaced with another one instantly, until the tactic it drives is achieved. Similarly, when a tactic is realised it should be replaced immediately, until the strategy it powers is fulfilled. This process continues until strategies need replacement, and objectives require updating. Thus an organisation never finishes a plan: strategies, tactics and activities should be like light bulbs—as soon as one goes out, it should be replaced with another. An organisation should never have to write a new plan; rather, the existing one should be updated by those implementing it on a weekly basis. We have termed this process 'rotation planning', and it eliminates the traditional practice of reviewing plans at selected intervals, instead forcing them into almost daily awareness.

The 1 × 2 × 3 × 4 model

This approach is best used by small profit-seeking organisations that have one *singular* objective, although it can be adapted according to need. In this case, two strategies are developed for the single objective, with three tactics for each of the strategies, and four activities for each tactic, culminating in a manageable total of 24 activities. (See Figure 3.4.)

Figure 3.4 The 1 × 2 × 3 × 4 model

Figure 3.5 The 4 × 2 (2 × 2 × 2 × 2) model

The 4 × 2 (2 × 2 × 2 × 2) model

For the small organisation that has only the services of part-time administrators, but pursues two objectives, we recommend the 4 × 2 model, which produces just 16 activities. This is the approach we would recommend for organisations such as the Bennetswood Rugby League Club. (See Figure 3.5.)

5 Strategic evaluation

Evaluation of a plan's success is the easy part, because, if the other components have been properly constructed, performance measures are tangible and easily identifiable. At a micro level, all activities can be assessed on the basis of whether they have met a standard and been completed on time, at the right cost and by the intended person. The purpose of these micro performance measures is to provide constant feedback concerning action, to indicate when activities need to be replaced. They do not, however, measure the effectiveness of the strategic plan.

The strategic plan is evaluated on the basis of whether an organisation's objectives have been met. Of course, each objective has a built-in measuring device: key performance indicators. When an organisational objective has been achieved, as measured by equalling or exceeding a key performance indicator, then the strategic plan supporting that objective may be considered successful, and should be updated. The process starts again.

STRATEGIC AND VISIONARY THINKING

All good sports administrators think about the future. This looking ahead is usually known as strategic or visionary thinking, and involves the ability to assess the marketplace and the internal and external environment in order to anticipate change and opportunity. In practical terms, managers must be able to constantly anticipate changes while maintaining an understanding of where to take their organisation and how to get there. In some ways it's like a perpetual SWOT analysis. Thus managers must continually attempt to maximise strengths, minimise weaknesses, capitalise on opportunities and neutralise threats.

An organisation's strategic plan is, in fact, only the 'coal face' of the strategic thinking operation. As Gary Hamel[26] explains, planning is about programming, not discovering, and is the domain of the 'technocrat' rather than the dreamer. The more elusive 'soul' of plan making is strategic thinking, where managers apply what they have learned from experience and observation, as well as from market research and quantitative data. According to Henry Mintzberg,[27] strategic thinking is about synthesis, as well as analysis, and involves intuition and creativity. The essence of Mintzberg's comment, from our perspective, is that there are no limitations or boundaries on how options or strategies may be translated into tactics and activities. Sometimes the steps are obvious and easily documented, and other times they are subtle and intuitive. Thinking strategically, therefore, is inseparably linked with creativity because complex and far-reaching problems necessitate innovative and powerful resolutions. Thus the best strategies, tactics and activities are the culmination of both 'hard' analytical skills and the 'soft' improvisation of inventive artistry. Mintzberg captured the creative component of the strategy-making process when he described it in terms of a craft rather than exclusively a rational and systematic process.[28]

Table 3.7 Generating visionary strategies by using strategic problem solving

Technique	Explanation	Practical application
Evolutionary refinement	Strategies developed from evolutionary refinement involve three properties: ■ they must be functional ■ changes and improvements are introduced incrementally ■ complexity develops from the strategy's creation e.g. Writing a procedures manual	■ Develop a strategy by starting with a broad idea that emerges as a result of operational necessity ■ Strategy is subsequently improved gradually and step by step, becoming more detailed and complex over time ■ Strategy develops in a logical, not linear, manner
Formal analogy	A formal analogy aids in retrieving from memory a case that is similar to the one presently faced. It works by using solutions to similar problems from unrelated areas e.g. Building a house and constructing a business process	■ Recognise that few problems are genuinely unique ■ Determine what types of problems have already been solved—may be relevant to components of the current problem
Detective model	The detective model identifies and lists potential 'suspects' in solving a problem and gathers information on each until the solution is determined. It is best used to create strategies to combat puzzling problems or situations e.g. To determine the causes of poor performance in athletes	■ List all possible 'suspects' in causing a problem ■ Gather detailed information on each area ■ Successively eliminate 'suspects' based on facts until one is remaining, and a solution can be traced
Classification	Sorting and distinguishing on the basis of processes, sub-processes and causal factors into component factors e.g. A specific service can incorporate dozens of steps	■ The customer point is that the solution to a problem may require a re-sorting into different classes ■ Decompose problem or process into its constituent parts and solve each separately
Scenarios	A scenario is an ordered sequence of events that either happens in order, or represents a sequence of events toward a goal e.g. Study hard → get a good job → make money	■ Determine the causal linkages of events including the possible consequences resulting from certain strategies ■ Select strategies that are anticipated to result in an ultimately desired outcome
Solution construction	Solution construction represents the difference between where the organisation currently is and where it would like to be e.g. To reach the goal of being a sports administrator, a precondition may include university education	■ Establish the end solution ■ Work backwards to the current position from the goal, and trace the necessary paths and preconditions for success

Table 3.7 (cont.)

Technique	Explanation	Practical application
What if?	In the 'what if?' approach, a standard rule or law of operation is assumed changed, and consequences are traced out e.g. What if we combine soccer with netball?	■ Eliminate traditionally held views or laws concerning operations/functions/processes ■ Trace new solutions to current problems if the 'what if?' is held to be true
Failure analysis	Developing a solution to a problem, product, plan or system on the basis of previous or potential failures e.g. Testing sports shoes for defects	■ Determine the critical failures or pathways for failure ■ Develop specific strategies to combat each individual failure
Cycles and spirals	Using natural business cycles to organise information and anticipate future changes e.g. Using summary financial statements at the end of the financial year	■ Recognise the natural and forced cycles in the organisation ■ Study the cycles and learn to anticipate changes on the basis of natural fluctuations
Transformations	A transformation is a mental construct that converts one type of thing into another type e.g. Transforming an hierarchical organisational structure into a matrix form	■ Recognise where transformations occur ■ Recognise the power of transformations ■ Utilise positive transformations for success, and eliminate or counter negative transformations
Nets and webs	The networks and webs approach provides a useful method of distinguishing relationships within complex systems e.g. Factors that affect sport participation levels can be traced and charted as relationships	■ Establish all the factors that influence a problem, process or system. ■ Chart the relationships between all factors

This craft-like element of strategic thinking is an excuse for some managers to hide behind the facade of the 'commonsense' approach to planning, which in reality is little more than trusting to luck. As management expert Noel McInnes[29] noted, this is business, not gambling, and luck is manufactured through skill, energy, planning and preparation.

There is a wide variety of specific approaches to strategic thinking. Although we don't intend to explore them further here, for the interested reader we have adapted a range of techniques suggested by Craig Loehle in his excellent book *Thinking Strategically*.[30] They are outlined in Table 3.7.

SUMMARY

This chapter described the first core management function of strategic planning. We indicated that all successful planning requires five generic steps. First, a strategic direction is set by documenting a mission and vision statement, and setting specific organisational objectives. These statements and objectives provide focus and motivation for the organisation. Second, a strategic analysis is undertaken to consider the impact of internal organisational competencies and external environmental factors. This is accomplished through SWOT analysis, which identifies existing strengths and weaknesses and potential opportunities and threats, and through competitor analysis, which notes the effect of competing organisations. Third, strategic options are developed by formulating better methods of working (benchmarking), and by pinpointing differences between fulfilled objectives and the present situation (gap analysis) Fourth, the actual strategic plan is documented and actioned by creating strategies, tactics and activities that, when implemented, will culminate in the realisation of organisational objectives. Finally, once the plan has been implemented, outcomes are assessed by determining whether key performance indicators have been achieved. This assessment subsequently feeds back into a review of the strategic direction, and the process continues.

FURTHER READING

Argenti, J. (1992) *Practical Corporate Planning*, Routledge, New York.
Australian Sports Commission (1992) *Planning in Sport*, ASC, Canberra.
Collins, J.C. and Porras, J.I. (1996) 'Building your company's vision' *Harvard Business Review*.
Jones, P. and Kahaner, L. (1995) *Say It and Live It: The 50 Corporate Mission Statements that Hit the Mark*, Doubleday, New York.
Porter, M.E. (1996) 'What is strategy?', *Harvard Business Review*, Nov–Dec.

4 Total quality management

After reading this chapter you should be able to understand the concept of total quality management (TQM) and its application to the delivery of a sports product or service.

More specifically, you should be able to:

- explain the notion of quality and of total quality management
- outline the philosophy, principles and tools of TQM
- devise an organisational strategy for quality service
- employ the tools of process analysis and total quality control (TQC), brainstorming, 'imagineering' and quality circles or teams

WHAT IS QUALITY?

Quality of service has five dimensions:

- consistency
- physical quality
- trust
- reaction
- caring

Consistency of quality refers to the ability of an organisation to deliver services that are dependable and reliable, i.e. that can be expected to be the same, or at least of a comparable quality, every time they are measured. Consistency has become a hallmark of the Hanshin Tigers of Nippon (Japan) professional baseball, who have established rigorous standards for service delivery in areas such as ticketing, merchandise and information.

Physical quality relates to the 'actual' or tangible quality of the service; obviously it is of no benefit having a uniformly poor level of quality unless that is what customers have been promised as part of a 'budget' service. Thus physical quality measures the overt and material physical aspects of the service or the product, like the desirability of facilities, the standard of coaching or umpiring, the condition of equipment or the appearance of personnel. The Sterling brand of ropes, for example, has for sporting rock climbers long been associated with durability and safety, the high physical quality ensuring a prominent market share as well as an impressive level of brand loyalty.

Trust quality refers to the degree of faith customers have in the products or services provided, and includes the ability of an organisation's representatives to convey assurance, confidence and competence to the extent that customers associate reliability and dependability with the organisation. Few teams can rival the entertainment dependability of rugby union's answer to American basketball's 'dream team', the New Zealand All Blacks.

Reaction quality is an organisation's ability to respond to customers' needs and is gauged by promptness and responsiveness. Members belonging to the world's most sought after club, the Marylebone Cricket Club at Lord's, report an unusually strong alignment between their views and the policies of the club. When an organisation reflects its customers' needs, a bond sealed with reaction quality is formed.

Caring quality is the ability of an organisation's employees to foster a sympathetic attitude to their customers via individualised attention and mindfulness of details. Sports clothing and equipment retailers often excel in this aspect of quality service, one example being Fila, which emphasises the importance of personalised and responsive customer service.

TQM: A WAY OF ACHIEVING HIGHER QUALITY

Total quality management is a collection of philosophies, principles and management tools that emphasise product and service *quality* and *delivery*. As all products and services have processes involved in their creation and delivery, TQM revolves around streamlining and continuously improving these processes. The guiding premise on which quality management is based is that developing and maintaining quality is not costly but rather the opposite; quality makes money and saves resources. It centres on doing the job properly the first time, and satisfying customers, while simultaneously fostering a committed and happy workforce. TQM is virtually unchallenged as the most effective method for consistently delivering higher quality products and services.

For TQM to be effective it must become interwoven into the strategic process and implemented uncompromisingly and unreservedly. It is related to every other management area: the delivery of quality services is both a primary function of all sports management operations and a core ingredient in the recipe for long-term success. TQM is particularly appropriate to the special features of sport addressed in Chapter 2, since it combines creativity, passion and rational thinking into 'a coherent and humane way of managing in chaotic times'.[1]

PHILOSOPHY, PRINCIPLES AND TOOLS

Most management literature credits the conception of TQM to W. Edwards Deming and, to a lesser extent, Joseph Juran, acting in response to American General Douglas MacArthur's request for assistance in the revitalisation of the devastated Japanese economy following World War II. Although there is some evidence[2] that the concepts were not entirely new, there is little doubt that the two men's ideas had a profound effect, not only on the performance of Japanese manufacturing industry, but also on management thought and practice throughout the world. However, it wasn't until the 1980s that the philosophies of TQM were widely adopted in Western nations, ironically as a means of competing with a booming Japanese economy that specialised in quality performance driven by *kaizen*, or continuous improvement.[3] Unfortunately, while the concepts of TQM have now become so commonplace that they tend to stimulate a yawn from big business, they have yet to be integrated into the standard practices of sporting organisations.

Sport has reached a crossroads. Products and services in the general commercial sector and even in government are being delivered with an unprecedented level of quality. The adoption of quality management practices in the wider community highlights the fact that sporting services are often substandard. Employees are more productive than ever before, technology is prevalent in even the most rudimentary transactions, and competition for the same discretionary leisure dollar is unparalleled. No longer is close enough good enough. If sporting organisations do not embrace the dogma of TQM with almost a fundamentalist fervour, then over the next decade clubs, leisure centres, recreational services and associations will experience a level of demand to rival Swiss watches in Japan and the Hills Hoist in Hong Kong.

The philosophy of TQM holds that an organisation cannot depend upon a goal at the final 'whistle' if it is to win. Product and service delivery must improve incrementally and constantly, which is achieved through efficient and effective work practices, where the day-to-day operation of the organisation can be improved. In essence, it is a 'work smarter not harder' approach. This notion of continuous improvement is supported by a number of interrelated principles. While originally numbering fourteen in the form of Deming's famous points,[4] these have, over time, been whittled down to six or eight, the precise number depending on the 'expert' proposing them. We will limit our examination of TQM principles to six:

- customer focus
- management leadership
- employee involvement
- organisational culture of quality
- fact-based decision making
- partnerships with suppliers

Figure 4.1 The TQM process

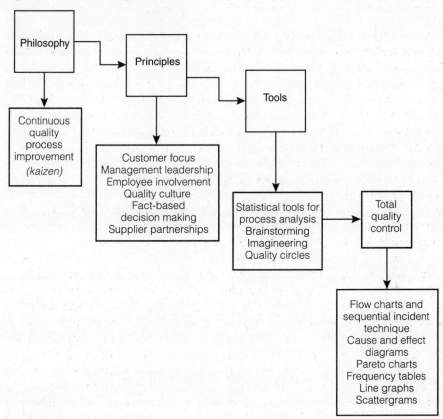

As well, there are a number of TQM tools. Again the range varies, but there are four broad types that tend to be used. They are:

■ statistical tools for process analysis, or total quality control (TQC)
  – flow charts and the sequential incident technique
  – cause-and-effect diagrams
  – Pareto charts
  – frequency tables
  – line graphs
  – scattergrams
■ brainstorming
■ 'imagineering'
■ quality circles or teams

The philosophy, principles and tools of TQM are illustrated in Figure 4.1.

TQM in a service industry

TQM emerged in manufacturing industries and its application to service industries has been slowed by a lack of attention.[5] As a result, it is sometimes difficult to see how certain TQM approaches might apply, particularly when they involve statistical significance and variability. Also, service organisations rarely distribute products with exact specifications, and they have a strong customer presence and rely on a delivery system that provides 'perishable' commodities. However, both manufacturing and service industries can apply the principles of TQM. As Frederick Reichheld and W. Earl Sasser[6] commented, service businesses have their own kind of scrap heap: customers who do not come back. Thus the service equivalent of the popular TQM manufacturing catchcry—'zero defections' (instead of 'zero errors')—is to retain every customer that can be profitably served.

An explanation of the most commonly used tools may help you see how TQM may be applied in everyday management.

THE TOOLS OF TQM

In the discussion to come (later in the chapter) about applying the six essential principles of TQM, we will refer to the tools that can be used in each case. Accordingly, we look at these tools first, beginning with the approach known as process analysis.

Statistical tools, or total quality control (TQC)

Sporting organisations are full of examples of employees who apparently work very hard but ultimately add little or nothing to the value of the services provided to members or customers. It is not uncommon to encounter marketing managers in both profit-seeking sports businesses and non-profit sports associations and clubs who have difficulty generating even the value of their own salaries. Process analysis is about decreasing and eventually eliminating inefficiencies—because only results are paid, not effort. Examples of inefficiency or waste can be found in the form of unnecessary meetings, double-handling of paperwork, lost opportunities, sloppiness and so on. Inefficiencies within the system are reduced through a clear definition of the product or service delivery process, using a simple tool known as process analysis, which establishes priorities and paves the way for continuous improvement. (See Figure 4.2.)

The first step in any analysis is to *understand the process*. Three questions must be answered fully:

■ How does the process presently operate?
■ What is it supposed to accomplish, i.e. how does the result fit into customer needs?
■ What is the best way known at the moment of carrying out the process?

Figure 4.2 Process analysis

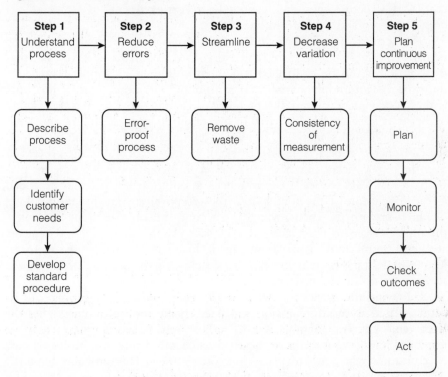

These questions can be resolved by utilising the techniques of TQC, described next, such as flow charts and cause-and-effect diagrams. However, the three questions can be also answered in at least a rudimentary way without the aid of any tools. For example, a ticketing system for a sporting facility may be described as operating between the hours of nine in the morning and five in the afternoon, with two receptionists taking orders and feeding them into a computer. The service itself is obviously relevant to the needs of the facility's customers and may presently operate in an efficient manner. But this is just the beginning.

After the process is described in a step-by-step fashion, it should be clear exactly who works on the process, what material and information goes into it, what skills and knowledge are required, and what happens in between. Identifying customer needs and concerns focuses the organisation on the fact that the purpose of the work is to benefit the customer. Thus, if the process doesn't directly benefit the customer, it should be scrapped altogether; there's no point improving what isn't contributing to the successful accomplishment of organisational objectives. Finally, the development of a standard procedure is the culmination of an intricate understanding of the system, and in standardising the process, it becomes duplicable. Standards are the walls of the TQM structure, but they cannot be constructed until the process has been 'error-proofed' and streamlined.

The second major step involves *eliminating errors*. The simple premise is that everyone makes mistakes and every system contains mistakes, but that these mistakes can be controlled and often prevented by simple changes to the process, commonly termed 'error-proofing'. In other words, not only is the process made more efficient but it is changed so that mistakes *cannot* occur, or at least are less likely to. In our ticketing example, the receptionists may point out that sometimes, through a typing error or a misunderstanding, the customer is allocated incorrect tickets. In this second step the process of over-the-phone ticket purchase may be reconsidered so that errors are prevented or at least reduced. For instance, an additional step could be added at the conclusion of the transaction: the receptionist confirms the booking or purchase with the client, which is a simple and obvious step. But unless the time is taken to chart the process, these plainly apparent improvements are never introduced. There is no magic involved in quality management, just an understanding that the existing systems for the delivery of goods and services are not necessarily the 'best'.

Following the extrication of errors, a *streamlining* of the process can be contemplated as the third major step. Here processes are tightened and the slack removed. For example, consider how our ticketing system may be improved by allowing recorded messages to be left during non-business hours by customers who wish to place their orders then. This probably wouldn't be a large process improvement, but may add value to the existing service in a small, bite-sized step: the heart of *kaizen*.

The fourth major step involves the reduction of *variation*. Here accuracy and consistency of performance measurement are vital. In our ticketing example, if a customer calls on one day to order a ticket and waits on hold for ten seconds, then on the following day waits two minutes, and then two weeks later gets through immediately, there is considerable variation in the consistency of the service. However, the only way this variability can be reduced is to have accurate data concerning the date, time and duration that customers are put on hold. Once this data has been collected, it can be reproduced in the form of a Pareto chart or a scattergram (these tools are explained below). This data should indicate the primary causes of customer waiting (e.g. a shortage of reception staff during lunch hours) as well as highlighting any relationships such as a positive correlation between the number of calls received and the proximity of a major event.

Finally, in step 5, to complete the cycle, continuous improvement must be planned. Here the process outcomes are monitored with a view to adopting tactics and activities that emphasise quality management and continuous improvement. In practical terms, the manager responsible for ticketing may review, with the help of his or her reception staff, one basic process a week: a commitment of probably no more than fifteen minutes.

In addition, the manager may request the reception staff to collect specific information for consideration on following weeks.

Flow charts

At the heart of TQM is the continuous improvement of processes and, since all services have a delivery system, sporting organisations are full of processes that can be streamlined to enhance quality. However, it is first necessary to understand and map every specific component, which is most easily and accurately achieved by using a chart. This is a diagram that shows the documentation, analysis and evaluation of a system, and it is effective because it makes functional relationships clear. Although not strictly necessary, there are a number of useful symbols that can be used in constructing a chart (see Figure 4.3).

John McConnell,[7] in his excellent book on total quality control, cautioned that it is unwise for one person to prepare a chart in isolation, as it is rare for one individual to fully understand an entire process. In addition, every employee takes a different perspective depending on their role in the process, which means that they each would very likely construct a different chart for the same system. For example, a retail salesperson in a sports shop may have a different perception of the process of selling a tennis racquet than the marketing manager who designed the pricing and promotional strategy for that racquet.

Keeping in mind that the whole point of flow-charting is to understand processes better so that they may be improved, each step in a process should be analysed by the people involved in it. According to McConnell, the question 'How effective and efficient is this process?' needs to be asked at every step. Specifically, questions should include:

Figure 4.3 Conventional flow chart symbols

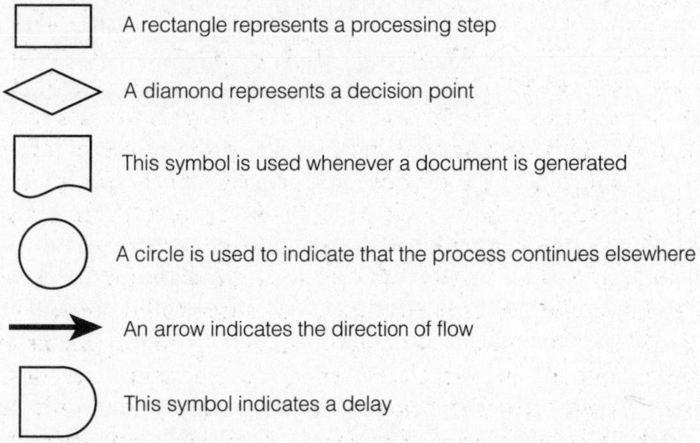

A rectangle represents a processing step

A diamond represents a decision point

This symbol is used whenever a document is generated

A circle is used to indicate that the process continues elsewhere

An arrow indicates the direction of flow

This symbol indicates a delay

Figure 4.4 Flow chart: process for new members to join a gymnasium facility

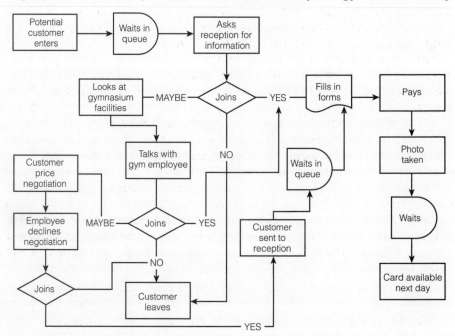

- What kinds of things go wrong?
- How often?
- What are the causes?
- What are the problems that occasionally occur?
- How much time is spent fixing problems that occasionally occur?

An example of a chart for the delivery of a leisure service appears in Figure 4.4.

This relatively simple chart illustrates a process that is rarely considered in leisure facilities—how potential customers become members—but is elementary for successful customer service. Flow charts are effective in reducing service inefficiencies and variability, and remain a core tool of process analysis and *kaizen*.

Sequential incident technique

Another form of process analysis and mapping is known as the sequential incident technique (SIT), which evolved as a marketing tool in order to capture customer opinions concerning service delivery.[8] Although used primarily as a market research method, the SIT is nonetheless a process-driven activity.

Traditionally, customer responses to delivery effectiveness are measured using an 'attribute'-based approach. That is, customers will rate specific service functions like the knowledge of a guide, friendliness of an usher or the efficiency of a catering service. In contrast, the SIT takes an 'incident'-based approach, where customers are asked to identify favourable and unfavourable 'experiences'. With this method, service processes are divided into discrete events or episodes, which comprise a cluster of experiences or incidents. These episodes and incidents are compiled to produce a service map and customer path, which are represented in the form of a flow chart.

The most significant difference between the standard flow chart process analysis and the SIT centres on how the information is gathered. The data used to form flow charts are obtained from those delivering the service, while the data used to compile SIT maps are obtained from those receiving the service. This is why the SIT can be so useful for market research. Thus participants, visitors, spectators, audiences, fans or spectators are selected as informants and are guided along the customer path, retelling the episodes or incidents that were positive or negative. For example, for a spectator attending the Australian Open Tennis Championships, the following episodes may have been mapped:

- travel from home to venue (positive—arrived on time, train not overcrowded)
- arrival and move to venue (negative—no signs, went to the wrong gate)
- entry point (neutral—waited, but only for a few minutes)
- admission (positive—price represented good value and ticketing operator was efficient)
- purchase of program and contact with usher (positive and negative—usher polite, but program expensive)
- movement to courts and seats (neutral—crowded, but moving quickly)
- seating and viewing (positive—comfortable seat, with excellent view of court)
- game quality (positive—overall, entertaining)
- movement around venue (positive—easy access to toilets)
- food and drink (negative—poor selection and expensive)
- exit (negative—crowded and slow)
- return home (positive—trains running regularly)

These negative and positive incidents are tabulated, and frequently cited episodes are highlighted. However, charts and the SIT only identify problem areas, they do not solve them. Cause-and-effect diagrams can take the diagnosis and eventual 'treatment' one step further.

Cause-and-effect diagrams

Cause-and-effect (or fishbone or Ishikawa) diagrams were developed by Japanese TQM guru Kaoru Ishikawa[9] in 1943, and since have become a standard TQC tool. Like flow charts, cause-and-effect diagrams can

Figure 4.5 Cause-and-effect diagram: gymnasium facility

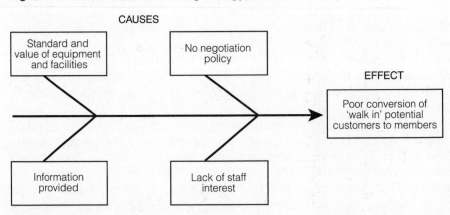

be underrated or overlooked because of their simplicity, but are useful for identifying the causes of variation or lapses in consistency or quality, and are best used to build on the information obtained from flow chart analysis.

For example, to continue the theme generated from the earlier flow chart, the operators of a leisure facility may contemplate why their conversion of 'walk in' potential customers to members is poor. In this case, this is the *effect* that they wish to examine. Based on the flow-charted process only, their next step is to establish possible causes. Their cause-and-effect diagram may look like Figure 4.5.

The next step in the analysis is to rank the perceived contribution of each of the 'causes' to the 'effect'. For example, if the people involved in the delivery of the process report that potential members want to feel as if they have 'earned' themselves a special deal via negotiation, then it may prove profitable to give them exactly that. In practical terms, that may translate into giving the gym staff the authority to negotiate a customer service arrangement, and perhaps even to make it a standard policy. In other words, sometimes when potential members enter the gym, the gym staff could offer them an 'on-the-spot' special discount of 10 or 15 per cent if they join immediately. Or better still, they may obtain a 20 per cent discount if they bring along a second person to join within twenty-four hours, with both parties to receive the discount. This simple remedy may make more impact than a costly equipment renovation. The key is to determine what are the most important causes of problems; this can be achieved through the development of a Pareto chart.

Pareto charts

'Pareto charts' are a fancy name for standard bar charts. They are a tool used to indicate where a problem should be most effectively attacked. They are

Figure 4.6 Pareto chart: causes of complaints in the 'Strikers' Soccer Club

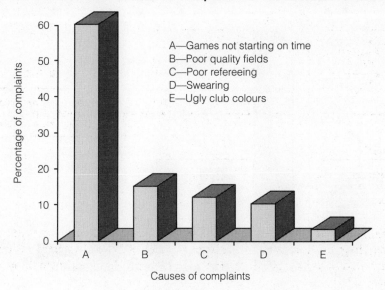

A—Games not starting on time
B—Poor quality fields
C—Poor refereeing
D—Swearing
E—Ugly club colours

Percentage of complaints

Causes of complaints

named after an eighteenth century Italian scholar, whose 'Pareto principle' noted that 80 per cent of the wealth in Europe was held by 20 per cent of the people. The term was popularised by Joseph Juran who suggested that approximately 80 per cent of managers' time is spent on 20 per cent of the range of work, and that 80 per cent of problems are caused by 20 per cent of the causes.[10] The purpose of applying the Pareto principle is therefore to distinguish pivotal problem areas from trivial ones, so that resources can be allocated accordingly. An example of a Pareto chart is given in Figue 4.6.

Figure 4.6 illustrates the causes of complaints within a local soccer club. It clearly demonstrates that the primary cause of customer dissatisfaction is 'games not starting on time'. It thereby indicates which area requires the most urgent attention. Like all TQC tools it won't fix the problem for you, but it can ensure that resources are put to best use by locating the heart of the problem.

In a slightly different application of a Pareto chart, assume that a State sporting organisation is struggling with cash flow due to an abundance of overdue memberships. Without the benefit of a Pareto chart, most organisations would probably pursue the payments that were the longest overdue. A logical approach, but absolutely disastrous. If they were to chart the number of outstanding membership payments in dollar terms, they would probably discover that the majority of outstanding accounts are in fact the least overdue, and resources should be channelled accordingly. (See Figure 4.7.)

Figure 4.7 Pareto chart: overdue membership payments by dollar value and time

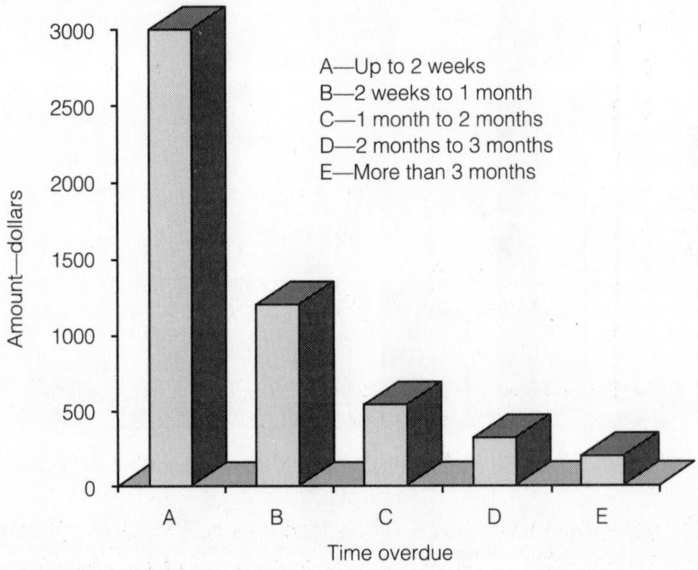
3000
2500
2000
1500
1000
500
0
Amount—dollars
A—Up to 2 weeks
B—2 weeks to 1 month
C—1 month to 2 months
D—2 months to 3 months
E—More than 3 months
A
B
C
D
E
Time overdue

Frequency tables

Frequency tables, also known as check or run sheets, are used to chart the frequency of certain processes, practices or occurrences. They are simple to construct and easy to understand, but it is important to ensure that they *help* employees to give service, and don't confine them to some rigid schedule. Keeping the customers delighted by always maintaining an appropriate level of cleanliness, for example, is a better employee responsibility than meeting the requirements of a prosaic chart of cleaning operations. Remember, delivering quality service should always remain the focal point with all administrative 'tools'.

Line graphs

Line graphs are the easiest and most common of all TQC tools and are used to highlight the relationship of two series of data. They are especially useful in establishing trends and can instantly show up fluctuations. An example is a graph plotting player participation rates over time.

Scattergrams

A scattergram or correlation chart is used when attempting to establish a direct link between two variables. For example, you may want to know the relationship between the weather and the number of people that play golf on Sunday mornings at a particular public course. If you have collected data

Figure 4.8 Scattergram: market research correlation

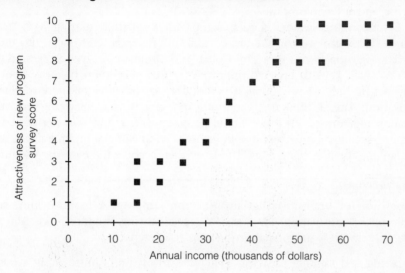

on, say, the air temperature and on the green fees received, then a scattergram will help you establish whether there is a relationship between weather conditions and the number of people attending. Similarly, Figure 4.8 illustrates the relationship between the attractiveness of a potential new service (e.g. a yachting marina) and the incomes of potential customers. In this *hypothetical* situation, data have been collected via market research in order to establish whether the new service is likely to appeal to a specific segment of the community, using income as an indicator. As can be seen by the positive gradient (slope or angle of the line), there is a positive relationship between income and interest in the service. In practical terms this means that the organisation should concentrate its resources on marketing the new service to higher income earners and not advertise in media directed at low income earners, such as certain magazines or television programs.

Other tools

Brainstorming

The tools examined thus far focus on problem identification. Brainstorming, imagineering and quality circles are, in contrast, more about problem solving.

Like many TQM and TQC concepts, brainstorming—a meeting of people in which ideas or solutions are freely floated—isn't new but is an old approach used in a 'new' context. Since TQM is about continuous improvement, tools for generating ideas are essential and brainstorming is one such (underappreciated) tool. However, brainstorming is often misunderstood and misused, commonly mistaken for an 'all-in verbal interchange' that is loose and informal, whereas in reality it is a formal and structured process with specific and inflexible rules.

Brainstorming sessions should begin with a question starting with 'how', such as 'How can we convert more "walk in" potential customers into members?', and go on from there. Phil Cohen and Onno van Ewyk[11] suggested that the two main keys to brainstorming are (i) free generation of ideas from all participants, and (ii) no appraisal or criticism of other people's ideas. Speed, innovation, lateral thinking, variation, spontaneity and quantity are other common ingredients. All ideas should be documented, and *following* the brainstorming session all members should be involved in eliminating impractical ideas and ranking the remaining ones. The latter then become the basis for a solution.

Imagineering

A variation of brainstorming, imagineering employs a brainstorming-style environment, comparing new ideas with the existing situation. According to John Blakemore,[12] imagineering involves four steps:

- listing and ranking ideas (as generated from the brainstorming session)
- analysing the actual situation
- noting the differences
- ranking the differences

Thus, once some ideas have been listed and ranked as a result of a brainstorming session, they are compared with the existing situation. A form of gap analysis (see Chapter 3) is completed, with the differences between the ideas and reality recorded. Of course, imagineering doesn't necessarily need to be preceded by brainstorming. For example, a flow chart may immediately highlight weaknesses and inefficiencies in a process, thus providing the catalyst for a new imagineered flow chart that illustrates how the process would look if it was running perfectly. As a result, the differences between the imagineered process and the actual process can be analysed and ranked, providing a central focus for problem solving.

For instance, consider the following imagineered steps in a 'perfect' player recruiting system:

- player identified as a junior by talent scout
- observation and recording of player performance
- player meets predetermined statistical standard of performance
- talent scout observes player and confirms talent
- talent scout approaches player
- player invited to train with team coach on trial
- player recruited, or player rejected and continues to be observed

However, the reality of the situation may typically proceed as follows:

- player identified as a junior by talent scout
- observation of player intermittent and inconsistent; no firm data recorded

- talent scout observes player and is convinced of 'winning' talent
- player approached by talent scout
- player invited to train with team coach on trial
- player recruited, or player rejected and ignored (possibly recruited by competition)

Even though this example would benefit from a flow chart representation, the difference between the 'perfect' recruiting system and the actual system can be clearly observed, even in point form.

The next task is to rank the areas in which the 'actual' sequence does not match the 'desired' sequence. Thus, in our example, we have:

- lack of independent and consistent data collection
- lack of observation of the player after initial rejection

These points represent problem-solving possibilities, which are explored in the final stage of the exercise.

Quality circles or teams

Teamwork is another essential ingredient in TQM. It has been popularised in the form of quality circles, a staff participation system that is designed to improve service delivery systems by bringing employees involved in the same work processes together in a formal but innovative way. Donald Dewar[13] defined a quality circle as a small group of people who voluntarily meet to identify, analyse and solve quality problems in their work area and then implement and monitor solutions, by applying TQM continuous improvement principles and total quality control techniques. In other words, quality circles harness the power of groups of people, rather than relying on management or individual employees exclusively. The dynamics of teamwork are complex and demanding[14] and are not discussed in detail here. However, Dewar's concept of how quality circles operate is flow-charted in Figure 4.9.

In a practical example, a suburban netball club may form a quality circle to combat a problem of decreasing player participation. In this case, the base data from the club president (posing as a specialist or expert) may simply show declining membership numbers. Other members of the circle, such as the team captain, club secretary, membership manager etc., may specify potential causes of the problem, like increased compulsory local school sport or an increase in the popularity of other leisure activities. These problems are discussed, solutions brainstormed, improved methods imagineered, and recommendations made to the club management committee, which ultimately reviews the recommendations and makes policy decisions.

Figure 4.9 Quality circle operation

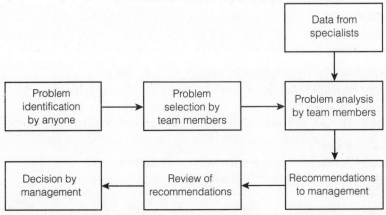

A STRATEGY FOR QUALITY SERVICE

We turn now to the application of the six essential principles of TQM, in the form of a strategy for quality service. The strategy involves the use of a variety of tactics and activities, along with appropriate tools. The tactics and activities suggested are not exhaustive, nor are they necessarily in a form useful for direct duplication in any particular organisation. The purpose is simply to demonstrate how to use TQM techniques in a practical way; so don't get too caught up in the specifics, just note how the ideas can be applied.

Customer focus

As a starting point, suppose that the core of our strategy is to deliver quality service on every occasion. Our 'standout' TQM principle is to take a *customer focus*.

An organisation must always recognise and understand the needs of its customers, and these needs must be reflected accurately in the specification and delivery of services. First, before anything can be undertaken, the customers must be defined (see Chapter 8); second, their needs must be determined; and third, services must be changed, modified or enhanced to suit those needs. Although this last point may sound like a 'selling' approach in which administrators design various persuasive techniques to push services on to different customer segments, quality management is not about manipulating the customers to suit the service but about changing the service itself to suit the customer.

We list below a variety of tactics and activities, some of which have been adapted from an excellent book, *Quality Customer Service*, by William

Martin.[15] Remember that activities should be timed, measurable and cost-based, and there should be an indication of who is responsible for their implementation.

POSSIBLE TACTIC
Generate and project an appropriate and professional image and attitude.

Possible activity (1)
Ensure that all staff maintain a professional appearance (e.g. hair, clothes).

Suggested tools:
■ generate standard—quality circles
■ new ideas—brainstorming, imagineering

Possible activity (2)
Establish standards of body language for dealing with customers (e.g. smiling and eye contact).

Suggested tools:
■ generate standard—quality circles
■ new ideas—brainstorming, imagineering

POSSIBLE TACTIC
Determine and anticipate the needs of customers.

Possible activity (1)
Conduct rigorous market research on the services customers require.

Suggested tools:
■ data gathering—frequency tables (also refer to Chapter 8 on marketing and market research)
■ process analysis—flow charts, SIT, cause-and-effect diagrams
■ data synthesis—Pareto charts, line graphs, scattergrams.

Possible activity (2)
Conduct rigorous market research on what customers expect from services offered, for example:
   – how they feel understood
   – how they feel welcome
   – how they feel important
   – how they feel comfortable

Suggested tools:
■ data gathering—frequency tables (also refer to Chapter 8)
■ process analysis—flow charts, cause-and-effect diagrams
■ data synthesis—Pareto charts, line graphs, scattergrams.

POSSIBLE TACTIC
Meet customer needs on the basis of results from market research.

Possible activity (1)
Establish time standards for dealing with customers:

- customer to be greeted in . . . time
- initial membership paperwork to be completed in . . . time
- follow-up paperwork to be completed in . . . time
- information requests to be handled in . . . time
- telephone to be answered in . . . rings
- customers to be notified of delays in . . . time

Suggested tools:
■ data collection—market research, frequency tables
■ process analysis—flow charts, cause-and-effect diagrams
■ data synthesis—Pareto charts, line graphs, scattergrams;
■ standards generation—quality circles
■ new ideas—brainstorming, imagineering

Possible activity (2)
Introduce standard procedures and statements for dealing with customers in every situation:
- standard telephone answering procedure
- standard 'over the counter' sales and information delivery procedure
- standard voice tone and loudness
- standard customer complaints procedure
- standard contingency plans for equipment failure, staff illness, fire, theft etc.

Suggested tools:
■ data collection—market research, frequency tables
■ process analysis—flow charts, cause-and-effect diagrams
■ data synthesis—Pareto charts, line graphs, scattergrams
■ standards generation—quality circles
■ new ideas—brainstorming, imagineering

Management leadership

Our second principle is to ensure active *management leadership*. According to TQM architect W. Edwards Deming,[16] having a TQM program driven by the top management is essential for its success. As well as the chiefs' active interest and participation, as Joseph Jablonski[17] pointed out, their preparedness to commit the organisation's resources is fundamentally important. Roy Fox[18] identified the top management role in TQM as being essentially a fourfold one:

■ developing a vision for the future
■ setting specific quality goals
■ establishing the budget for quality
■ providing leadership

Since the first two points were dealt with at length earlier, we concentrate here on the second two.

POSSIBLE TACTIC
Establish a specific budget for implementing and maintaining TQM.

Possible activity
Determine how much a quality service is worth to the organisation (how much it will save or make within a specific period, e.g. the financial year). Consider:
- – cost of failure (repeating the same service when not done right)
- – administration costs of market research already done
- – preventative costs (in total approximately 10–30% of turnover[19])

Keep in mind the degree of quality already existing in your organisation, and the fact that implementing a quality program is costly early in the piece and pays off later.

Suggested tools:
- ■ imagineering (conduct a gap analysis)
- ■ set quality budget at a percentage (e.g. 50%) of the amount that quality will make or save the organisation.

POSSIBLE TACTIC
Management to 'lead from the front' in establishing quality in organisation.

Possible activity
Construct and lead quality circles.
Provide constancy of purpose and consistency of decisions by:
- – motivating staff;
- – directing and delegating
- – providing training on quality
- – counselling and listening to staff

Employee involvement

Our third principle is to ensure *employee involvement* by continually consulting the people at the 'coal face'. It is essential for all employees to be involved in the quality management process for two reasons. First, no administrator or manager can possibly have a complete understanding of all processes, and employees can provide valuable information concerning quality improvements. Second, involvement in the decision-making process is intrinsic to job satisfaction, making employees happier.

Sporting organisations attract many committed and knowledgable employees, particularly considering the number of volunteers who dedicate their valuable time. The key then is to harness employees' energy, enthusiasm and expertise by managing them intelligently. As Myron Tribus[20] argued, real employee involvement requires a redefinition of the manager's job: employees work in a system, and the job of the manager should be to manage the system with the help of the employees—*not* manage the employees with the help of the system. This fits well with what has become known as the 'Juran rule', after Joseph Juran, and is an offshoot of the Pareto principle. It states that, whenever there is a problem, 80 per cent of the time the cause will be the system and 20 per cent of the time it will be the employee. In other words, employees generally have their hands tied by the system, unless managers are able to improve it, and improving the *system* is what TQM is all about. Thus the process of employee involvement should be focused on using employees (and voluntary workers) to help managers improve the system.

POSSIBLE TACTIC
Set and document operational standards as determined by the employees who work in the system.

Possible activity (1)
Employees set procedures to control, design, review and verify the processes involved with service delivery.
Employees set procedures for identification and evaluation of service delivery problems.
All operational standards are documented by employees in the form of a quality manual.

Suggested tools:
■ data collection—market research, frequency tables
■ process analysis—flow charts, cause-and-effect diagrams
■ data synthesis—Pareto charts, line graphs, scattergrams
■ standards generation—quality circles and teams
■ new ideas—brainstorming, imagineering

POSSIBLE TACTIC
Give employees authority to change processes as well as responsibility for them.

Possible activity (1)
Employees are not required to obtain approval to change processes in which they are involved.
Employees are considered experts on their specific areas and are trusted to employ the 'best practice' approach as determined by their own expertise.
In relevant areas, employees are provided with budgets and are trusted to use it without approval or supervision, and are also provided with consultation, guidance and support as required.
Employees are encouraged to become involved in the management and change of their own workplaces.

Possible activity (2)
Employee teams to analyse and discuss working conditions and recommend improvements.

Suggested tools:
■ employee teams
■ brainstorming
■ imagineering

> Eliminate individual performance measures. Judge performance on a team basis, by the achievement of organisational objectives.
> Use quality circles and other employee teams to construct the parts of the business plan that they will implement.
>
> *Possible activity (3)*
> Allow employees in work teams to set the strategies, tactics, activities and performance measures that they will have to implement.
>
> Suggested tools:
> ■ employee teams
> ■ brainstorming
> ■ imagineering

Organisational culture of quality

Our fourth principle is to generate a climate of 'quality service' throughout the organisation. Managing *organisational culture* is so important that we dedicate the next chapter to it. An organisation's culture is the set of values, beliefs and behaviours that form its personality and identity, and distinguish it from others. Many companies and businesses, including sporting organisations, have a history of excessive rigidity and hierarchical relationships, often manifested in the form of dangerous mistrust between management and 'labour'. However, establishing an open culture of quality is becoming more widely accepted as a necessity. Such a culture is the culmination of a successful quality management strategy, and means that all members of the organisation accept the importance of quality service.

The United States General Accounting Office,[21] which was commissioned to study the common features of high performing companies that had incorporated TQM systems, reported four elements of a culture conducive to quality management:

■ widespread information sharing
■ few formal barriers between employees
■ a spirit of innovation
■ a high level of employee satisfaction

The following tactics and activities may be utilised to create a quality sporting culture.

> POSSIBLE TACTIC
> Deploy all organisational information to employees.
>
> *Possible activity*
> Share all organisational performance data with employees; for example, financial data and membership/participation figures.

Share the results of market research and customer-focused studies with employees.

Share results of employee surveys.

Share information concerning remuneration of all staff, including top management. No secrets!

POSSIBLE TACTIC
Eliminate as many formal and informal barriers as possible.

Possible activity (1)
Remove management or chief executive 'perks' like parking spaces, expensive offices and furniture. What's good for the employees should be good for the boss.

Organise quality circles and work teams, to be arranged according to processes; that is, teams should be cross-functional and focused on solving problems.

Change the physical work environment as much as possible to reflect openness and flexibility. Keep office doors open and avoid segregating organisational members.

POSSIBLE TACTIC
Build a spirit of innovation into the work environment.

Possible activity
Recognise suggestions for quality improvements.

Support team and individual efforts to improve quality by bolstering partially developed ideas with financial and technical resources.

Allow employees and groups time away from 'normal' duties to develop and consider new opportunities and ideas.

POSSIBLE TACTIC
Focus on improving morale.

Possible activity
Publicly associate quality improvements with the effort and skill of employees.

Survey employees' morale levels and discuss the results in quality circles and teams.

Chief executive and/or top managers to concentrate on improving the system, not the people.

Fact-based decision making

Our fifth principle is to make *decisions based on facts*, with no more 'guesstimates'. One of the interwoven principles of TQM is that hard evidence should be used instead of tradition, instinct, 'commonsense' or the way that competing organisations do something. Because the concept of TQM is based on continuous improvement, or *kaizen*, it is necessary to embrace a systematic procedure to constantly measure and evaluate the quality of existing processes and to make changes when appropriate.

POSSIBLE TACTIC
Make no decisions about customer service systems without facts generated from actual performance.

Possible activity
Monitor variations in customer service on the basis of data such as complaints and customer satisfaction surveys.
Use TQC tools to highlight problem areas.

Suggested tools:
■ charts, cause-and-effect diagrams, Pareto charts, frequency tables, line graphs, scattergrams

Partnerships with suppliers

Our sixth principle is to make *suppliers our partners*. Manufacturing industries have typically established minimum specifications and selected their suppliers on the basis of the lowest price. However, the TQM approach to suppliers is not to award business based on price but rather to form closer, long-term partnerships based on high quality standards. In the TQM case, cheaper is rarely better.

A similar approach can be applied in service industries which, although not manufacturing a physical product, do require 'material' supplies. For example, the Victorian Baseball Association faced a difficulty with the variability of competition baseballs. Some clubs, whose strengths included power hitting, used harder balls at their home games, because they could be hit further than softer balls. On the other hand, clubs whose primary strength was pitching would use soft balls at home games to their advantage. The result was inconsistent quality of performance and an unfair advantage for the home team, which could decide which type of ball to use. By establishing a standard quality of ball, and forming what TQM advocates would describe as a 'supplier partnership' with a suitable manufacturer, the Association found a compromise between the two extremes, thereby ensuring a standard and fair competitive environment for their customers, the clubs and players.

A second view of customers, involving an internal dimension, is also promoted by TQM theory. The concept of the 'internal customer' holds that even if a particular employee does not deal directly with a paying customer, he or she provides a service to someone who does. Furthermore, there are numerous levels of customers, and although some are 'hidden' or distant, they must all be recognised.

A useful tool for highlighting customer/supplier relationships is a customer/supplier map, which is nothing more complex than a flow chart describing the process of delivering a service within a consumer 'hierarchy'. Figure 4.10 provides an example.

Here are some specific tactics and activities by which the strategic aim of meeting different customer expectations can be met.

Figure 4.10 Customer/supplier map: Australian Football League

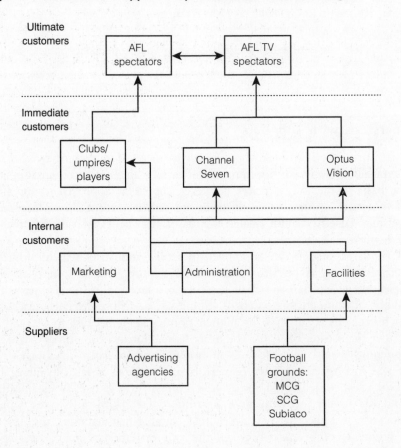

POSSIBLE TACTIC
Establish formal and documented supplier standards.

Possible activity
Allow the employees who deal with the supplied products or services to determine the exact standards required.
Approach suppliers with exact standards. Negotiate on quality first, then price.

Suggested tools:
- quality circles and teams
- brainstorming
- imagineering

POSSIBLE TACTIC
Ensure that suppliers are aware of how their products or services are being employed.

Possible activity
Invite suppliers to participate in quality circles to discuss how they might provide a more appropriate service or product.
Invite suppliers to review or experience the services provided by the organisation, so that they may better understand what their products are used for and also make suggestions on more effective use.

TQM IN ACTION: AN EXAMPLE

This example demonstrates how TQM can be used to solve a customer problem in a leisure services organisation where the reception service is not working properly.[22]

The overall objective is to build the customer base by 15 per cent by the beginning of the 2000 financial year. In this case the objective is supported by one strategy, which is to deliver quality service on every occasion. The strategy in turn is pursued through one tactic, which is to meet customers' needs on the basis of evidence obtained from market research (fact-based decision making).

The market research shows that 80 per cent of customers become irritated when they have to wait on the phone longer than thirty seconds, and 20 per cent hang up.

It is decided to focus on one activity:

introduce standard procedures to reduce the number of customers waiting on the phone (for more than thirty seconds) by 50 per cent by 1 September 1999 (three months away).

STEP 1
Question: Why are customers waiting longer than 30 seconds?
Form a quality circle of all people involved in answering the phone; brainstorm the possible causes of delays.

Action: Use a cause-and-effect diagram to illustrate the results (see Figure 4.11).

Figure 4.11 Cause-and-effect diagram: 'Why customers have to wait longer than 30 seconds on the phone

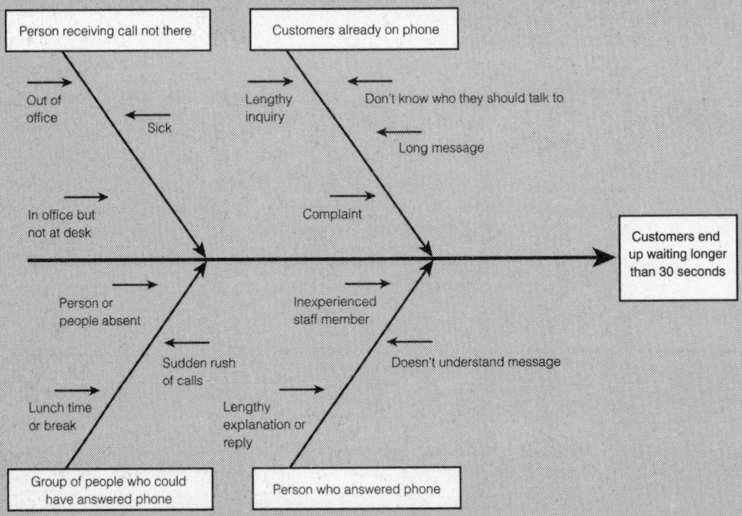

STEP 2

In, say, the first two weeks of July, collect data to determine the relative importance of each possible cause identified by the quality circle.

Action: Use a frequency table to collect data (see Table 4.1).

Table 4.1 Frequency table: 'Why customers have to wait longer than 30 seconds'

July	A	B	C	D	E	F	G	H	I	J	K	L	M
1	IIII	I	II	I			I	I	II	₩		I	
2	II	II	I				II		II	₩ I			
3	IIII	I	I	I	I				III	IIII			
4	III		I	I					I	₩ II	I		
5	₩ I	I		II			II			₩			
6	II		II						II	₩ II			
7	₩		I				I		I	₩			
8	III		II					I		₩			
9	₩ II	I	I							IIII			
10	IIII		II				I			IIII			I
11	II		I			I			II	II			I
12	III	II	I	I				I		₩ I		I	I
13	II		I						I	III			I
14	I		I	I			III			₩ II			
TOTAL	48	8	17	6	2	1	10	3	14	70	1	2	4

Note: Causes are recorded in tally form; data for two weeks prior to the intervention.

Key: A   Out of office
          B   Sick
          C   In office but not at desk
          D   Lengthy inquiry
          E   Don't know who they should talk to
          F   Long message
          G   Complaint
          H   Person or people absent
          I   Sudden rush of calls
          J   Lunch break
          K   Inexperienced staff member
          L   Doesn't understand message
          M Lengthy explanation or reply

STEP 3

Display the data using a Pareto chart (see Figure 4.12).

Figure 4.12 Pareto chart: 'Why customers have to wait longer than 30 seconds'

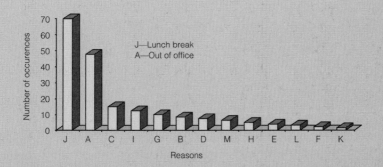

STEP 4

Bring the quality circles together again.

Action: Brainstorm and imagineer solutions for the two major problems indicated: lunch breaks; and receiving party being out of the office.

STEP 5

Implement the solutions revealed by brainstorming and imagineering; for example:

■   rotate lunch breaks so that only one person is off at one time;
■   reduce lunch break from one hour to 30 minutes, to be compensated

for by either another 30 minute break or two 15 minute breaks during the day

■ bring in an additional person from the administrative staff to cover for 30 minutes when a receptionist is at lunch

■ ask all employees to make suitable arrangements at reception when they will not be at their desk or in the office

STEP 6

In, say, the first two weeks of August, monitor the procedures introduced, collecting data in a frequency table and comparing it with the original data (see Table 4.2). The two sets of data can also be displayed together in a Pareto chart, providing an easy visual means of comparison.

Table 4.2 Frequency table: evaluation (comparison of data before and after the intervention)

Jul	Aug	A	B	C	D	E	F	G	H	I	J	K	L	M
1	1	IIII	I	II	I			I	I	II	||||/ II		I		
2	2	II	II	I				II II		II I	||||/ I I				
3	3	III I	I	I	I	I				III	IIII I				
4	4	III		I I		I		I		I I	||||/ II I I				
5	5	||||/ I I	I	I II				II I		I	||||/				
6	6	II I		II I		I		I		II I	||||/ II				
7	7	||||/ I		II I I		I		I		I I	||||/				
8	8	III I		II I		I			I I	I	||||/ I				
9	9	||||/ II III	I	II I I		I			I	I	IIII				
10	10	IIII II		II I	I			I		I	IIII I				I
11	11	II		II I I	I		I			II I	II I			I
12	12	III II II		I II I I				I I I		I	||||/ I I		I	I
13	13	II		II I	I					I I I	III I			I
14	14	I I		I I I I		I		III		I	||||/ II			
TOTALS		**48** 13	**8** 8	**17** 12	**6** 5	**2** 5	**1** 0	**10** 8	**3** 3	**14** 12	**70** 12	**1** 0	**2** 0	**4** 0

Key: A   Out of office
           B   Sick
           C   In office but not at desk
           D   Lenghty inquiry
           E   Don't know who they should talk to
           F   Long message
           G   Complaint
           H   Person or people absent
           I   Sudden rush of calls
           J   Lunch break
           K   Inexperienced staff member
           L   Doesn't understand message
           M   Lengthy explanation or reply

STEP 7

Evaluation: Table 4.2 shows that before the intervention (the July data) customers waited more than 30 seconds on 186 occasions. After the intervention (the August data) customers waited more than 30 seconds on only 78 occasions. In other words, on this measure the reception service improved by more than 50 per cent.

Other things being equal, the procedures introduced should be maintained.

BUSINESS PROCESS RE-ENGINEERING

Business process re-engineering (BPR) is one of the management buzzwords of the 1990s, a concept originally developed by Michael Hammer and popularised in a bestselling book,[23] co-written with James Champy, focusing on process redesign. In this sense it is a second cousin of TQM, which is driven by continuous improvement of processes. By contrast, though, BPR involves complete process redevelopment rather than mere improvement. At the heart of BPR is what Hammer and Champy term *discontinuous thinking*, a mode of thought that allows the identification and abandonment of the 'outdated rules and fundamental assumptions' that underpin business operations. In other words, they advocate a complete departure from existing methods—rebuilding processes from scratch. They define re-engineering as the fundamental rethinking and radical redesign of business processes to achieve dramatic improvements in critical contemporary measures, such as cost, quality service and speed.

Being a comparatively new management practice, BPR has little in the way of formal methodology, but among its features are:

■ several jobs are combined into one; usually into a team- or task-structured form

■ processes are performed in a logical order; they are undertaken where they make most sense

■ processes often have several versions; for example, in sport there may be one process for registering clubs and a separate process for registering individual players

■ quality control checks and measures are minimised as quality improves

■ an organisational infrastructure can change according to the processes: it can sometimes be centralised and sometimes decentralised

■ strong use of technology to support new processes

■ workers are empowered to make decisions; job satisfaction is improved because processes are arranged into multiple tasks

■ management style is based on 'coaching' rather than supervising

Hammer and Champy vehemently argue that BPR is not related to TQM (or to the common 1990s practice of downsizing, which involves the 'shrinking' of processes and personnel for the sake of efficiency). Yet we believe that it is appropriate to include BPR within a broad quality strategy. We preach no particular loyalty to either TQM or BPR; we're interested in what works, and see no reason why process analysis can't incorporate the re-engineering of processes in certain circumstances. BPR should be used when a process requires such an improvement in performance that only a radical redesign will do the job. But there's little point in starting again from scratch if the process is more than about 75 per cent right.

Whatever approach one uses, it can mean a visible and significant addition to the way business is done and services provided. Quality development is particularly important in the sporting world, since so much current practice is framed by tradition and history. The question that should always be asked is: *Is there a better way?*

SUMMARY

This chapter explained the second core management function, total quality management (TQM). The underpinning philosophy of TQM is continuous improvement, which can be achieved by adopting six principles of quality management. First, management must adopt a customer focus, allowing the organisation to behave responsively to their consumer's needs. Second, there must be management leadership, so that delivering quality becomes an overt commitment. Third, employee involvement should be fostered, to allow decision making and responsibility to be undertaken by the staff that are involved in the production or delivery of the product or service. Fourth, an organisational culture of quality should be established, so that the importance of quality outcomes becomes integrated with the values and beliefs of employees. Fifth, decision making should be based on 'hard data', increasing the probability of making decisions that are conducive to quality. Finally, partnerships must be created with suppliers, so that managers can focus on value and quality instead of exclusively on price.

A number of tools to assist in the delivery of quality were highlighted in the chapter. These were the statistical techniques of total quality control, which help to identify quality problems; and brainstorming, 'imagineering', and quality circles, which assist in generating solutions to quality problems. The technique of business process re-engineering used to radically redesign quality management processes was also discussed.

FURTHER READING

Deming, W.E. (1982) *Out of the Crises*, MIT, Cambridge, Mass.

Hammer, M. and Champy, J. (1993) *Reengineering the Corporation*, Nicholas Brealey Publishing, London.

Longman Group (1992) *Quality First: Quality Management in the Leisure Industry*, Longman, UK.

Martin, W.B. (1993) *Quality Customer Service*, Crisp Publications, Ca.

5 Organisational culture and change management

After reading this chapter you should have a clear understanding of what organisational culture is, and be able to explain how the culture can be changed and managed in order to optimise the performance of a sporting organisation.
More specifically, you should be able to:

- identify the building blocks of organisational culture
- outline approaches to understanding an organisation's culture
- map the culture of a sporting organisation
- use a change management process in moulding a new culture

GOOD CULTURE, BAD CULTURE

Organisational culture can be viewed as a pattern of beliefs and expectations common to members of a social unit, and which set the behavioural standards or norms for new members.[1] In all organisations, individuals are exposed to what may be termed 'culture-revealing' situations, which include artefacts (e.g. photos, honour boards and other memorabilia on show), the observable behaviour of members (e.g. highly masculine or 'blokey' ways of communicating) and work methods (e.g. multiskilling and project teams as a norm). Shared values and common understandings constitute the foundation of organisational culture.[2]

While the management of organisational culture is fairly well understood in the commercial and government sectors, it is frequently overlooked and often misunderstood in the sporting domain. This is unfortunate, since corporate culture is a powerful determinant of behaviour, and the ability to reshape and foster a strong and appropriate culture is a vital means of improving performance. As well, organisational culture is an integral consideration in organisational change, since it is impossible to change anything in an organisation without also affecting its central 'feel' or personality. Change management is built upon culture management, which makes it sensible to address the two issues at the same time.

As we have noted, many sporting cultures have been less than conducive to best practice management. A club or association that, for example, is sceptical of the value of sports science, fails to properly train its casual and volunteer staff, encourages hypermasculine leadership or discourages the full involvement of women is unlikely to prosper or achieve its full sporting potential. However, it is not easy to change the culture of a sporting organisation, since sport is by nature a conservative institution that values its traditions and history highly. (This feature was discussed in detail in Chapter 2.) Sometimes a sporting organisation's current values and practices are based upon the way things were done more than 100 years ago—test cricketers wear all-white 'neck to ankle' uniforms because that is the way it has always been. Yet change is essential if sporting organisations are to meet the challenges and opportunities of today. It is not unreasonable to suggest that the membership problems faced by lawn bowls clubs are largely the result of being caught in a 1950s time warp. When image is now nearly everything, that of lawn bowls is seriously flawed, as the sport is unable to shake off the perception that it is dominated by traditionalist administrators who value a weighty set of dress and game rules over a pleasurable pastime.

The purpose of this chapter is twofold. The first task is to explain how culture can be described, analysed and ultimately modified to best 'fit' an organisation's environment. The second is to examine how change management can be used to 'realign' or 'reposition' the operations and culture of a sporting organisation to more adequately meet its strategic vision.

EXPLORING ORGANISATIONAL CULTURE

Organisational culture is a 'slippery' concept, one in which everything seems to be connected to everything else and in which 'cause' and 'effect' are never completely clear. Nonetheless, organisational culture's impact is significant and it can profoundly influence both an enterprise's behaviour and its strategic planning.[3] Just as nations have a culture that dictates how their citizens will act toward each other and to outsiders, organisations have a culture that governs how their members behave. Culture 'conveys' assumptions, norms and values, which in turn impact upon activities and goals; the process orchestrates the manner in which employees undertake their work and determines what they view as significant within the workplace. Culture has been related to performance and excellence in the marketplace,[4] as well as to employee commitment, co-operation, efficiency, job performance and decision making.[5]

While organisational culture has been described in many ways, there are a number of recurring themes:

■ left to itself, it tends to be inflexible
■ the members of the organisation play a large part in generating it

- the members share it
- despite this, its *core assumptions* are frequently hidden from most members.[6]

Another recurring theme throughout studies of organisational culture is the notion that it should be appropriate to the environment or context in which the organisation functions—and that effective strategy is dependent upon the degree to which the culture supports the organisation in its relations with shareholders or other outside stakeholders.[7] Senior management should therefore foster the development of cultural traits that are consistent with (or fit) the challenges and expectations of the external environment.[8]

A further theme, the strength of a culture, has also been associated with corporate performance. Strength refers to intensity or pervasiveness—the degree to which organisation members embrace the prevailing assumptions and values. It has been argued that a strong culture leads to unity, commitment and co-ordination, thus contributing to enhanced performance throughout an organisation.[9] However, Schneider and Rentsch,[10] caution that a strong organisational culture can prove in some circumstances to be a debilitating hindrance, such as when it fails to align with (or fit) the operating environment; most notably when a business operating in a constantly changing industry is resistant to change. Figure 5.1 lists the factors that need to be addressed when managing organisation culture.

Impact of organisational culture

An organisation's culture is important because it can affect all management functions and decision-making processes, as outlined in the following list.[11] Here the functions are divided into the traditional areas of planning, organising, leading and controlling. In the case of planning, for example, the organisational culture will help to determine the degree of risk that is acceptable to the organisation, and whether it is prepared to look ahead to the longer term or not. In each of the other functions, beliefs and values will be reflected in the way things get done. Some examples are listed below.

- Planning
  - degree of risk contained in the plan
  - emphasis on long or shot term
  - level of employee involvement
  - whether employees should have clear and tangible goals
  - degree of influence that organisational members/stakeholders have in determining objectives
- Organising
  - degree of authority delegated to subordinate managers
  - degree of freedom and flexibility inbuilt into employees' jobs
  - degree to which procedures, policies, rules and regulations are enforced

Figure 5.1 Organisational culture management

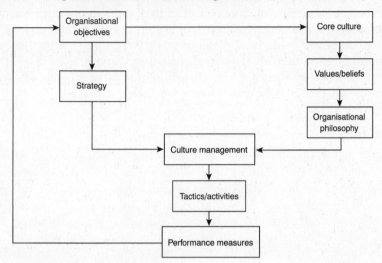

- Leading
  - motivational incentives in use
  - appropriate leadership styles
  - degree to which disagreements are accepted
- Controlling
  - degree to which employees are allowed to control their own actions
  - degree of externally imposed controls
  - criteria emphasised in employee performance evaluations
  - repercussions as a result of extending beyond the standard range of control (e.g. exceeding the budget)

BUILDING BLOCKS OF ORGANISATIONAL CULTURE

History and ownership of the organisation

History and ownership form the first cultural building block. History is particularly relevant in many sporting organisations, where traditions, myths and ritualised behaviour are embraced, old memories cherished and frequently relived, and change feared and avoided. The length of time an organisation has existed is critical, as older organisations tend to have more entrenched 'philosophies' and underlying assumptions about how things are done.

Ownership and the type of organisation also have a significant impact upon the culture. For instance, national sporting organisations (NSOs) and State sporting organisations (SSOs) are likely to have a different cultural composition from that of national league clubs. Clubs tend to have 'stronger', more pervasive and better established cultures than NSOs and SSOs, as their members are bound to the organisation in a powerful sense of identity and ownership. The ownership of clubs can affect the culture in other ways as well. Privately owned leisure and recreation facilities do not often seek direct input from their customers in decision making, in the way that membership-based clubs might. Nor do they always mould their organisational culture to attract volunteers, or rate autonomy and team-based decision making highly. For them, cost savings and productivity enhancement are central issues.

Resources

The source and availability of resources, both human and financial, can also affect the culture. For example, the composition of externally generated resources, either from government grants or commercial sponsorship, can affect policy decisions and consequently cultural values and beliefs. An organisation that is plagued with financial woes may undertake decision making with considerably more hesitation and anxiety than an organisation with sufficient monetary support. As a result, its culture may come to reflect an unadventurous and cautious outlook, in contrast to a bold, risk-taking philosophy.

Employees

Employees play an enormous part in creating, maintaining and changing an organisation's culture. There are two categories of employees: administrative employees, who deal with the organisation's customers and are judged according to their competence and personality; and players, who represent an organisation in contests, and are judged according to their achievements and win–loss record. While administrative employees are influential in the establishment of the office culture of an organisation, players can be influential in the public arena. For example, Mark Taylor, captain of the Australian cricket team, has valiantly tried to civilise his team-mates by weeding out the intimidation and sledging that characterised teams of the past.

In fact, players can demonstrate a club's character in one action viewed by hundreds or thousands of spectators who then translate that action into a 'stereotype' for the team. The team's perceived character is then imposed on the whole organisation to which it belongs. It is the same for umbrella sporting organisations. Many of us remember the Korean boxer who won gold in the 1988 Seoul Olympics, despite clearly losing to his superior American opponent. From that one action, many people branded the South Korean Boxing Federation as corrupt!

Products and services

Differences in culture can also be apparent depending on whether an organisation is orientated towards spectators or towards participation. The primary service delivery component of the former type of organisation is the quality of the match or game played; whereas in the latter case game quality is often incidental. Participation-oriented organisations emphasise support services, comfortable clubrooms and a variety of social activities. It is left to the participants to determine their own quality of game.

In addition, the intrinsic nature of the sport can affect an organisation's culture. A chess club and an amateur boxing club are likely to have different underlying assumptions and values. Also, aggressive sports such as rugby league and kickboxing are more likely than others to have aggressive managers implementing aggressive administrative policies (because the organisation is likely to have former players employed in an administrative capacity, or because the sport itself influences otherwise placid managers). While our own research[12] supports the claim that different sports promote different values and practices—such as aggression and masculinity in AFL football—it also suggests that even different clubs in the same sport can have significantly different cultures.

Environment

A further 'building block' of organisational culture is the impact of the political environment. For example, government policies on sports funding and the relative importance of *elite success* and *participation* rates can influence sporting organisation values and beliefs by rewarding certain behaviours. Other external influences are international trends and fashion, industry competition and employee law.

Organisational objectives

Organisations seeking elite success are likely to have different cultural characteristics from those pursuing 'grassroots' participation. A profit-seeking enterprise may be different again, being more 'rationalist' in its professional approach than, say, a community recreation club that focuses on local involvement.

ANALYSING AND UNDERSTANDING AN ORGANISATION'S CULTURE

If we are to shape and develop an organisation so that it performs better, we must properly understand its culture. A major problem in this is the difficulty of teasing out hidden cultural aspects. A quantitative approach using questionnaires and scaled responses to generate data from sporting club officials, players and members is not likely to be sufficient. Only a detailed *qualitative* examination of an organisation, using 'deep' interviews, close but discreet observation of behaviour and the systematic analysis of statements and documents will do the job. At the same time, it is clear that the culture of a sporting organisation is manifested in every aspect of its existence. All the actions undertaken by an organisation are rich in symbolic meaning and must be addressed.

Figure 5.2 Jungian model of organisational culture/'personality'

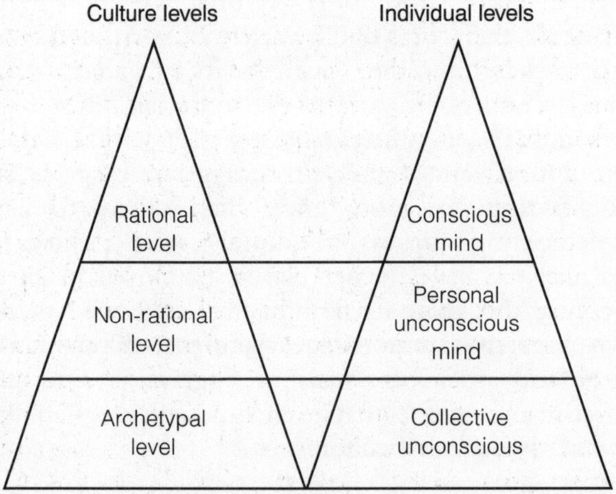

Culture levels   Individual levels

Rational level

Conscious mind

Non-rational level

Personal unconscious mind

Archetypal level

Collective unconscious

The rationale for the use of qualitative methods in organisational culture analysis is that there are elements of culture of which individuals are only partially aware—for example, assumptions, values and beliefs. While exposing the depth of organisational culture is a formidable task, it is the only way in which a clear understanding of a sporting organisation's practices can be obtained.

Approaches to analysing an organisational culture

Culture can be described as the 'personality' of an organisation, representing a shared value and belief system which tempers all organisational activity. However, this deceptively simple but succinct description camouflages a number of complex ingredients. There are several ways of exploring them.

A Jungian approach

The eminent psychologist Carl Jung provided a useful construct for the contemplation of cultural meaning—a three-tiered pyramid (see Figure 5.2). The highest level of the Jungian pyramid represents the individual person's conscious mind: the totality of the person's thoughts and cognitive experiences. This corresponds to the first level of culture in an organisation, the rational level.

The rational level includes those readily apparent and observable characteristics of a sporting organisation, such as the physical environment, the public statements of officials, the way individuals communicate, the form of language used, what clothes are worn, and the memorabilia that fill the rooms and offices. One of the most important observable characteristics is the place of sporting heroes. Heroes give a good insight into the culture of an organisation because they are 'selected' by both the rank and file and the bosses and powerbrokers. In addition, they indicate those qualities for which individuals are respected and admired by a wider audience. The hero is a powerful figure in a sporting organisation, and may be simultaneously an employee and an ex-player.

By understanding the orientation of heroic figures, both past and present, it is possible to map cultural change. Heroes can be reactionary or progressive. A hero may reinforce the dominant culture by manifesting the values and attitudes that that culture emphasises. On the other hand, a hero who transcends the dominant culture may be a catalyst for change in the behaviours and values of the club. Often a hero is the most powerful medium for successful change management. For example, the success of the AFL's anti-vilification rules were in large part due to the powerful supporting public statements of senior Aboriginal players like Michael Long and Nicky Winmar.

Tradition is another window into the culture of an organisation. Like heroes, traditions are readily observable via document analysis or the investigation of memorabilia. They are also observable in club rites, which may take the form of trophy presentations and award functions, roasts and barbecues, guernsey presentations, or even wakes that follow dramatic failure.

For such observable characteristics to be usefully employed in understanding organisational culture, meanings must be attached to them. This requires more than a superficial level of analysis.

The second, and middle, level of the Jungian model is the personal unconscious. This is perhaps better known as the 'subconscious', and frequently governs individual behaviour. It corresponds to the non-rational level of an organisation's culture, which incorporates values, beliefs, attitudes and behaviours. Making an accurate assessment of this level of culture is both difficult and potentially risky, even for an expert. How employees, for example, say they behave, and what they say they believe, must be compared to their actual behaviour if the true state of affairs is to be properly understood.

Finally, at the deepest level of the psyche, according to Jung, is the collective unconscious. This is an innate, primal, virtually inaccessible level of the mind, which humans are born with. It corresponds to the archetypal level of culture in organisations. This is revealed in the traditions, legends, myths and stories of an association or club, which are in turn a reflection of deeply held views about the meaning of sport and its social and communal significance. An investigation at this level can, for example, expose core assumptions about manliness, the role of women, leadership, competition and aggression. The paradox with this level is that it is similar in some ways to the most superficial layer, the rational level. However, the difference is that, at the rational level, cultural traits are accepted at face value, whereas at the unconscious level these same cultural traits are just the iceberg's tip. They are a physical manifestation of a deeper and intensely more complex phenomenon.

Analytical models

In order to make sense of the complexities of cultural practices, some researchers have attempted to construct 'ideal' categories or cultural types.

Figure 5.3 Harrison/Handy model

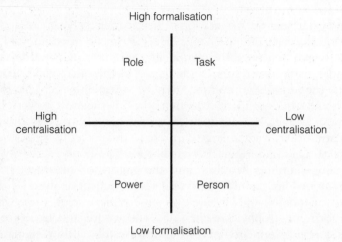

Source: Handy, C. (1987) *The Goals of Management*, Souvenir Press, London; Harrison, R. (1972) 'How to describe your organisation', *Harvard Business Review*, Sept–Oct.

Although often simplistic and narrow, these models can brighten our understanding of the culture conundrum. Let's look at two of them.

Harrison/Handy model

Roger Harrison, who pioneered the analysis of organisational culture, sought to identify values and styles of behaviour found in an organisation. He argued that within each organisation there is likely to be a combination of *four* major 'organisation ideologies' or cultures, one of which may predominate. He termed them *power*, *role*, *task* and *person* cultures.

Charles Handy used Harrison's four types of culture to develop a detailed analysis of organisational structure and behaviour. (Figure 5.3 sets out the four types in relation to two major dimensions of organisational life, centralisation and formalisation of control.) According to Handy, each type of culture produces specific organisational outcomes.

The *power* culture originates from a central source—much like a spider's web—and provides excitement and exhilaration for some and discomfort and intimidation for others. In a power culture, the organisational structure is centred on a select few, including a strong leader to manipulate and orchestrate all activity. In many cases, the power leader is surrounded by technical specialists who provide advice and guidance, further enhancing the leader's omnipotent image. Power-centred organisations depend heavily upon the quality of individuals in the central roles, decision making being undertaken by these select few, whose power base lies in resources rather than expertise. Consequently, the decision-making process is rapid, suited to a competitive, risk-taking environment, capable of undertaking considerable change quickly, and concentrated on results, irrespective of means. In organisations typified by this culture there are few written rules and procedures—low formalisation—with control being exercised centrally. Power organisations' 'heroes' traditionally involve larger-than-life inspirational and entrepreneurial leaders who lead 'from the front'. The weaknesses of such an organisation are that it has difficulty accommodating to growth in size and relies too heavily upon the abilities of the select few individuals.

A power culture is frequently found in small entrepreneurial organisations, occasionally in trade unions, and may also be found in some sporting organisations. One might imagine that a sporting organisation led by a Ron Barassi, a David Hill or a Bob Simpson would display elements of a power culture. Such a culture puts faith in the individual, judges by results, and is tolerant of rule breaking as long as things get done. Unfortunately, the loss of a power leader might cause strong reverberations, which may partially destroy the organisation. It is possible, for example, that the loss of David Hill as president of Soccer Australia may allow the chronic tensions that characterise Australian soccer to resurface.

The *role* culture is, by contrast, highly bureaucratic. It features functional specialisation, control, rules and procedures, and hierarchy. The main function of senior management is co-ordination and direction rather than adventurous decision making. In this case, decisions are based upon lengthy formal procedures, culminating in predictable, low-risk strategies. Concomitantly, managers of role-centred organisations are reluctant to undertake change to accommodate environmental variables. The major orientation of the role culture is the job to be filled rather than the individual who is to fill it. The allocation of work and responsibility determines the efficiency of the culture rather than individual ability. As a consequence, there are few heroes in organisations in which role culture predominates, with its strengths being its stable, secure and predictable outlook and its weaknesses being its inflexibility and protracted change processes.

The role-orientated organisation needs a stable environment in which to function. The public service, automobile and oil industries, life insurance and banking contain examples of role culture. Again, it may be applicable to sporting organisations; an example might be England's Marylebone Cricket Club, or the Australian Cricket Board prior to Kerry Packer's intrusion in 1977. In a sporting organisation, bureaucracy may impede rapid decision making. For instance, the inability of the English cricket authorities to determine a single squad from which to draw Test players during the mid-1990s may be explained by a breakdown in the role culture of the MCC board.

The *task* culture is job or project oriented and, because of this, decision making tends to be undertaken by specialists rather than those in power positions. The predominant style in task culture is to work in team settings, which encourages a flexible attitude toward projects. Formal roles have little meaning in task groups and procedures are adaptable and pliant. Task cultures are cohesive, innovative and competitive, with the ability to conform where appropriate. The group dynamics are complex and can be difficult to control. Heroes in these types of organisations are rare, and the focus is on groups of individuals and team accomplishments. Task culture organisations (assuming they have adequate time and resources for their work) are often successful.

However, when speed is of the essence, and resources become difficult to acquire, the management begins to feel the need to control methods as well as results. As a result, task culture can readily change to role or power culture. Task cultures are frequently seen in sporting organisations, because influence is widely dispersed and effectiveness must rely on overall team strength. Outcomes depend upon team members subsuming their individuality, particularly status and power, to the common good. There are signs that as sporting organisations become more complex the need for high performance work groups becomes greater. Indeed, we argue that task cultures, where project teams provide the management energy, are the future for successful sports administration. This point is addressed in more detail in Chapter 12.

The *person* culture exists to serve the individuals in the organisation. As a result, the organisational structure, rules, procedures and roles are formulated according to the requirements of the individual members. Decision making can only occur with the mutual consent of all members, and can, therefore, be tentative. Similarly, high-risk activities are rarely pursued because consensus is difficult to achieve among individual members, leading the organisation to resist change and encourage stability. While person-orientated cultures aim to be co-operative, they also allow individual members to be elevated to hero status by their peers, and admired for their individual accomplishments. The strength of a person-orientated culture is its solidarity, which can unite its members against management. However, it can also create control difficulties for management. Advertising agencies, hippie communes, fundamentalist religious groups, welfare agencies and families often have this 'person' orientation. If this type of culture exists in sporting organisations, then it resides with the amateur clubs and those individuals who gather together to play their sport in their own way. They lack the formality to undertake serious training, and indeed, such sporting clubs rarely have a paid coach or any work-like structure. On the other hand, sociability and conviviality are often highly valued.

Goffee/Jones model

A more recent model of organisational culture has been offered by Goffee and Jones, who focus on two determinants: sociability, a measure of friendliness among members of an organisation; and solidarity, a measure of an organisation's ability to pursue a common objective. These two behavioural dimensions are combined to produce the typology shown in Figure 5.4.

'Networked' organisations are high in sociability but low in solidarity,

Figure 5.4 Goffee/Jones model

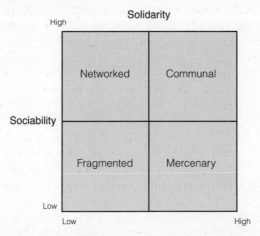

Source: Goffee, R. & Jones, G. (1996) 'What holds the modern company together', *Harvard Business Review*, Nov–Dec.

which means that they focus on personal relationships rather than organisational objectives. They possess formal hierarchies, but also informal methods of getting around them. In this model, the opposite type is the '*mercenary*' organisation, which is typified by a lack of interest in interpersonal relationships, and by a focus on business performance. At the other extreme, the '*fragmented*' organisation is low on both scales, and reinforces an 'every person for themself' attitude. Finally, the '*communal*' organisation is high on both scales, reinforcing the importance of both organisational goals and kinship.

The Goffee/Jones model, like all analystical approaches, has its strengths and weaknesses. While all such models gloss over the differences between organisations and fail to account for the needs of different members and for different environmental demands, they help to reveal the complexity and subtlety of the determinants of organisational culture.[13]

MAPPING THE CULTURE OF AN ORGANISATION

Understanding a culture stems from successfully translating information into meaning. Every aspect of an organisation is symbolically representative in some way of its culture. All information is not equal, yet all possible data must be analysed in order to establish a holistic representation of the existing culture. Organisational culture is classically defined in management literature as shared values and beliefs that are taken for granted and are located beneath the surface of organisational life. This makes culture a more complex issue to study. In order for a culture to be created and bolstered the shared values and beliefs must in some way be conveyed to organisational members, especially new members. The following list[14] sets out the types of things that communicate culture, and which can be used in mapping a sporting organisation's culture.

■ *Artefacts:* Material objects manufactured by people to facilitate culturally expressive activities.
■ *Environment:* Those things that physically surround people.
■ *Gestures:* Movements of parts of the body to express meaning.
■ *Language:* A particular manner in which members of a group use vocal sounds.
■ *Symbol:* Any object, act, event, quality or relation that serves as a vehicle for conveying meaning.
■ *Folktale:* A completely fictional narrative.
■ *Story:* A narrative based on true events—a mix of facts and fiction.
■ *Legend:* A handed-down narrative of a particularly significant event that has a historical basis but has been embellished with fictional details.
■ *Saga:* A historical narrative describing (usually in heroic terms) the unique accomplishments of a group and its leaders.
■ *Myth:* A dramatic narrative of imagined events, usually used to explain origins or transformations of something.
■ *Ritual:* A standardised, detailed set of techniques and behaviours that help one to manage anxieties.
■ *Rite:* A relatively elaborate, dramatic, planned set of activities that combines various forms of cultural expression.
■ *Literature:* Any written document produced for the purpose of communication or expression of meaning.

While the range and diversity of information available for cultural analysis is profound, many cultural studies ignore all but the most apparent and accessible data. A holistic cultural analysis will utilise every available piece of information, with the more obvious elements becoming vehicles for the transmission of less tangible but often more revealing values and beliefs. The difficulty in any cultural investigation is translating the data into meaningful categories, patterns and themes.

Cultural mapping in a sporting context

In sport there are as many organisational cultures as there are sporting organisations; and they cannot always be generically categorised or neatly slotted into one simple grouping. Nor can they be fully described by looking only at the observable characteristics of an organisation. As we have said, sporting clubs are typically immersed in tradition and related myths. These symbolic conveyors of the culture are often more important indicators of a club's real mission and purpose than the readily observable features such as the organisational structure, the physical facilities and the types of services offered.

A cultural map seeks to incorporate these symbolic indicators as well as the overt features, and provides a means by which data can be collated and interpreted. The accompanying box gives an example of a cultural map that may help in documenting and assessing organisational culture. Used with the second and third columns blank, it can be applied to a sporting club of your choice.

ALLENWOOD RUGBY UNION CLUB: EXAMPLE OF A CULTURAL MAP

Cultural features	Existing nature	Cultural meaning
Physical environment	Old and new together, clean, neat, well designed and cared for, roomy, good facilities	Indicates a willingness to embrace the new as well as valuing the old
Public statements	Brief, concise and succinct	No-nonsense image
Documents	n.a.	
Communication	Management: polite but to the point Coaching staff: often impolite and to the point	No-nonsense image Lack of subtlety
Language/jargon	Full of colloquial expressions, rugby jargon, swearing	Direct and unpretentious behaviour is admired
Artefacts (memorabilia)	Trophy cabinets, medals, pennants, team and individual pictures from games and social events	Winning is of the highest importance
Heroes	All male, tough rather than skilful, uncompromising, 'team' players	Masculinity and teamwork to win
Values/beliefs/ assumptions/ habits/attitudes/ behaviours	Rugby is one of the most important things in players' lives Important to be tough and 'manly' Strength and victory are pursued Fear and failure are to be avoided	Masculinity and victory of the highest importance Discipline is highly valued

Cultural features	Existing nature	Cultural meaning
Rites/rituals/ ceremonies	Rites of initiation: getting a guernsey Social rites: drinking, swearing, bragging Playing rites: being given specialist position Rites of victory: drinking, celebration	Bolsters sense of belonging and importance of victory
Traditions/myths/ legends/stories	Emphasise toughness, extremities, great wins, playing under adverse conditions, injuries, heroes, pre and post match superstititions	Masculinity and victory are of the highest importance Women excluded
Organisational structure (centralisation/ formalisation)	Flat	Structure is less important than performance
Degree of risk taking	On-field: high Off-field: low	Players take risks but the organisation doesn't
Adaptability to change	On-field: high Off-field: low	Players are flexible but the organisation isn't
Major orientation/ organisational objectives (solidarity v. sociability)	On-field performance	Winning is everything
Resources	Poor, membership-driven	Attitude that cost is everything
Employees	Volunteers	Unresponsive and overworked but well-meaning
Services	Narrow	Lack of interest in quality or provision of alternative services
Role of rules and procedures	On-field: high Off-field: low	Outcome of game is more important than anything else

While organisational culture is troublesome to reveal, and difficult to manage, it remains the cornerstone of any successful change strategy. Despite the conceptual messiness that surrounds culture, a detailed cultural map is the most effective tool for coming to grips with the culture of a sporting club or association. Some cultures are clearly engines of energy and innovation, but others can be negative, distorted and even dysfunctional. While it was once believed that a strong culture is a good culture, this is no longer the case. For culture to be useful and productive, it must be appropriate to the circumstances as well as strong.

Of course, changing an organisation's culture can be very difficult. It is therefore important to develop a sound understanding of the change process, and of how change management skills can be employed to re-energise a sporting group.

CHANGE AND ITS MANAGEMENT

Organisational changes are departures from the status quo or from traditional ways of doing things.[15] In the simplest possible terms, if we alter something, whether it is habits, customs, attitudes, systems or processes, we are practising organisational change. In order for change to be successful and permanent, the change process must be both *understood* by members of the organisation and *agreed* to. Moreover, the types of changes, and what and how to change, must also be very clearly revealed and explained.

Aspects of change

Belden Menkus[16] highlighted five aspects of change that need to be appreciated if change is to be undertaken successfully:

- *Change does not equal progress:* It is important not to confuse *change*, which is simply an act of making things different, and *progress*, which implies positive and inexorable advancement. The point is that change is not valuable in and of itself—particularly if frequent and arbitrary changes in procedures and systems are an indication of unstable or incompetent management. Progress *should* be the outcome of thoughtful change management, but that is not always the case.
- *Change is 'linear' in nature:* There is no turning back once a change program has begun.
- *Change is traumatic:* It is a human disposition to experience discomfort as a result of change. This discomfort is particularly acute when people feel that change is being forced upon them.
- *Change is most powerful when it is simple:* Small changes are more likely to be accepted than big changes, particularly when they can be easily understood and assimilated into current work processes and systems.

Unfortunately, organisations become overzealous, and attempt to make radical changes rapidly. Although sometimes this is appropriate, most often change is better approached incrementally.

■ *Change can only be considered successful when it results in added value:* No change may be considered effective unless its end is the creation of 'something' better.

Types of organisational change

Organisational change may be classified on the basis of four characteristics: planned or unplanned; internal stimulus or external stimulus.[17] If we put these together in the form of Figure 5.5, we see that four *types* of organisational change are possible.

A *Type 1* change (a planned change that originates internally from management) may come in the form of new programs or services, a streamlining of procedures or even a complete redesign of the organisation's structure.[18] Examples of Type 1 change are the replacement of an 'old' senior coach with a younger one from a rival team, or the move to a summer soccer season from the traditional winter months. Such changes are typically initiated by an organisation in a stable environment.

A *Type 2* change (in which organisational modifications follow unforeseen internal events) may transpire as a result of an unexpected turnover of key members of the board or management committee of a sporting organisation, or from a sudden change in the ownership of a private facility or business.

A *Type 3* change involves a planned response to external developments. The introduction of automated ticketing at venues in the light of improved technology would constitute such a change.

Finally, a *Type 4* change occurs when unforeseen external circumstances

Figure 5.5 Types of organisational change

Nature of change

	Planned	Unplanned
Internal	Type 1	Type 2
External	Type 3	Type 4

Stimulus for change

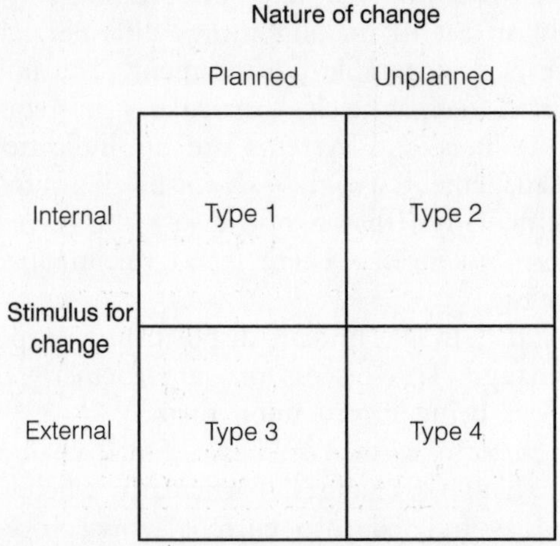

force an ad hoc organisational response. The formation of World Series Cricket nearly two decades ago and, more recently, the advent of Super (Rugby) League are two such events, in which the environment was for a time clearly unstable.

What and how to change

While categorising the types of organisational change is enlightening, it does not tell us when change is needed or how to undertake it. Frank Blount, chief executive officer of Telstra, recommends a simple but powerful matrix (see Figure 5.6) to indicate when change should occur, and how to go about it when it is needed.

The matrix divides functional activity within an organisation into what is done and how it is done. 'What' refers to the products or services offered to customers, while 'how' refers to the systems and processes that are in place to deliver those products and services.

The upper left quadrant combines *'what' right* with *'how' right* to describe an organisation that essentially requires no change because it is providing what is wanted by the customer and doing it in a competent and correct manner (how). In this case the group has no fundamental problems.

The upper right quadrant represents an organisation that provides the appropriate products or services (*'what' right*), but does so inefficiently and poorly (*'how' wrong*). In other words, it knows what its customers want, but fails to provide the necessary quality of response. Here the matrix indicates the appropriate change remedy for this situation. An organisation that has got its products or services right, but needs to improve its delivery of them, should implement a quality program covering this part of its operations.

Figure 5.6 What and how things are done: the cultural perspective

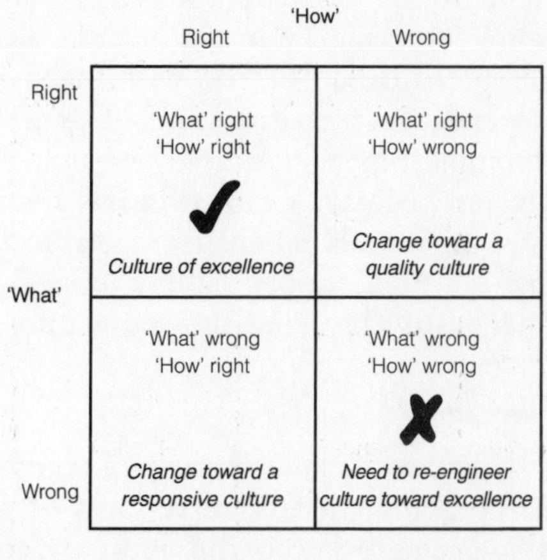

Many sporting organisations are in this position. For example the game has many attractive qualities, but is delivered through inferior facilities.

The bottom left quadrant presents the combination of *'what' wrong* and *'how' right*. This means that an organisation is supplying *unwanted* products or services with high quality delivery, which is obviously pointless. The only possible change remedies are to radically modify the products or services or to market the existing products or services to a totally different (and more receptive) market segment. Organisations with this sort of problem will not survive without prompt change management.

Finally, the bottom right quadrant depicts a combination of *'what' wrong* and *'how' wrong*. There is little need to explain that this equals disaster, and the only way out is to initiate a severe and radical change management program immediately. A case in point is a prominent leisure centre which decided, without any market research, to put its resources into European handball, but found, among other things, that it could not attract players or enough trained referees.

Radical change management

Once the decision makers in a sporting organisation recognise that substantial change is needed as soon as possible, they are faced with the daunting question of where to start. Frank Blount has highlighted four factors that need to be in place before change can be made successfully. Let's look at them in turn.

1 Large-scale dissatisfaction with the organisation

The bottom line here is that change will not and cannot take place until the people who constitute the organisation—its board or owners, managers, employees, volunteers and members/customers—are dissatisfied with the current situation. In many cases this is a massive hurdle, particularly as sporting clubs often tend to be stuck in their traditional operations and structures, like pylons in concrete. Thus the board's first and overriding concern is to *create* widespread dissatisfaction with the status quo. How this is best accomplished depends on the situation, but generally it will require enormous effort in communicating with employees and customers, either in person or via market research. Daryl Conner[19] used a single word for this prerequisite for successful organisational change: *pain*. In other words, there must be an impending sense of 'doom' and a critical mass of relevant information that together justify breaking the status quo.

2 A shared vision of the future

Once dissatisfaction is widespread, there must be a common view of where the organisation should be going; that is, there must be a shared vision for the future. Again, this will require purposeful and energetic leadership, as it rarely occurs naturally. To become a common view the vision, once created, must be communicated throughout the organisation.

3 Ability to make the change

For change to be successful, even if the first two factors are in place, there must be systems that will support the change in a practical, day-to-day manner. Thus the architects of the change program must identify the skills, roles and processes that must be undertaken, and provide appropriate education and training to bolster these systems. In real terms, this means that the rank and file employee, player and volunteer has to know exactly what they are going to do differently on Monday morning—compared to the week before. Change cannot proceed unless the infrastructure is there to uphold it.

4 'Actionable' first steps

The organisation's leaders must take the first steps, overtly demonstrating that the change process has actually begun. These actions must be direct and clearly related to the resolution of the difficulties faced.

The initial step must establish a sense of urgency along with the element of dissatisfaction.[20] Although it may seem that dissatisfaction with the status quo may be sufficient to overcome the organisational inertia associated with ingrained and traditional practices, the reality is that many employees are going to be preoccupied with their own activities and agendas. Thus getting a change program to gather momentum requires aggressive and proactive effort and commitment. The key to organisational transformation, therefore, lies with the management leadership's ability to empower others to act on the vision and, once they have established new policies and procedures, to anchor these into the organisation's culture.

The most effective method of facilitating the change process is to set up a change management project team. This is essential in order to provide guide-rails for employees who have been 'empowered' but do not know what to do. The team must have both authority over the change process and accountability for its success, allowing for responsive and decisive action when necessary. According to Daniel Duck,[21] a change management team has eight primary responsibilities:

- *Establish context and provide guidance:* Ensure that the change process remains consistent with the vision, and that all employees are aware of that vision.
- *Stimulate communication:* Establish alternative and non-traditional informal communication networks that work top-down and bottom-up.
- *Provide appropriate resources:* Change is rarely inexpensive. The change management team must make sure the organisation 'puts its money where its mouth is'.
- *Co-ordinate projects:* Task and project groups must work synchronously

to ensure that every component of the organisation is working toward the vision.

■ *Ensure congruence of messages, activities, policies and behaviours:* The change team must be vigilant in eliminating anything that is inconsistent with the vision.

■ *Provide opportunities for joint creation:* The change team is responsible for ensuring that *everyone* is involved in the change process, and that it proceeds as a partnership rather than through one-way orders.

■ *Anticipate, identify and address people problems:* Change is not easy on people; it will undoubtedly lead to stress and discomfort. It is therefore vital that someone on the change team be skilled in diagnosing, anticipating and addressing human relations issues.

■ *Prepare and maintain the critical mass:* For the change process to be a success, the organisation requires a minimum number of 'converts' among the staff. It is the job of the change team to win over or recruit these pivotal staff members.

Understanding culture's role in change

Having discussed the four factors that must be in place for change to be successful, the question arises as to what happens when any one of the factors cannot be implemented. For example, it is easy to say that large-scale dissatisfaction exists and must be attended to, but sometimes it will seem impossible to go any further than that—core parts of the organisation will not only resist change but vehemently deny that it will improve performance. In some extreme cases they may go so far as advocating a return to past policies and traditional practices.

What needs to be understood is that attitudes to change are 'mediated' by the personality or culture of an organisation, which is formed from the collective values and assumptions of individuals. Accordingly, change teams must work closely with key influential people—at all levels of the organisation—in order to bring about a more receptive mood concerning change. Then the question of changing the work processes and ultimately improving the organisation's performance can be tackled.

When it comes to specific organisational variables, a chart like that shown earlier (in the box headed Allenwood Rugby Union Club) can be developed to assist in mapping the culture and devising change strategies. Although cultural maps are best constructed according to the specific needs of an organisation, there are certain central components usually worth including. For example, a good starting point is to give special attention to the values surrounding quality management. These values, which are discussed in detail in Chapter 4, are:

■ customer focus
■ management leadership

- employee training and development
- fact-based decision making
- partnerships with suppliers

More detailed cultural maps can be created for every category in the Allenwood template. They can be used to reveal those aspects of culture that are holding a club back, and to endorse cultural values like team building, inclusive decision making and continual improvement.

SUMMARY

This chapter introduced the reader to the concepts of organisational culture and change management, which is the third core management process. We highlighted how organisational culture influences the behaviour of sporting club officials, members and fans, often without them being conscious of it. While organisational culture is not something that is written down or that can be always clearly articulated by its members, it can be easily revealed by talking to anyone who is closely connected to a club. You can, for example, get a good picture of the culture of an organisation by asking officials what they value about the organisation, what unwritten rules guide their administrative procedures, and what is expected of them. Culture is also expressed through artefacts, ceremonies, rituals and day-to-day practices.

Cultures can be strong or weak, but strong culture may not always be good or productive. For example, sporting clubs have a history of keeping women in subordinate positions, under-utilising their management skills and making decisions without prior review or consultation. This is no longer an appropriate cultural trait for a sporting organisation.

Finally, we link change management to culture, since any effective and lasting change requires an equivalent change in culture.

FURTHER READING

Huber, G.P. and Glick, W.H. (1993) *Organisational Change and Redesign*, Oxford University Press, New York.

Kotter, J.P. (1996) *Leading Change*, Harvard Business School Press, Cambridge.

Ott, J.S. (1989) *The Organisational Culture Perspective*, Brookes-Cole, Pacific Grove, Ca.

Schein, E. (1992) *Organisational Culture and Leadership*, Jossey-Bass, San Francisco.

Senior, B. (1997) *Organisational Change*, Pitman, London.

Smith, A.C.T. & Stewart, R. (1995) 'Sporting club cultures: An exploratory case study, *Australian Leisure*, December, pp. 31–7.

6   **P**layer management

After reading this chapter you should have a broad appreciation of key issues in player management.

More specifically, you should be able to indicate how administrative processes can strengthen crucial elements of:

- coaching
- medical support
- conditioning
- recruiting

INTRODUCTION

For most people, winning is important. In sport it is often pursued with an obsessive passion. Age and gender are no barriers to the need to do better. It goes without saying that one of the core responsibilities of a sporting club is to help boost the athletic performance of its members, irrespective of their ability or motivation for playing or taking part. Indeed, most club mission statements have something to say about development, excellence and achievement.[1]

This responsibility is enacted through 'player management', which involves the provision of support and guidance for teams and individuals in order to enhance their athletic experiences and achievements. Most sports managers are at some stage involved in the management of players, and although the size and type of organisation may vary substantially—from, say, New Zealand's Otago Car Club to the South African cricket team—the principles applied remain standard. Nor does it matter for our purposes that one national sporting organisation manages Olympics-bound cyclists from an impressively resourced sports institute, while another lesser known national sporting organisation co-ordinates its highest level of competition in high school gymnasiums. The principles of player management hold irrespective of context, and constitute a fundamental part of a sporting organisation's mission and vision.

ELITE SUCCESS AND GENERAL PARTICIPATION

It is indicative of our broad approach to sports management that the playing dimension represents only one part in eight of our overall operational management system. In reality, of course, support for 'on-field' performance generally ranks highest of all the functional management arms when athletic success is paramount. Some organisations are dependent on their competitive success at an elite level for continued funding, their successes also driving their popularity and exposure. Australian Swimming Inc. and Athletics Australia rely heavily on their Olympic and Commonwealth Games medal tallies for both their funding and their media coverage. As well, the Australian Soccer Federation reportedly invested $400 000 in obtaining the coaching talents of Terry Venables, the former England manager, in an attempt to improve the national team's chances in the 1998 World Cup. In short, a sporting organisation's investment in performance management will be commensurate with its commitment to a performance priority, which will usually be revealed in its mission and objectives.

At the same time, while elite success may be a central objective of bodies like national sporting organisations (NSOs) and State sporting organisations (SSOs), they frequently have the added task of increasing participation rates in their sports. Apart from special programs, 'participation' is generally administered through junior and senior programs. Junior performance is usually measured by the number of young people participating, and senior performance is measured in terms of the number of adult participants and the number and location of competitions and clubs involved.

Elite success and general participation are thus two major components of player management in its widest sense. This is indicated in Figure 6.1. Although the chart appears complex, it is worth studying because it presents a complete picture of what we call player management. In the remainder of this chapter we will concentrate on four elements—coaching, medical support, conditioning and recruiting—and their application to elite performance and general participation.

FOUR CRUCIAL ELEMENTS

Coaching

Coaching competence is vital in both team and individual sports. The performance measures for coaches are usually clear and concise, since they relate to actual achievements—for example, medals and rankings. Martin Leech, coach of the Australian weightlifting squad, was considered successful because of the squad's impressive World Championship and Commonwealth Games results during the 1990s. The success of Australia's swimming team

Figure 6.1 Player management: context and elements

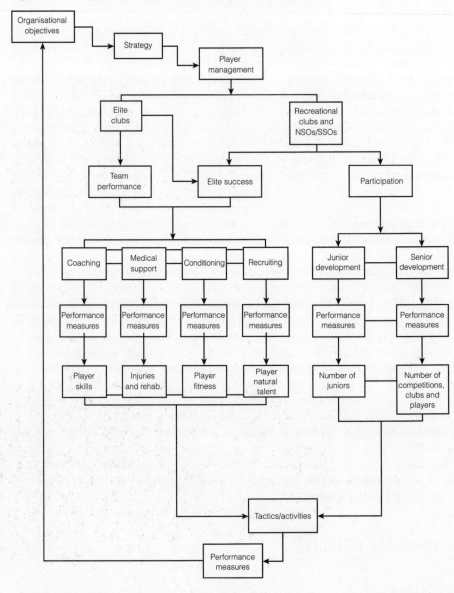

at the 1996 Atlanta Olympics reflected well not only on the swimmers but on the coaching staff, who basked in the shared glory.

Unfortunately, the quality of coaching is not usually seen as a management responsibility. Traditionally, the management role has been restricted to selecting a coach and coaching staff, and then 'handballing' them all the responsibilities. While we are not suggesting that administrators, whether paid or voluntary, should interfere in the training programs instituted by coaches and related staff, we do insist that their responsibilities include the provision of adequate support systems and the objective evaluation of coaches.

Management support for coaching and coaches

It is often difficult to establish responsibility in sporting organisations: rarely do job specifications provide details on precisely where coaches' duties end and those of administrators begin. Although we address the need for accurate and detailed job specifications in Chapter 10, the truth is that the level of management support for coaches is often dependent on personality rather than position, and decided more by trial and error than by thoughtful consideration. Beyond the obvious, there are typically no rules concerning who should do what. We recommend that the duties of the coaching staff, even in local, community and recreational clubs, be documented and followed, at least broadly.

Coaches and administrators need to come to clear arrangements concerning their mutual involvement in the functional areas of scheduling, training facilities and equipment, and information distribution.

Schedules

Appropriate and accurate schedules and timetables are critical to the effective management of team performance. Irrespective of who develops the schedule—although it is best accomplished with the coaching staff driving the process and the administrators tempering their decision making in the face of practical restrictions—it remains the central tool for co-ordinating a large group of players, athletes and support staff. The success of a schedule lies in detail and flexibility: if there is insufficient detail, it is almost worthless; and if it is discarded when something goes wrong—which frequently happens—then it is not going to be in use for long. Finding the balance between detail and flexibility is the key, and it is not necessarily dependent on the size or importance of the organisation or event. As the accompanying box—a week in the life of the New York Giants gridiron team—shows, a detailed schedule provides an excellent picture of the work requirements of both core and peripheral club staff.

NEW YORK GIANTS: WEEKLY SCHEDULE			
Day	Time	People involved	Activity
After previous match		Doctors report	Review injury list Diagnosis and treatment

Day	Time	People involved	Activity
Day 1	8:45	Offensive and defensive staff meet	Video review of past game
			Video preview of last game of next opponents
	11:00	Head coach	Video preview of next opponents
	Noon	Offensive coaches	Tactics development
	3:00	All coaching staff	Review opponents coaching
	4:00	All coaching staff	Plan training to the minute
Day 2	6:45	Defensive coaches	Review all past opponent's games
	10:30	Offensive coaches	Development of tactics based on opponent's strengths and weaknesses
	Noon	Head coach and all players	Discussion of general tactics
	12:30	Head coach and quarterback	Press conference
	12:30	Specialty teams	Specific game tactics
	4:00	All players and coaches	Specific skills training
	5:00	Head coach	Deals with correspondence and phone messages
	5:30	All coaching staff	Review day's activities and plan next day's training
Day 3	6:30	All coaching staff	Refine tactics
	9:00	All players	Team meeting to explain general tactics
	9:35	Offensive and defensive coaches	Review tactics
	11:00	Specialty teams	Review skills
	11:30	All players and coaches	Lunch
	Noon	All players and coaches	Walk through set plays
	Noon	Head coach and selected players	Press conference
	12:30	Defensive players	Video of opponent's offense
	1:30	All players and coaches	Skills training and conditioning
	4:30	Players	Players rest or go home
	5:00	All coaches	Working dinner

Day	Time	People involved	Activity
	6:30	All coaches	Review day's activities and plan next day's training
Day 4	7:15	Defensive coaching staff	General defensive tactics
	7:30	Offensive coaching staff	General offensive tactics
	7:45	All coaching staff	Tactics
	9:30	All coaches and players	Tactics
	9:40	Specialty groups	Specific tactics
	11:30	All coaches and players	Lunch
	12:30	Defensive coach and players	Tactics
	2:00	All coaches and players	Skills and conditioning
	5:00	All players	NFL commissioner answers questions
	5:30	All coaches and players	Dinner
	6:00	All players	Players go home
	7:00	All coaches	Coaching staff go home
Day 5	6:30	Offensive coaching staff	Review video of opponents
	7:00	Head coach and offensive coaching staff	Finalise tactics
	8:00	Defensive coaching staff	Review video of opponents
	9:30	Specialty teams	Refine tactics
	1:00	All coaches	Travel to game location
	5:30	Coaches and players	Coaches arrive at hotel and players travel
	9:00	Players	Players arrive at hotel
	9:05	All coaching staff and players	General theme of game and situational variables
	9:15	Specialty groups	Finalise tactics
	10:00	All players	Retire to sleep
Game day	9:30	Head coach	Arrive at venue
	11:00	Players and support staff	Arrive at venue
	12:15	Players	Drills and warm-up on ground
	12:40	All coaches and players	Main tactical points and motivation
	1:00	All coaches and players	Game starts

We do not suggest that you necessarily follow the New York Giants' format, which is very detailed, but it will give you a picture as to what must be done when, where and by whom if there is to be a co-ordinated and efficiently run program. You may wish to adapt it in constructing your own coaching schedule.

Training facilities and equipment

The second area requiring organisation and management from both the coaching staff and administrators concerns facilities and equipment. It is not unusual to hear conflicting arguments about use of venues, particularly during season transitions between football and cricket, or in overlaps between rugby and soccer, where grounds have been damaged by or maintained for one sport despite several sports' needs. These logistical problems are not only prevalent at local and regional levels but also occur at 'semi-professional' and elite levels. Council restrictions on lighting and noise, ground quality, grass length, and renovations are common concerns for outdoor sports, while double-bookings, inappropriate or limited seating, and unclean or non-standard facilities are often disputed in indoor sports.

These occasional but typical difficulties should be predicted and managed by good coaches and administrators. Nothing special is required to ensure that players have the appropriate facilities and equipment, beyond rudimentary administrative care and a thorough review of what needs to be done. A useful tool for training or competition is a checklist, to ensure that nothing is overlooked. Table 6.1 gives an example for competition purposes.

Information distribution

The final responsibility held jointly between coaches and administrators is concerned with information distribution, which is clearly linked to the above two areas. When done properly, a detailed schedule and a completed checklist will provide the essential information that players and support staff require. Additional information, such as timetable and venue changes, should always be documented and distributed as early as possible. A distribution 'system' is the most effective method of ensuring that the necessary information reaches players and support personnel, who in many cases include volunteers, parents, friends and supporters in addition to paid professionals. The system need not be complicated; as long as the appropriate people receive the information in an agreed form, at an agreed time, then problems should be minimised.

Performance measurement

Performance appraisal is a human resources issue and is discussed in Chapter 10. We repeat that performance cannot be managed unless it is first measured, so we briefly note here the way in which performance measurement occurs. All 'employees', paid or voluntary, honorary or appointed, should have their performance evaluated or measured in some way. It does not matter what type of sporting organisation it is, ultimate authority and responsibility for the organisation's performance is held by members, supporters and other stakehold-

Table 6.1 Facilities and equipment checklist

ITEM	CHECK	
	✔	✘
Facility		
(Indoor)		
■ Quality of playing/competition area		
■ Change-rooms		
■ Ventilation		
■ Lighting		
(Outdoor)		
■ Quality of playing surface		
■ Shade		
■ Standard markings/size		
General		
■ Access to food		
■ Access to phones		
■ Accredited umpires/referees		
■ Cleanliness		
■ Comfort		
■ Convenience/accessibility		
■ Designated drivers		
■ Doctor to attend		
■ Price		
■ Proximity to hospital		
■ Proximity to social facility		
■ Route to hospital		
■ Safe and adequate parking		
■ Safety		
■ Spectator area		
■ Sports trainer/s to attend		
■ Toilets		
■ Value		
■ Other essential personnel:		
_____		
_____		
_____		
_____		
Equipment		
■ Emergency money		
■ First aid kit		
■ Fluid replacement drinks		
■ Line marking chalk		
■ Mobile phone		
■ Phone card		
■ Social drinks		
■ Spare shoes/boots		

ITEM	CHECK	
	✔	✘
■ Spare team clothing ■ Sports equipment (club kit) ■ Sports tape ■ Stopwatch/timer ■ Whistle ■ Witches hats/cones ■ Other:		
Documentation ■ Certificates/trophies/awards ■ Copies of schedule ■ Insurance ■ Lists of participants ■ Participant medical histories ■ Participant playing records ■ Registration information ■ Statistics ■ Other:		
Minors ■ Liability/negligence/duty of care ■ Medical information release forms ■ Medical release forms ■ Names and phone number of parents or next of kin		

ers. Indeed, it is the customers who determine the fate of board or committee members, as was dramatically illustrated with the sacking of the Hawthorn Football Club's board of directors at the conclusion of the 1996 season. Similarly, the declining attendances at Australian Rugby League matches throughout 1996 and 1997, as a result of Super League–induced disillusionment, demonstrated how significant fans can be in changing the direction of a sporting competition. But it does not end with members giving the 'thumbs up' or 'thumbs down' to a management proposal. While customers and members have the ultimate role in performance appraisal, they do not in most cases directly appoint and dismiss staff. In most cases the board or committee judges the performance of the chief administrator and coach, the chief administrator evaluates paid employees' performance, and the coaching staff evaluate players' performance. Figure 6.2 illustrates this hierarchy of performance appraisal.

A coach's performance can be monitored by the use of objectively established performance indicators determined by the board or committee.

Figure 6.2 Hierarchy of performance appraisal

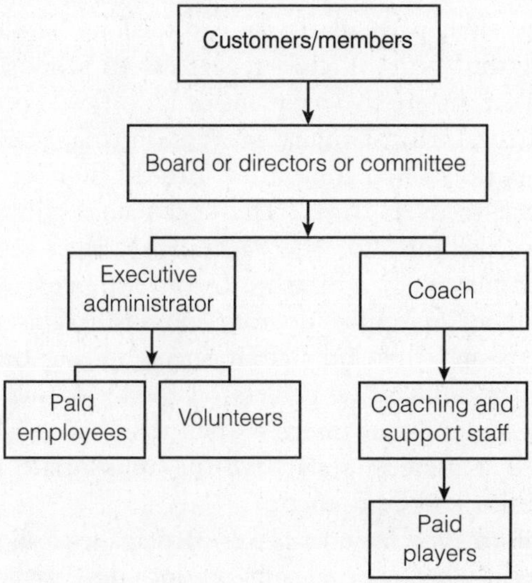

Performance reviews of staff are discussed in greater detail in Chapter 10. The indicators can be established in consultation with the coach and should reflect the organisation's priorities, such as performance at one extreme or participation at the other.

Tactics and activities

Systems should be put in place to ensure that the coaching staff are able to work to their potential. The following items indicate the kind of steps involved in a coaching support program.

POSSIBLE TACTIC
Provide quality organisational and managerial support to coaching personnel in order to bolster the performance of individuals and teams.

Possible activities
Create and circulate a detailed schedule of all activities, venues, times and personnel involved.
Use checklists to ensure that equipment and facilities are satisfactory, and that all appropriate documentation is available.
Create a simple and standard system for information dissemination that is easily and reliably duplicated.
Board (committee) to evaluate coaches on the basis of objective performance criteria such as player skill and win–loss record (depends on level of competition)

Medical support

Medical support is vital, particularly for 'professional' athletes, who may be seen as 'assets' of the sport or club regardless of whether they are on an employment contract, or are the recipient of an official sponsorship. Medical support comes in the form of injury prevention, management and rehabilitation. Standard performance indicators include number of injuries, their seriousness and the recovery time. The speed and skill with which Errol Alcott, chief physiotherapist for the Australian cricket team, can treat and rehabilitate injured players is a measure of his competence.

Medical staff may comprise doctors, physiotherapists, sports trainers, sports psychologists and first aid practitioners, among others. Their job is to advise coaches and athletes or players on the avoidance of injury and the handling of stress, and to treat injuries when they occur. The administrator's role is to ensure that medical staff have the appropriate information, legal support, and facilities and equipment.

Appropriate information includes player/participant profiles, medical histories and details of special needs. Legal support includes player and organisation insurance (legal issues are examined in more detail in Chapter 11).

The checklist in Table 6.2 details the basic items that should be available to the medical staff. Further information can be obtained from Sports Medicine Australia (SMA), which conducts regular sports trainer accreditation courses.

Table 6.2 Medical and first aid checklist

ITEM	CHECK	
	✔	✘
Information		
(Contact numbers)		
■ Ambulance		
■ Dentist		
■ Doctor		
■ Eye and ear hospital		
■ Head trainer		
■ Local general hospital		
■ Parents or next of kin		
■ Specialty hospitals		
■ Sports medicine clinic		
■ Team headquarters		
(Documentation)		
■ Injury forms		
■ Instruction sheets for common and severe injury		
■ Medical history forms		
■ On-duty forms		

ITEM	CHECK	
	✔	✘
■ Participant medication lists		
■ Treatment forms		
Legal support		
■ All medical support accredited and qualified		
■ Organisation insurance		
■ Player insurance		
Facilities		
■ Clean		
■ Close to change rooms		
■ Close to playing area		
■ Electricity outlets		
■ Entrance large enough for stretcher and wheelchair		
■ On ground floor		
■ Privacy		
■ Running water		
■ Sufficient lighting		
■ Telephone		
■ Temperature control		
Basic equipment		
(Medical supplies to be determined by doctor)		
■ Antibiotic ointment		
■ Antiseptic		
■ Bandaids		
■ Blankets		
■ Bowls		
■ Broom		
■ Bucket and mop		
■ Clock		
■ Cotton buds		
■ Disinfectant (for cleaning)		
■ Elastic bandages		
■ Eyewash		
■ Eyecup		
■ Garbage bins		
■ Heel and lace pads		
■ Jordan frame		
■ Mirror		
■ Razor		
■ Scissors		
■ Slings		
■ Soap		
■ Sterile gauze		
■ Sterile pads		
■ Stretcher		

ITEM	CHECK	
	✔	✘
■ Sunblock		
■ Tape		
■ Tape adherent		
■ Tape cutters		
■ Thermometer		
■ Tongue depressors		
■ Towels		
■ Tweezers		
■ Underwrap		
■ Vaseline		
Useful extras		
■ Adhesive-backed foam		
■ Air splint		
■ Antacid tablets		
■ Anti-fungal powder		
■ Anti-glare ointment		
■ Assorted bandaids		
■ Assorted tape		
■ Crutches		
■ Eyepads		
■ Heel cups		
■ Massage lubricant		
■ Micropore tape		
■ Padding		
■ Panadol and aspirin		
■ Pillow		
■ Scales		
■ Steri-strips		
■ Tape remover		
■ Waterproof tape		

Performance measurement

Whatever method is used, evaluation should involve objective criteria related to the organisation's area of sport. In the case of a team, the performance indicators are likely to include frequency, type and duration of injury.

Tactics and activities

Administrators should put in place a management support system which enables the medical and paramedical staff to provide quality service. A generic approach is as follows:

POSSIBLE TACTIC
Provide quality organisational and managerial support to medical personnel in order to bolster the performance of individuals and teams.

Possible activities
Use checklists to help ensure that medical personnel have the necessary facilities and equipment.
Use checklists to help ensure that medical personnel have all appropriate information at their disposal.
Use checklists to help ensure that the legal support medical personnel require in place, in order to protect them as well as the organisation (more detail on legal support is contained in Chapter 11).
Evaluate the performance of medical personnel on the basis of objective performance criteria.

Conditioning

Conditioning is concerned with developing strength, flexibility, agility, speed and endurance. It is often co-ordinated and directed by specialists rather than by the skills coaches. Conditioning is an essential part of team preparation, being vital in gaining a competitive advantage over opponents. Capable fitness coaches are in high demand.

Administrators have an overall responsibility for the quality and appropriateness of conditioning equipment and facilities, nutritional supplements needed by players or athletes, and information concerning fitness needs. While direct initiatives in this area are usually taken by the coaching staff, administrators need to appreciate the requirements of conditioning personnel and to be sensitive to the rapid technological change going on in this field.

Performance measurement

The conditioning staff's performance is typically measured in terms of the fitness and performance of players or athletes. Again the specific indicators should be developed in conjunction with those to whom the service is supplied—the coaches and players.

Tactics and activities

A generic approach is as follows:

POSSIBLE TACTIC
Provide quality organisational and managerial support to conditioning personnel in order to bolster the performance of individuals and teams.

Possible activities
Provide appropriate equipment and supplements for players as determined by the coaching staff and conditioning personnel.
Develop a system for providing the necessary information to conditioning staff concerning the needs of players.
Evaluate the performance of conditioning personnel on the basis of objective performance criteria.

Recruiting

Recruiting involves identifying sporting talent and attracting it to a team or to a sport. Performance indicators include the relative talent of the players or athletes and the proportion of those 'discovered' who are ultimately successful. The Australian Institute of Sport can measure the success of its junior talent identification programs by simply counting the number of competitors who make the transition to senior events.

The ultimate indicator is overall performance in competition—win–loss records, titles, premierships, medals and rankings.

Since recruiting and talent identification officers usually report directly to the coach, they tend to rely on the coaching panel for information and resources. In practice, this may leave the humble administrator with a 'fill in the gaps' role. Nevertheless, good administrators, even if they are not required to directly provide any resources or information, should know the infrastructure that must be in place for recruiting to proceed successfully.

The information that recruiting officers require includes statistics on fixtures and games, the recruiting 'systems' available to them, the success of previously used methods, the player draft in regulated leagues, and the playing needs of the team. Additional resources include access to computers, video equipment and statistical software. Again, a checklist approach is recommended. Ideally, it should be developed by the coaching staff and recruiting officers in consultation with administrators. Good recruiting is resource-dependent. Experience and intuition is no longer sufficient.

Performance measurement

Recruiting officers are usually evaluated on the basis of the quality of their selections. They provide a service to the coaching staff, and it is therefore axiomatic that the coaching panel be involved in the review process. This is a good example of how 'internal' customers' needs must be considered (see Chapter 4).

Tactics and activities

To achieve success in recruitment, appropriate support must be made available. The following generic approach will assist in this.

POSSIBLE TACTIC
Provide quality organisational and managerial support to recruiting and talent identification officers in order to bolster the performance of individuals and teams.

Possible activities
Provide the appropriate resources to recruiting officers as determined by the coaching staff and office bearers.
Develop a system for providing the necessary information to recruiting officers.
Evaluate the performance of recruiting officers on the basis of objective performance criteria.

SUMMARY

This chapter addressed the pivotal administrative support measures that comprise player management. Player management has four dimensions. First, a broad base of coaching support must be available. This includes the formulation of detailed training and player activity schedules; the provision of appropriate instruction, facilities and equipment; and the effective distribution of information to staff and players. Second, quality medical support must be provided. This requires the acquisition of vital medical data; a knowledge of legal responsibilities; an injury and fitness dossier; and the availability of essential treatment, facilities and equipment. Third, conditioning is essential to the physical development of players. This requires the supply of quality equipment, nutritional supplements and professional advice based on sound scientific research. Finally, recruiting systems must be designed and implemented extensively. These should focus on systematic 'market' surveillance, in which player and league information is collated and analysed.

FURTHER READING

Day, R. (1994) *Management Strategies in Athletic Training*, Human Kinetics, Champaign, Ill.
Parcells, B. (1995) *Finding a Way to Win: The Principles of Leadership, Teamwork and Motivation*, Doubleday, New York.

7 Financial management

After reading this chapter you should be able to understand and practise the preparation and analysis of financial statements
More specifically, you should have a general grasp of how to:

■ record financial events in journals and ledgers
■ develop income and expenditure statements and balance sheets
■ create cash flow statements
■ use financial ratios to analyse financial positions
■ practise the essentials of budgetary control

INTRODUCTION

Money is not everything, but for many organisations it can be the deciding factor in their success. In this chapter we aim to demonstrate and explain how financial management should be approached in sporting organisations. We do not provide a recipe for maximising income, but we do identify guidelines and procedures for the proper financial management of an organisation and its activities.

The central components of financial management are set out in Figure 7.1.

BASIC CONCEPTS AND REQUIREMENTS

Dollars and cents are literally the 'bottom line' for profit-seeking sporting franchises and some leisure-based businesses, but the importance of formal financial management for sporting clubs and associations is frequently underemphasised. Although clubs and associations are generally not profit-seeking, and are not encumbered with the complexities of some commercial businesses, they have no excuse for poor financial operation. A well-documented and systematic scheme for managing an organisation's money and other assets is essential, because it:

Figure 7.1 Central components of financial management

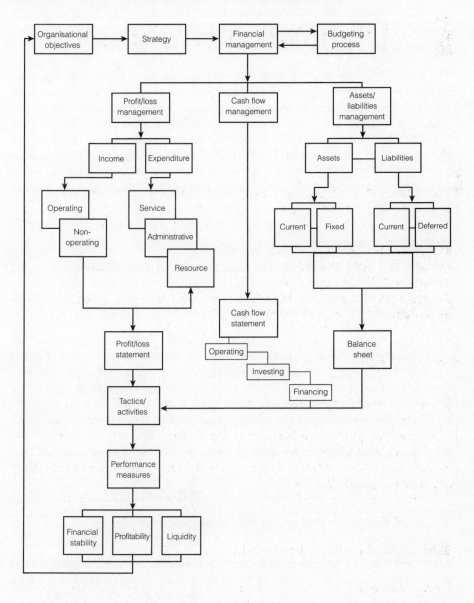

- can inform the committee or board of management as to the financial position of the organisation at any one time
- helps staff to anticipate any impending problems and to take steps to avoid them

- provides a basis for forward planning by detailing information concerning anticipated income and expenditure.

Wealth versus profits

The financial health of a sporting organisation can be diagnosed in the same way as in any other organisation. However, many people are confused by the difference between a wealthy club and a profitable club. Wealth is calculated by comparing the difference between the total asset value and the total liabilities at a particular time. In other words, what is owned is contrasted with what is owed. Profit is calculated by identifying the difference between total earned income for a period and the total expenses incurred in generating that income. All other things being equal, increasing profits will lead to an increase in wealth.

Role of the treasurer

In clubs and associations, the treasurer has the responsibility for managing financial affairs, although often in larger organisations this is at least partially delegated to paid administrators or accountants. The role typically involves three duties:

- *Maintaining custody of the organisation's funds:* The treasurer should aim to deal with all organisational funds in accordance with the entity's constitution and the legitimate wishes of the members. Thus the primary role of the treasurer is to keep accurate records concerning sources of income and areas of expenditure.
- *Reporting to members:* The treasurer must report the organisation's financial affairs to the members, including detailed financial statements.
- *Dealing with money responsibilities promptly:* Treasurers should ensure that transactions are recorded immediately; the least useful trait of a treasurer is procrastination.

Rules of financial operation for non-profit sporting organisations

Maintaining and presenting financial records is one of the most important tasks in the administration of a sporting body, from both an operational and a legal viewpoint. It is therefore common for financial procedures to be defined in the organisation's constitution or by-laws. Such matters typically include:

- authorisation of office bearers to operate the organisation's bank accounts (usually this requires the signatures of several office bearers)
- limits on expenditure that may be authorised by the treasurer or the chief executive without reference to the full committee or the general membership

- dates of the organisation's financial year
- audit requirements

What is expected from an organisation's accounts?

Accounting is concerned with identifying financial information, expressing it in quantifiable terms and communicating it to interested parties. Bookkeeping constitutes the base information for accounting reports and is sometimes referred to as financial 'scorekeeping'. It involves the basic but essential tasks of cash recording and bank reconciliations.

As far as reporting is concerned, section 30(3) of the *Associations Incorporation Act 1981* in Victoria, for example, requires an incorporated body to submit statements of income and expenditure, assets and liabilities, mortgages, charges and securities, and details of trusts. Other Australian States have similar reporting requirements for incorporated clubs and associations. Further details on incorporation are discussed in Chapter 11.

The financial matters of an organisation do not have to be complex, but they should be accurate, consistent, timely and reported regularly to the management committee. It is also important that all monetary matters be dealt with in accordance with the rules of the organisation. Financial reports are not confidential or secret documents; they are the public property of the organisation, not the private property of the treasurer and management committee.

Auditing a non-profit sporting organisation's accounts

It is in the interests of a sporting organisation to have its financial records audited on at least an annual basis. This may be a legal requirement under the constitution of some organisations and/or under State legislation. In some circumstances, such as in an unincorporated club, it may be legally acceptable for the auditor to be a member of the organisation, but the legislation applying to incorporated bodies commonly requires that the responsibility for auditing be assumed by an independent person or firm. This may need to be done under a professional arrangement, with an audit fee incurred. While auditors must be independent of the treasurer with respect to carrying out the audit, they can advise the treasurer on how the financial records should be maintained. An inexperienced treasurer may find a certified auditor a valuable source of advice.

METHODS OF ACCOUNT RECORDING

The particular form that a non-profit organisation's financial management system takes will vary according to the size of the organisation, its range of programs, services and activities, and whether or not it is incorporated. There are two recognised methods of account recording:

- cash accounting
- accrual accounting

Cash method

Some small organisations use the cash accounting method, in which receipts and expenses are reported when they are actually received (banked) or paid. In this case the revenue and expense patterns of the organisation form an exact match with the cash flow pattern. In other words, what is spent by and paid to an organisation is exactly what is recorded at the time. However, while the cash method is uncomplicated and logical, it leaves something to be desired as a means of measuring the organisation's performance over time. Because the cash system is based on cash as it is spent or received, it is simply not appropriate for most organisations. It is often not in their best interests to record a payment or receipt when it actually occurs. Instead, it should be recorded for the appropriate *financial period* in which it is earned or incurred. For example, if an organisation were to pay an insurance premium on behalf of its members on 30 June 1999, it would be recorded in the 1998/99 financial year despite the fact that the benefits would be obtained during the 1999/2000 financial year. Similarly, the purchase of a computer would be recorded in the year it was bought, even though it would provide benefits in many subsequent years as well. The only official assets that an organisation using a cash-based accounting system possesses are cash and shareholders' equity or capital (what the owners or members have contributed out of their own pockets to start the organisation).

Accrual method

In contrast, the accrual system is based on the notion that expenses and revenues need not involve cash at the immediate moment of transaction, but rather when the resources acquired have been used. So revenue is recognised when it is earned, instead of when it is collected, and expenses are recognised when assets or benefits are used, instead of when they are paid for. The accrual system provides more accurate details on the financial status of an organisation than the cash-based system, and therefore is of more use for management decision making. However, it's also more complicated, requiring what's known as a 'matching' of expenses to revenue.

As noted, under the accrual method expenses and revenues are identified independently of when cash is actually received or paid. The problem with this approach is that revenue earned during a specific period must be 'matched' with the expenses linked with that revenue, thus making revenue the driving force dictating the documentation of expenses. The chief purpose of the matching procedure is to ensure that a true net profit or loss is reported, because if revenue is matched directly to its accompanying expenses, then a surplus represents a profit and a shortfall a loss. In order that the matching process be as accurate as possible, numerous recording 'adjustments' are made prior to the preparation of financial statements.

Before we turn to the adjustments needed, we must take a brief look at the recording of transactions.

Recording of transactions

The whole point of keeping records on financial transactions is to monitor the organisation's performance and provide a summary of its financial affairs. For some small sporting organisations there are few financial transactions, leaving cash receipts and cash payments as the only details to consider in calculating overall financial performance during a given period. However, other organisations are faced with a large number of daily transactions, particularly profit-seeking enterprises like leisure centres and non-profit but 'surplus-seeking' professional clubs such as those in national sports leagues. In these situations, the documentation process involves recording transactions on a daily basis in journals which are subsequently totalled into ledgers, which in turn are compiled to form trial balances which form the basis for financial statements. Figure 7.2 illustrates this process.

Journals

Transactions are recorded in chronological order in journals, which are simply books or computer files. Although financial events can be documented in

Figure 7.2 The accounting process

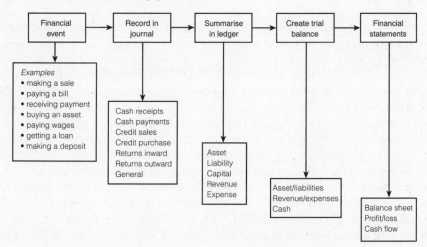

one all-encompassing journal, there are several useful subdivisions that can be used to record specific transactions. They involve:

- cash receipts journal: records all cash received
- cash payments journal: records all cash paid
- credit sales journal: records all sales of goods or services that are paid for by credit
- credit purchase journal: records all purchases of goods or services bought with credit
- returns inward journal: records reimbursements of goods or services to customers that were purchased using credit
- returns outward journal: records reimbursements of goods and services bought by the organisation on credit
- general journal: records purchases of assets other than stock on credit, and any other transactions not entered elsewhere.

No financial event should be recorded in more than one journal.

In many situations all these subdivisions are unnecessary, but the theory of record keeping remains fixed. The accompanying box contains simple examples of two of the types of journal.

AUSTRALIAN INDOOR WINDSURFING ASSOCIATION: CASH PAYMENTS JOURNAL

Event	Details	Amount $
1	Office stationery	25
2	Advertising	156
3	Postage-paid envelopes	1 500
4	Staff T-shirts	225
5	Promotional caps	300
	Total	2 206

PARADISE CITY LEISURE CENTRE: CREDIT SALES JOURNAL

Event	Details	Amount $
1	P. Johns—full membership	590
2	I. Lills—swim suit #23	45
3	A. Gleeson—gym membership	295
4	Brisbane City Council—corporate membership	40 000
5	J. Hamad—protein powder #1456	36
	Total	40 966

Ledgers

The totals from the journals are transferred to a ledger, which is simply an account of debit and credit, typically summarised by using a T-account. The T-account includes debits on the left side and credits on the right, as can be seen in the illustration below.

Name of account

Debits	Credits

In order to understand financial recording using the T-account—also referred to as double-entry bookkeeping—it is first necessary to purge your mind of the traditional notion of debits and credits: that of increasing and decreasing an account, respectively. Accounting convention holds that debits refer to the left side of an account, and credits to the right. From now on, consider debits and credits to mean no more than left and right.

There are five standard groups of accounts:

■ asset accounts
■ liability accounts
■ capital accounts
■ revenue accounts
■ expense accounts

The most important rule in recording information on a ledger is that for every debit there must be a corresponding credit, and for every credit there must be a corresponding debit. (Hence the name, double-entry book-keeping.) This is accomplished by recording opposing effects on opposite sides of the ledger. All financial recording can be summarised using a simple equation:

$$A = L + P$$
$$\text{where } P = [C + R - E - D]$$

Thus assets or items of value owned (A) is always equal to liabilities or amounts owed to others (L) *plus* proprietorship (P). Proprietorship consists of the owner's equity or invested capital (C) which is in turn affected by revenue (R), which boosts the equity. But expenses or costs (E) associated with earning revenue, and withdrawals or owners' drawings from equity (D), must be subtracted from the equity.

For the non-accountant, the easiest way to cope with the peculiarities of financial recording is to follow the 'rules' listed in Table 7.1.

You might observe from these rules that increases in assets and expenses normally have a debit outcome, while increases in liabilities, capital and revenue usually have a credit outcome. Note how this rule is effected in the

Table 7.1 Financial recording rules

Account	Increase	Decrease
Asset	Debit	Credit
Liability	Credit	Debit
Capital	Credit	Debit
Revenue	Credit	Debit
Expense	Debit	Credit

example ledger for Greenwood Tennis Club. To keep matters simple, we have constructed the ledger from a single general journal (see below). Account symbols (refer above equation) are included in brackets.

GREENWOOD TENNIS CLUB: GENERAL JOURNAL

Date	Particulars	Debit $	Credit $
July 1	Cash at bank (A—increases)	20 000	
	Capital from membership (C—increases)		20 000
	New members pay 'joining fee'		
3	Office equipment (A—increases)	1 800	
	Accounts payable (L—increases)		1 800
	Purchased computer and printer on credit		
4	Office supplies (A—increases)	140	
	Accounts payable (L—increases)		140
	Purchased office supplies on credit		
5	Insurance (E—increases)	12 000	
	Cash at bank (A—decreases)		12 000
	Paid members' insurance		
7	Accounts receivable (A—increases)	450	
	Service revenue (R—increases)		450
	Invoiced members for racquet restringing		
11	Cash at bank (A—increases)	3 000	
	Service revenue (R—increases)		3 000
	Payment for coaching clinic		
20	Advertising (E—increases)	400	
	Cash at bank (A—decreases)		400
	Advertising payment in cash		
25	Cash at bank (A—increases)	50	
	Office equipment (A—decreases)		50
	Cash sale of photocopier		

Date	Particulars	Debit $	Credit $
July 29	Office equipment (A—increases)	2 500	
	Accounts payable (L—increases)		2 500
	Purchased photocopier on credit		
30	Utilities bills and rent (E—increases)	2 500	
	Cash at bank (A—decreases)		2 500
	Cash payment for utilities and rent		

Transactions, July

1st Deposit of $20 000 from members joining fee in business cheque account.

3rd Bought computer and printer for $1800 on credit.

4th Purchased office supplies (staplers, scissors etc.) on credit for $140.

5th Paid insurance for members of $12 000 in cash.

7th Invoiced members for racquet restringing to the value of $450.

11th Received payment for coaching clinic completed on the 1st, to the value of $3000.

20th Paid for advertising in local paper for $400 in cash.

25th Sold photocopier for $50 cash.

29th Bought new photocopier for $2500 with credit.

30th Paid utilities bills totalling $1500 and rent of $1000.

GREENWOOD TENNIS CLUB: LEDGER

Date	Particulars	Debit $	Credit $	Balance $
July	**Assets**			
	Cash at bank			
1		20 000		20 000DR
5			12 000	8 000DR
11		3 000		11 000DR
20			400	10 600DR
25		50		10 650DR
30			2 500	8 150DR
	Office equipment			
3		1 800		9 950DR
4		140		10 090DR
25			50	10 040DR
29		2 500		12 540DR

Date	Particulars	Debit $	Credit $	Balance $
July 7	Accounts receivable	450		12 990DR
	Liabilities			
July 3	Accounts payable		1 800	11 190DR
4			140	11 050DR
29			2 500	8 550DR
	Capital			
1	Members' equity		20 000	11 450CR
	Revenue			
7	Accounts receivable		450	11 900CR
11	Coaching revenue		3 000	14 900CR
	Expenses			
5	Insurance expense	12 000		2 900CR
20	Advertising expense	400		2 500CR
30	Utilities and rent expense	2 500		0

As can be seen in the ledger, all financial events have been summarised directly from the general journal, with debits and credits balancing exactly. As a result, the balance column equals zero at the end. Don't worry too much about the exact meaning of each heading—they can be determined by your accountant. Rather, concentrate on understanding the process.

Trial balances

The next step is to create a trial balance for Greenwood Tennis Club. This is simply a verification that equal debits and credits have been recorded in the accounts (see over). Trial balances are generally completed at the end of each month, and form the basis for the annual financial statements.

GREENWOOD TENNIS CLUB: TRIAL BALANCE (TOTALS)		
Account title	Debit $	Credit $
Assets		
Cash at bank	23 050	14 900
Equipment	4 440	50
Accounts receivable	450	
Liabilities		
Accounts payable		4 440
Capital		
Members' equity		20 000
Revenue		
Accounts receivable		450
Coaching revenue		3 000
Expenses		
Insurance	12 000	
Advertising	400	
Utilities and rent	2 500	
	42 840	42 840

What to do and when

Table 7.2 provides a general guide for keeping financial records up to date.[1]

Adjustments

As mentioned earlier, there are a number of so-called balance day adjustments, which affect both the income and expenditure statement and the balance sheet. The point of these adjustments is to make certain that accurate records are kept concerning transactions that might otherwise go unrecorded. There are five possible adjusting entries that are recorded in the journal:

- record of accrued revenue: revenue earned but not yet received is recorded as an account receivable (money owing)
- record of accrued expenses: expenses incurred but not yet paid for are recorded as accrued expenses (money owed)
- record of prepaid expenses: expenses such as utilities and insurance which are paid prior to their consumption are recognised as assets
- record of revenue received in advance: payment for goods not yet supplied or services not yet performed are recorded as liabilities
- depreciation: recognition that fixed or long-term assets do not hold their cost value over time

Table 7.2 Recommended documentation for financial record keeping

Daily	Weekly	Monthly	Annually
Total up cash	Review accounts	Balance cheque	Prepare income
Record income	Review accounts	accounts	and expenditure
Record payments	payable	Total all ledgers	statements
Enter deposits	Prepare payroll	Reconcile petty	Prepare balance
	Deduct items sold	cash	sheets
	from stock	Review inventory	Prepare cash flow
			statements

Depreciation

Any system of financial management will involve a detailed set of principles by which assets are valued and depreciated. This process is more formally known as amortisation. The generally accepted accounting convention is to enter a non-current (fixed or long-term) asset in the journal at an 'historical' or cost price, although sometimes it may be recorded in terms of a replacement or market value. As a rule, accounting tradition tends toward conservatism and therefore undervaluation. Also, the cost of an asset can often be more than the purchase price. For example, if a club purchased a personal computer, software and printer for $5000, and incurred freight and installation charges of $500, then the cost of the computer system would be $5500. Assets may also be revalued up or down during their lifetime.

Depreciation is based on the principle that all non-current assets represent a store of 'service potential' that the organisation intends to use over the life of the asset. Assets have a limited life as a result of wear and tear and obsolescence. Accounting for depreciation is the process whereby the decline in the service potential of an asset, such as a motor vehicle, is progressively brought to account as a periodic charge against revenue. In simple terms, an asset is devalued in response to its market or real value, and offset against income. In order to allocate the cost of the asset to the period in which it is used, an estimate must be made of the asset's useful life. This will usually be less than its physical life. For example, in the case of a motor vehicle, it may be decided that after three years it will not be operating as efficiently and therefore will be worth less after this period, even though it is still running. If an asset has a residual, or resale, value, then this amount will be subtracted from the asset cost to establish the actual amount to be depreciated.

The simplest method for depreciating an asset is the straight line or prime cost method. This method allocates an equal amount of depreciation to each full accounting period in the asset's useful life. The amount of depreciation for each period is determined by dividing the cost of the asset minus its residual value by the number of periods in the asset's useful life. Depreciation for each year is calculated as indicated in Table 7.3.

Table 7.3 Recording depreciation

Cost – Residual value = $30 000 – $2000 = $28 000

Useful life = 7 years

= $4000 annual depreciation for 7 years.

A journal entry to record this depreciation might look as follows:

Date	Particulars	Debit $	Credit $
Aug 23	Depreciation expense: Motor vehicle (E—increases)	4000	
	Depreciation: Motor vehicle (A—decreases)		4000

COMPUTER ACCOUNTING

Accrual accounting has traditionally been the domain of wealthier sports clubs and associations which have simply hired accountants to maintain their financial records. However, in the last decade accrual methods have become increasingly accessible to small, under-resourced sporting organisations via computer accounting software.

Popular small-business accounting packages such as Quickbooks and MYOB remove the confusion from the double-entry bookkeeping system. Transactions are simply entered as they occur in 'idiot-proof' pro formas. The software calculates and updates journals, ledgers, trial balances and all financial statements at the whim of the user. For a small financial investment and a couple of hours practice, accounting software is a must for even the smallest sporting organisation. Accounting software can even analyse financial statements for you; and statement analysis is instrumental to successful financial management.

FINANCIAL STATEMENTS

Financial statements exist to provide information about the financial status of an organisation to those outside its administration; in this case members, government and commercial sponsors. In the commercial world, there is only one way to keep score in a business: in dollars and cents. And while making a profit is not an objective for many sporting organisations (though achieving a surplus may well be a valid strategy), complete and accurate financial records are the key to the financial health, and ultimately the continued existence, of any organisation.

Income and expenditure (profit and loss) statement

This statement records the results of operating a business, and under normal circumstances it is formally documented on an annual basis.[2] Income, or revenue, includes any earnings associated with the operation of the organisation. Expenditure consists of the costs or expenses incurred as a result of operation. Revenues in sporting organisations are generally obtained from the provision of services, and in providing these services there are certain costs. The income and expenditure statement gives a *breakdown* of the various revenues and costs associated with service delivery. It is useful for an organisation to keep track of the *areas* of primary income and expenditure as well as establishing whether it has operated with a surplus (profit) or with a deficit (loss).

The accompanying box contains an example of an income and expenditure statement.

QUEENSLAND AERIAL TENNIS ASSOCIATION PTY LTD

Statement of income and expenditure for the year ended 31 July 1999

	1999 $	1998 $
INCOME		
Operating		
Membership fees	15 000	15 800
Corporate sponsorship and licence fees	5 000	5 000
Donations	2 100	1 000
Fund raising	1 500	2 400
Grants		
Federal—Australian Sports Commission	2 000	1 500
Investment	200	245
Non-operating		
Asset sales	340	
	26 140	25 945
EXPENDITURE		
Service		
Program services	6 700	8 000
Insurance	3 200	3 500
Administrative		
Wages (masseurs and umbrella holders)	1 400	2 500
Utilities and rent	3 000	3 200
Stationery and printing	1 135	2 245
Resource		
Sunscreen	356	500
	15 791	19 945
Surplus (Deficit)	10 349	6 000

Incomes

Income is typically classified into either an operating or a non-operating category. Operating income is ongoing and provides the necessary funding for the organisation's continued functioning, while non-operating income is 'out of the ordinary' and is infrequent and irregular. Non-operating income may include the sale of assets such as unneeded equipment or, in some cases, the transfer of players. Normally non-operating income is negligible, but in the case of clubs competing in unregulated leagues it can be considerable as a result of player transfers. Operating income is derived from three sources:

- members and the public: membership fees, payment for specific services, gate receipts, sale of promotional material and merchandise
- government: grants
- sponsors: money exchanged for sponsor 'exposure' and other tangible and non-tangible benefits

Expenses

Usually expenses are classified on a functional or operational basis. They can be grouped as:

- actual service costs
- administrative costs
- resource costs

Actual service costs include the expenses incurred as a direct result of services delivered, such as program costs, facility hiring fees and referees' pay. Administrative costs are those generated from the general operation of the organisation, such as salaries, office lease, utility bills and stationery. Resource costs are the expenses generated as a result of the external acquisition of resources; for example, interest paid on bank loans, or resources committed to sponsorship agreements, such as the provision of seating, tickets or personnel that would normally be occupied elsewhere. In addition, resource costs can be incurred by allocating money, time and personnel in satisfying the policies and political whims of government agencies and other sponsors.

Balance sheet

The balance sheet indicates an organisation's 'balance' of economic resources in the form of assets and liabilities, and provides a 'snapshot' of its financial position at any time. Assets are items of monetary value owned by the organisation or owed to the organisation. Liabilities are the amounts owing to creditors for goods or services received or borrowed. Balance sheets are not a measure of profits or surpluses. This is the function of income and expenditure statements. Balance sheets measure the wealth of a sporting organisation.

The common method of classification of assets is by liquidity, which is a measure of how rapidly an asset can be converted into cash. Assets can be *current*, which means they can be converted comparatively rapidly (in less than about one year); examples may be debts owed to the organisation and stocks. Or they can be *fixed* or *non-current* (the terms are used interchangeably). These are intended for continuing use instead of conversion to cash; examples are facilities and equipment.

Liabilities are classified according to the urgency with which they must be removed. *Current* liabilities must be discharged promptly; they include short-term loans, interest, bills and tax. *Deferred* or *non-current* liabilities are not urgent; they include debts owed by the organisation that do not require repayment within a year, such as mortgages.

The accompanying box sets out an example of a balance sheet.

PERFORMANCE PERSONAL TRAINING PTY LTD

Balance sheet for the year ended 30 June 1999

	$	$
ASSETS		
Current assets		
Cash in bank	5 000	
Money owed by clients	3 000	
Nutritional supplements stock	2 000	
		10 000
Non-current assets		
Motor vehicle	20 000	
Exercise equipment	10 000	
Office furniture	1 500	
Office equipment	2 500	
Sporting equipment	3 000	37 000
Total assets		47 000
LIABILITIES		
Current		
Bank overdraft	7 500	
Credit card debt	4 000	
Money owed to suppliers	2 500	14 000
Non-current		
Personal bank loan	18 000	18 000
Total liabilities		32 000
Net assets (before income tax)		15 000
Proprietorship (capital)	15 000	

Balance sheet details

Information used in the balance sheet can be obtained from the income and expenditure statement as well as from previous balance sheets.

Assets

Anything that is legally owned by the organisation or owed to the organisation is included under 'assets'. Always work with net values, which means that depreciation must be subtracted.

Current assets

- *Cash in bank:* this means what it says—the amount of cash in the bank, including checking accounts and savings accounts.
- *Petty cash:* funds held specifically for miscellaneous expenses.
- *Accounts receivable:* everything owed to an organisation for services or products already provided.
- *Inventory/stock:* raw materials and goods that are held by an organisation for sale.
- *Short-term investments:* interest or dividends that are expected to be converted to cash inside one year. Stock portfolios and time-deposit bank accounts that are anticipated to be soon converted to cash are examples. List these investments at either cost price or market value—whichever is less.
- *Prepaid expenses:* any goods or services that are paid for before they are used, such as insurance or rent.

Non-current assets

- *Long-term investments:* any long-term assets that are intended to be held for more than one year, which typically pay interest or dividends, such as stock and bonds.

Fixed assets

Includes all facilities, equipment and resources that a business owns or uses for use in its operations, and that are not intended to be sold. Remember to subtract depreciation.

- *Land:* value of land owned by organisation.
- *Buildings:* value of buildings owned by organisation.
- *Upgrades and improvements:* value of investment made in improving land or buildings.
- *Furniture:* value of office furniture.
- *Vehicles:* value of vehicles owned by organisation.
- *Specific equipment:* value of equipment used in organisations' services, such as cricket bats or weight-training equipment.

■ *Office equipment:* value of equipment used in administrative operation of organisation, like computers and printers.

Liabilities

The value of everything an organisation owes to others.

Current liabilities

■ *Accounts payable:* what is owed to suppliers for goods or services already received.
■ *Notes payable:* the principal of short-term debts from borrowed funds, such as credit cards and bank overdrafts.
■ *Interest payable:* Total of fees on all borrowed capital and credit.
■ *Taxes:* amounts of tax estimated by accountant.
■ *Payroll accrual:* total of salaries and wages owed.

Non-current liabilities

■ *Notes payable:* the principal of debts to be paid over a period greater than one year, such as bank loans and mortgages.

Net assets

The total amount an organisation is worth, calculated by subtracting liabilities from assets. The term 'net worth' can also be used to describe this relationship.

Cash flow statements

Cash flow is a measure of liquidity, rather than profitability. Traditionally cash flow statements have not been part of sporting organisations' financial statements. However, this has changed in recent years, particularly as asset-wealthy sporting organisations have discovered that they require a steady flow of cash to pay suppliers, creditors and employees. In addition, as sport clubs become incorporated, they are legally obliged to present cash flow statements. Liquidity is a particularly useful measure for many sporting organisations, because rarely do they have a constant or consistent cash flow. Instead, their income is predominantly acquired through lump sum payments at predetermined times in the year, correlating with membership payments, government grants or sponsorship revenue. The net result is that their 'turnover' or total or gross income can be sufficient, but their cash flow is irregular, and often generated over a period of several months. Consequently, administrators have sought to deal with the major expenses of their organisation at 'convenient' times of the year, but as the organisation has grown to meet the demands of increased professionalism their expenses have become more regular. Staff, for example, might expect to be paid fortnightly, and if the cash is not available there will be serious ramifications. To combat this problem, cash flow statements can be used to increase financial control.

It is possible for an organisation to be generating profits but still go into liquidation or become bankrupt. This arises due to a lack of cash flow planning. *Profit does not equal cash*. A cursory look at financial statements shows that cash and profit figures do not match in an accrual system; income earned is matched with the expenses incurred as a result of producing that income. A decrease in cash balance may occur at the same time as an increase in net operating profit for the period. For example, cash used for loan repayments and asset purchases does not affect profit. A cash flow statement, detailing month-by-month expected cash inflows, expected outflows and monthly cash balances, is required to determine whether the organisation will have sufficient cash flow to pay its debts when they fall due and, consequently stay in business.

Perhaps the easiest way to look at cash flow is to think of it in terms of three areas:

■ operating activities: activities relating to the delivery of goods or services
■ investing activities: activities related to the purchase and sale of non-current or fixed assets
■ financing activities: activities related to the type of finance that supports an organisation

An example of a cash flow statement is outlined in the accompanying box. Please note that outgoing cashflow is recorded in brackets.

BLACKSTUMP LEISURE CENTRE

Cash flow statement for the year ending 30 June 1999

	$
Operating activities	
Receipts from members	5 000
Interest received	150
Tax rebate	6 000
Investing activities	
Equipment	(10 000)
Sale of non-current assets	15 000
Financing activities	
Loan from bank	6 300
Repayment of overdraft	(2 100)
Net cash inflow or (outflow)	20 350

Table 7.4 Projected and actual cash flow proforma

	PROJECTED $	ACTUAL $
Operating activities		
Receipts from customers	—	—
Payments to suppliers	(__)	(__)
Payments to employees	(__)	(__)
Dividends received	—	—
Interest received	—	—
Interest paid	(__)	(__)
Tax paid	—	—
Tax refunded	(__)	(__)
Other operating payments (e.g. advertising or insurance)	(__)	(__)
Other operating proceeds	—	—
Investing activities		
Payments for facilities or equipment	(__)	(__)
Sale of non-current assets	—	—
Payments for non-current investments	(__)	(__)
Proceeds from non-current investments	—	—
Other investing payments	(__)	(__)
Other investing proceeds	—	—
Financing activities		
Proceeds from current investments	—	—
Payments for current investments	(__)	(__)
Payments for borrowings	(__)	(__)
Other financing payments	(__)	(__)
Other financing proceeds	—	—
NET CASH INFLOW OR (OUTFLOW)	—	—

Tactics and activities

Control of cash flow is so important for administrators that we detail here an approach you might take to ensure appropriate levels of liquidity.

POSSIBLE TACTIC
Manage and maximise cash flow by implementing control processes (leading to monthly cash flow statements).

Possible activities
Record all financial events in a journal and transfer totals to ledgers weekly.

Complete all financial documentation promptly (as recommended in Table 7.2 above).

Establish a performance measure by calculating and recording the quick asset ratio (see below) annually.

Streamline billing procedures using total quality management techniques to decrease payment delays for services and goods already delivered.

Keep stock to a minimum by controlling ordering with total quality management techniques.

Consider leasing rather than purchasing equipment and facilities wherever possible (this conserves cash, and monthly lease expenses are tax-deductible expenses, whereas owned resources are depreciated over time).

Use interest-free credit from suppliers wherever possible (the longer an organisation has to pay for its purchases the better for cash flow).

Get rid of unused assets or stock (if they cannot be sold, they should be donated for a tax benefit where the organisation pays income tax).

Take as long as is legally possible to pay taxes without incurring penalties, and file for refunds as soon as they're available.

Encourage members to pay their annual fees as early in the financial year as possible by providing discounts.

Invest membership and other income in short-term high interest accounts whenever the funds will not be needed for several months.

Record, predict and manage cash flow by projecting it using Table 7.4 as a guide.

FINANCIAL RATIOS

The data appearing in income and expenditure, balance sheet and cash flow statements are essential financial indicators, but in most cases financial ratios can provide additional information about the financial health of an organisation. Financial ratios are simply two figures that, when expressed as a relationship, provide another figure that can be used to quickly check financial performance and pinpoint any areas of concern. While the types of financial ratio used vary from industry to industry, the following should prove useful for most sporting organisations.

Gross profit and net profit ratios

The performance measure for the profit and loss status of an organisation is profitability. There are two useful ratios for profitability: gross profit to sales; and net profit to sales. In sporting organisations, these can be expressed as (respectively) gross and net operating surplus to annual income. When put in terms of a percentage, the higher the percentage, the greater the profitability. Of the two measures, *net* operating surplus divided by annual income is more practical, as it takes into account operating expenses. The resulting figure may be usefully converted into a percentage. (See example.)

EXAMPLE

Net surplus	Annual income	Net profit (surplus) ratio
$50 000	$500 000	0.1 (10%)

Current ratio and quick asset ratio

Also known as the working capital ratio, the current ratio is a measure of liquidity, or the ability of an organisation to pay its current debts by using its current assets. In other words, the current ratio indicates whether there is sufficient cash available to pay the organisation's immediate debts; the higher the ratio the more 'solvent' an organisation is. It can be derived from the balance sheet which, of course, lists all assets and liabilities. The current ratio is established by dividing current assets by current liabilities.

In general, a current ratio less than approximately 2:1, where an organisation owes more than half of its available assets, is an indication of trouble.[3] For example, if a club selling sportswear has cash at the bank of $50 000, debtors of $10 000 and stock of $40 000, its current assets are $100 000. If the same club owes creditors $40 000, the ratio is 100 000:40 000, which is 2.5:1. (See example.) In practical terms this means that for every dollar of debt the club has $2.50 to pay it, which is a comfortable position. Just as a ratio lower than 2:1 is a problem, so is a ratio considerably higher, which normally indicates that too much of the funds is tied up in cash or working capital.

EXAMPLE

Current assets	Current liabilities	Current ratio
$100 000	$40 000	2.5:1

The quick asset ratio, also known as the liquid ratio, is related closely to the current ratio, and is probably the best way to determine if an organisation could fulfil its financial obligations if it 'went under', or lost all revenue. This ratio omits stock from current assets as it is recognised that stock cannot provide *immediate* cash. Bank overdraft is subtracted from current liabilities as it is acknowledged that this is a normal way of financing business and is not likely to be called in for payment on demand.

If the creditors called for payment immediately, our sportswear organisation would have available $1.50 for every dollar of debt, which is obviously sufficient to clear its liabilities. (See example.) As a general rule, provided that the quick asset ratio is equal to or greater than one, the financial position of an organisation may be considered satisfactory.

Financial leverage ratio

The financial leverage ratio measures the extent to which an organisation is financed by external debt. The higher the ratio the greater the financial risk borne by creditors. The equation to determine financial leverage is shown in the box below, together with an example from the organisation's balance sheet (assets and liabilities).

FINANCIAL LEVERAGE RATIO

$$\text{Financial leverage ratio} = \frac{\text{Current and long-term liabilities}}{\text{Total liabilities} + \text{capital}} \times \frac{100}{1}$$

EXAMPLE

Creditors	$40 000
Mortgage	$55 000
Capital	$90 000
Total of the three items	$185 000

$$\text{Financial leverage ratio} = \frac{95\,000}{185\,000} \times \frac{100}{1}$$
$$= 51.4\%$$

In this case about half of the business is financed by external debt, and hence half must be financed by the proprietors (owners' equity/capital). If the leverage ratio is too high, a greater risk is endured by the creditors, leaving it difficult for the organisation to find additional finance. The financial leverage ratio gives an indication of the long-term stability of the organisation by focusing on its level of debt funding. In general, the higher the financial interest of the proprietors (or members/shareholders) the lower the financial leverage ratio, and the sounder the financial structure.

BUDGETING

The basic tool for financial planning is the budget, which is essentially a prediction of an organisation's financial situation for the coming month, year, or beyond. As well as being a valuable form of management control, the budget can also be important in communicating with members and customers, particularly if there is a need to justify increased fees and charges, or in assessing the financial implications of new development initiatives.

Budgeting is undertaken for two purposes:

■ to provide an organised estimate of future resource requirements broken down over a period of time
■ to provide a method of monitoring, controlling and evaluating an organisation's financial affairs

Budgets can take a number of forms including:

■ capital budget
■ revenue and expense budget, or operating budget
■ cash budget

Operating budgets are the most used, and provide an excellent framework for ensuring ongoing financial viability. Generally an operating budget shows a twelve-month projection of income and expenditure, although in fact it can cover any time period. An organisation may, for instance, prepare twelve one-month budgets at the beginning of the year in order to take account of any variations or fluctuations expected during the annual cycle. It is then a simple matter to convert the set of monthly budgets into an annual budget. The values for all revenue and expense items are aggregated to form the annual budget, with expected revenues compared with anticipated expenses. An excess of revenue over expenses would mean a satisfactory budget process outcome. However, if the budget process produced an excess of expenses over revenue, then it would be necessary to trim expenses or tease out some additional revenue.

Keep in mind that a budget deficit signals a problem that must be addressed. Budgets are a great antidote to wishful thinking.[4]

Variance analysis

Variance analysis, which focuses on revenue and expenses, is a simple but powerful technique for monitoring the financial progress of an organisation. Variance analysis can only be undertaken if a budget has been constructed. It is essentially an 'after the event' exercise where the *actual* revenue and expense figures are compared and contrasted with the *budgeted* items. The variance can be either favourable or unfavourable. For example, if a 'fun run' event recovered $3000 from entry fees, when the budgeted figure was only $2500, then the variance is favourable. That is, the entry fee revenue was greater than anticipated. Favourable variances are entered as a positive, while unfavourable variances are recorded as a negative figure. If the actual revenue was only $2000, then the variance is unfavourable. That is, the revenue was less than anticipated. The same principle can be applied to expenses.

Variance analysis can be used to closely monitor the ongoing financial operations of a sporting organisation. Monthly or quarterly reports can be constructed whereby all major expense and revenue items can be viewed in terms of actual versus budgeted. If an item like casual wages is consistently greater than the budgeted figure, then it is essential to review the casual staffing situation and to aim to staff the activity more efficiently. Otherwise you could end up with a seriously excessive wage bill and the possibility of a large operating deficit. This is why variance analysis is so important. It can show where costs are increasing too rapidly or, conversely, indicate where specific revenue items are lower than expected. Either way, it shows what needs to be done to ensure a profitable enterprise.

Break even analysis

Break even analysis (or cost-volume-profit analysis) looks at how costs, revenues and profits change in relation to changes in sales, membership or attendance levels. It is a valuable budgeting tool, and helps in financial planning and decision making. The break even point for sales, membership or attendance occurs where revenue equals costs. Below that point losses will be made, while above that point profits will result. Break even analysis is applicable particularly to event management. It answers the question 'what attendance level is needed to ensure a viable event?'. It shows the changes in profits and losses that result from changing attendance patterns and changes in prices. As a result, it quickly shows if an event is likely to be a commercial success.

There are three steps involved in identifying the break even point. The first step involves dividing costs into fixed and variable. Fixed costs are those costs that remain constant as sales and attendance levels change. They include the venue hire, lighting and power, insurance and the costs associated with core staff. On the other hand, variable costs will vary directly with changes in sales and attendance levels. They include things like casual staff, equipment and catering. The second step is to estimate anticipated revenue for every level of sales and attendance. These estimates are based on the expected attendance and the admission price. The third step is to compare and contrast total revenue and total cost for every sales or attendance level. The following case gives a succinct picture of how break even analysis operates.

BREAK EVEN ANALYSIS—SPORTS MANAGEMENT CONFERENCE

Fixed costs	Variable costs
■ lighting and power	■ additional staff
■ core staff	■ printing, stationery and supplies
■ venue hire	■ food and drink
■ guest speakers	
Total fixed costs = $1000	Variable costs estimated at $60 per person

Revenues

- number attending
- registration fee per person

Revenue (average admission) estimated to be $80 per person

Break even point = Fixed costs ÷ Contribution margin
(where contribution margin = average revenue − average variable cost)

In this case example the break even analysis is conducted as follows:

Fixed costs = $1000
Average variable costs = $60
Average revenue (admission price) = $80
Contribution margin = $80 − $60 = $20
Break even point = 1000 ÷ 20
= 50 attendees

If the attendance level falls below 50, then losses will occur, while for every attendee over the 50 cut off, profits will increase. It should be noted that any change in fixed costs, variable costs or admission prices will change the break even point.

Tactics and activities

The following approach can be taken in the interests of a sound budgetary process and to help prevent any budget 'blowouts'.

POSSIBLE TACTIC
Develop a carefully planned and closely monitored annual budgeting system.

Possible activities
Make allowance for likely changes in prices when budgeting, using Consumer Price Index (CPI) movements as an indicator.
Monitor and record financial information monthly (projected versus actual income and expenditure), using Table 7.5 as a guide. The monthly totals are compiled from records of income and expenses.
Conduct a variance analysis quarterly.

SUMMARY

This chapter provided a general introduction to the ways in which the financial affairs of a sporting club can be constructed, summarised, managed and monitored. We pointed out that while sporting clubs do not operate for profit, this is no excuse for sloppy bookkeeping and financial management.

Table 7.5 Income and expenditure proforma—monthly totals

Month	Projected income and expenditure	Actual income and expenditure	Variance
July			
August			
September			
October			
November			
December			
January			
February			
March			
April			
May			
June			
Annual total			

The first step in designing an efficient financial system is to understand the basic principles that underpin financial statements. Therefore we discussed briefly the concept of accrual accounting, the use of journals and ledgers, the accounting equation, and the principles of double-entry bookkeeping. We then examined the ways in which the balance sheet, income and expenditure statement, and cash flow statement are constructed from 'raw' financial data. We stressed how important it is to use these statements to diagnose the financial health of a club or association, and introduced some simple ratio analysis to assist with this. We concluded with a detailed discussion of the budget process, highlighting the importance not just of creating statements of anticipated revenue and expenditure, but also of using variance analysis to monitor this revenue and expenditure.

FURTHER READING

Battistutta, S. & Duncan, S. (1998) *Accounting for Non-Accountants*, Nelson ITP, Melbourne.

Hey-Cunningham, D. (1998) *Financial Statements Demystified*, 2nd edn, Allen & Unwin, Sydney.

Straughn, G. & Chickadel, C. (1994) *Building a Profitable Business*, Bob Adams Inc., Holbrook, Mass.

8 Marketing management

After reading this chapter you should have an understanding of the tools and techniques of marketing, as applied to sports products and services.

More specifically, you should have a general grasp of how to:

- conduct market research
- audit the marketplace
- analyse market opportunities
- identify target markets
- develop positioning strategies
- construct a marketing mix
- gain a competitive marketing advantage
- create or augment sponsorship arrangements

INTRODUCTION

To some, image is everything. If you have been to Miami in the United States recently, you may have noticed that some of the homeless beggars wave glossy, professional-looking placards at passing pedestrians and motorists, requesting money. The slick plastic signs contain an endorsement at the bottom which explains that they were donated by the *Design Shoppe*, which can meet limitless (as well, apparently, as tactless) signage needs, along with the firm's phone number: 443-SIGN!

In some respects, sport has a similar concern with image. It has its symbols and heroic icons which are all powerful influences on sports followers. The Olympic rings and the Nike 'swoosh' are two of the most recognisable signs in the world and have become massively important selling tools.[1] Sporting celebrities have similar powers of persuasion. Shane Warne and Cathy Freeman have used their enormous public appeal to sell postal services, footwear, jeans and deodorant, as well as their sport itself. They, and many other sporting heroes, have become integral cogs in the sports marketing machine. At the same time, sports marketing is more than image building and celebrity endorsement.

The term marketing can mean different things to different people. To some it is the use of promotion and publicity gimmicks to generate greater awareness and attract more customers to a product or venue, while to others it is the use of particular techniques to identify specific market segments which can be exploited by the sale of customised commodities. Both views are correct as far as they go, but the theory and practice of marketing is much broader than these two examples. It is more than getting out a press release or lining up a sponsorship, and in the case of sport it is more than getting a few more people to join, play, watch or support a club or program.[2]

The purpose of this chapter is to explain the marketing process in sport, which is encapsulated in a strategy that uses the techniques and tools of marketing to:

■ promote an awareness of the organisation and its services
■ 'delight' customers via the provision of appropriate products or services
■ boost an organisation's income by introducing additional customers

Simply put, marketing aims to influence demand for what an organisation provides. It constitutes a systematic, 'scientific' method of selling products (or services) to customers. The fundamental tenet of marketing is that customers will only purchase products if they meet a need. Therefore, the central aim of a marketer's energies should be to clearly identify customer needs and design a product that satisfies and 'delights'[3]—or, in the words of Ken Blanchard, that creates 'raving fans'.[4] This is not as easy as it sounds, though, since the marketplace is made up of people with a wide range of demands and desires. In addition, people will respond to similar products differently. Some will put a high value on convenience, some might be seeking excitement and sensory stimulation, others will respond to low prices, and others again will prefer a quality, long-lasting product. In fact, there are good grounds for concluding that each customer has a 'unique' combination of wants and expectations.[5]

Marketing therefore involves looking at both the buying and the selling of products in order to establish, first, what sort of individual or group needs are reflected in the purchase of products and, second, what strategies can be used to stimulate customers to purchase one product or brand instead of another. At the centre of effective marketing is the capacity to 'listen acutely to the voice of the customer'.[6]

Figure 8.1 illustrates the 'demand side' and 'supply side' components of marketing management.

MARKET AND CUSTOMERS: THE DEMAND SIDE

Market research

On the demand side of the picture, information must be acquired concerning the market and the customers it contains. Market research is the process of

Figure 8.1 Components of marketing management

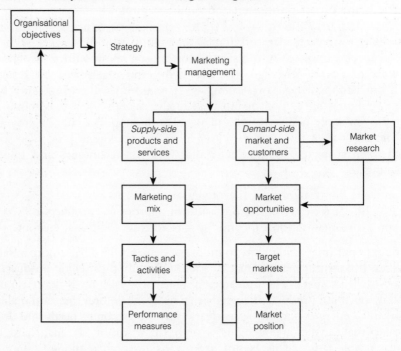

learning what customers want, listening to their desires and expectations, and determining how to satisfy those wants. In addition, it is used to assess whether customers have reacted to a marketing plan as expected. Thus market research is concerned with answering the following general questions about the market:

- Who are our customers and what do they want?
- In what manner and how often should we communicate with our customers?
- Which marketing strategies elicit the 'best' responses in our customers?
- What responses will each type of marketing strategy elicit?
- What mistakes have we made?

While these questions are a valid starting point, they are only a part of the big picture since market research can have far broader uses. Table 8.1 outlines the applications of market research.

The results obtained from these market research applications are sufficient to generate a marketing strategy, but the applications can be broken down into dozens of issues in order to generate greater detail. The more detailed the information the better and more effective the marketing program will be. However, there is a catch: the greater the detail the greater the cost of the market research. The difficulty facing small, 'resource-challenged' sporting

Table 8.1 Applications of market research

Market	Products	Pricing	Place	Promotion
■ customer profile ■ customer demographics ■ customer needs ■ demand for existing services ■ identification of market opportunities	■ customer satisfaction with existing services ■ testing new services ■ evaluation of potential services ■ studying the competition	■ identification of costs ■ identification of price elasticity ■ testing potential price strategies	■ identification of best facility design ■ testing effectiveness of distribution methods	■ testing customer response to advertising ■ testing effectiveness of various mediums ■ evaluating effectiveness of potential mediums

organisations is that market research is expensive, time-consuming and expertise-intensive. For these organisations, the trick is to find a simple and inexpensive approach while avoiding the pitfalls of poor research. Examples of poor research include:

■ using an unrepresentative sample
■ asking irrelevant questions
■ 'stacking' questions so that they force certain types of (biased) responses
■ ignoring answers selectively
■ failing to accept criticism from respondents

In general there are two broad types of market research: *quantitative*, which generates superficial data from a diverse and usually sizeable sample; and *qualitative*, which produces in-depth information from a narrow and relatively small sample. Figure 8.2 sets out the types of quantitative and qualitative research techniques.

Quantitative research

Quantitative market research allows responding consumers to answer questions within predetermined guidelines, enabling researchers to access a large sample within the population group and to analyse the results quickly with statistical measures. The style of question varies with the type of information sought. Some questions allow open and extended answers, encouraging elaboration and detail. Others restrict the respondent to short answers, sometimes in terms of a series of alternatives provided in the questionnaire. A scale may be used for a specific question such as: *How do you rate the seating quality at the Sydney Cricket Ground?* Answers on a scale may range from 'poor', with a rating of one, to 'outstanding', with a rating of ten.

Figure 8.2 Market research techniques

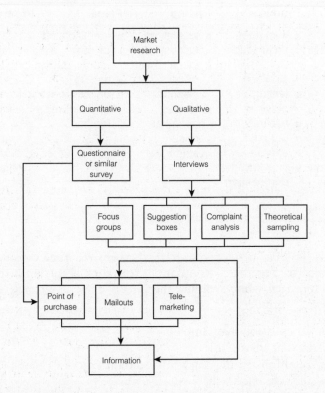

If sufficient responses are obtained from a well-designed survey, the results can be regarded as an accurate representation of customer perceptions in the entire target population group. For example, the results may translate into an 'average' rating, such as 7.8, indicating a positive view overall of the quality of seating at the SCG. On the other hand, a rating of, say, 2.5 would indicate a serious problem with the seating arrangements.

Questionnaires may be conducted via mailouts, one-on-one personal contacts or over the phone or Internet.

Floyd Fowler[7] listed three main steps in designing valid questionnaires. First, the questions must be selected to align with the research objectives. The second step involves testing to ensure that they can be asked and answered as planned. In the third step, the questions must be ordered in a format that maximises ease of response and subsequent interpretation. Fowler offers four criteria that all questions should meet:

■ Is this a question that can be asked the way it is written?
■ Is this a question that will mean the same to everyone?
■ Is this a question that people can answer?

■ Is this a question that people will be willing to answer, given the data collection procedures?

As you have probably guessed, designing good questionnaires requires considerable expertise. But when administered properly, to a well-drawn sample of the target population, they are incomparable for making *generalisations* about markets and consumer groups. For example, if a sporting organisation already knows that there are four general reasons why their customers use their services, they can use questionnaires to establish the relative importance of each.

However, few questionnaires are capable of reflecting the complexities underpinning consumer motivation and behaviour. Personal preferences, values and beliefs are intrinsically hidden and private, and cannot typically be accessed via the superficial and overt responses that surveys elicit. For this reason, an organisation may choose to undertake a qualitative approach as part of its market research.

Qualitative research

The premise supporting the qualitative approach is that it is impossible to separate the person responding to questions from his or her social context, so consequently the social context must be understood. In practical terms, this means that circling a number on a scaled response questionnaire or ticking a box on a survey form is inadequate for getting to the heart of consumers' opinions and behaviour. A survey may tell us that a married, middle-aged female player with three children plays netball because she enjoys the game, wants the exercise and is relatively happy with the quality of service at her club. However, it is unlikely to tell us that she is thinking about taking up chess for the reason that her kids play, that it is less stressful on her knees, that she can't play with the club next season because of a business commitment overseas, etc. Some of these issues may be revealed through surveys, but to assume that all will be is unrealistic, and to attempt to design a survey that covers every contingency is impracticable.

There are a number of effective and inexpensive approaches to qualitative market research that can provide rich and detailed data about the market, and which can subsequently be used to construct succinct questionnaires if necessary. Among them are:

■ focus groups
■ suggestion boxes
■ complaint analysis
■ interviews using theoretical sampling

Focus groups

The basic tool of qualitative market research is the interview, which can be applied in a variety of situations, with individuals or small groups. One potent method is known as the focus group, where a group of respondents from the population being studied are gathered in an informal setting and encouraged to talk about specific issues. The involvement of a moderator who can co-ordinate the group without inhibiting or leading the respondents is necessary, so that ideas are free-flowing and all opinions are expressed. Sessions should always be audio-recorded. The sequential incident technique (SIT) has its most effective application in focus groups (refer to Chapter 4, for more detail on the SIT). Further information about using focus groups can be found in Richard Krueger's excellent book on the subject.[8]

Suggestion boxes

A suggestion box is a simple tool that can work if taken seriously. In order for it to be successful, customers' suggestions must be read regularly and, more importantly, be *seen* to be read regularly. Furthermore, action must be taken in response to the suggestions received. Probably the best approach is to document all suggestions and the responses in a prominent place readily accessible to all customers. For example, place all incoming suggestions where everyone can see them (ensure that the identity of those writing is kept confidential) and provide detailed and professional answers. Don't simply make excuses if there is a genuine problem, and always state the measures taken.

Nothing is worse than a suggestion box with a rusty lock, so don't bother with this style of customer feedback if you are not prepared to deal with the suggestions promptly and systematically.

Complaint analysis

This method is cheap and relatively easy to implement. It involves encouraging customers to contact employees directly if they have a complaint. Respond to every complaint with a personal letter similar in content to the responses to suggestions, including thanks for highlighting the problem and giving information concerning its resolution.

Theoretical sampling

We believe that theoretical sampling for interviews is one of the most powerful weapons in the arsenal of qualitative market research. Although most people are unfamiliar with the technique, it is simple, inexpensive, and requires little prior expertise. Theoretical sampling refers to the selection of informants on the basis of issues or themes that emerge prior to and during data collection.[9] Its object is to uncover diversity. In other words, it seeks to facilitate the identification of a full range of possibilities that have proven to be theoretically relevant to the questions being asked.[10] For example, we may recognise that, in theory, males are biologically more aggressive than females and therefore will have a greater preference for contact sports than

Table 8.2 Theoretical sampling example

Age	20–35				36–50			
Gender	M		F		M		F	
Motivation	H	P	H	P	H	P	H	P
Sample group	1	2	3	4	5	6	7	8

females will. However, when the notion is explored, other factors such as class, income, occupation, geographic location, upbringing, nationality, sexuality and personality may also have an impact. The point is that we *don't know* until we start to gather information about the question. Thus, through analysis, the market researcher is directed to additional data which must be collected next in order to explore aspects of the working theory that have become important.[11] By using theoretical sampling, the data collection and data analysis components of the research are conducted simultaneously,[12] with each piece of analysed data providing information as to where to look next for further data.

As always, an example will explain, where prosaic principles fail. Let us assume that we are running a gymnasium, and conducting market research to gain insight into the basic question: *Are our customers satisfied with the service they are getting?* We want detailed responses, and we recognise that some of the information we require to improve our services may be elusive and difficult to extract by using 'number-crunching' methods. So the only way to gather the information is to talk to a cross-section of customers in an in-depth manner. The problem is: who do we talk to? Theoretical sampling provides the answer.

We know from membership records that our members are predominantly aged between 20 and 50, of both genders, and appear to use the gymnasium for either health and fitness reasons (H) or to bolster sports performance (P). These are our 'theoretical' starting points and can be expressed as in Table 8.2.

As the table shows, we have generated eight categories. The first is a male between the ages of 20 and 35 who uses the gymnasium for health and fitness reasons, while the second is a male between the ages of 20 and 35 who uses the gymnasium to enhance his sporting performance. Now we have a representative sample (in qualitative terms only—it is not statistically representative) to work with. A customer from each of these categories can be approached for an in-depth informal or formal discussion about their opinions, criticisms, ideas and lifestyle. Of course you cannot expect customers to reveal confidential details, but if treated with respect and courtesy most are prepared to discuss their needs frankly. How customers are 'enticed' into being involved in the process depends on the situation. In our gymnasium

Table 8.3 Data-gathering stage

Age	20–35						36–50					
Gender	M			F			M			F		
Motivation	H	P	S	H	P	S	H	P	S	H	P	S
Sample group	1	2	3	4	5	6	7	8	9	10	11	12

example, it is likely that staff members are already friendly with some of the customers—customers who would probably be willing to spend 10–60 minutes (depending on the detail required) in discussion while they did, say, their stationary cycling. Alternatively, small incentives such as a week of free solarium use or an extra month's membership would be sufficient to attract most.

The beauty of the theoretical sampling method is that it is intrinsically flexible: built into the model is the anticipation of discovering additional factors that may affect the original question. For example, after completing several interviews, it may become blindingly apparent that there is another motivation for attending the gymnasium that was previously overlooked: the social factor (S). In such case, the data-gathering process provides additional detail for a revised sample with twelve categories (see Table 8.3).

The theoretical sampling process should continue until no new factors are discovered. This may mean that repeat interviews are conducted in certain categories. When this saturation level has been reached, the information can be analysed on the basis of common themes and issues. In a gymnasium, you may find that safety, instructor qualifications, pool maintenance, reception staff and equipment variety are frequently mentioned, and need to be addressed by management. Techniques for sorting and coding the information are succinctly discussed by Miles and Huberman.[13] Mostly, however, the analysis merely requires logical thought and consistency.

Another benefit of theoretical sampling is that it enables you to build up a databank of client *types*.

Table 8.4 may help you in deciding when to use theoretical sampling and when to use other market research techniques.

Competitor analysis and position audit

As we discussed in Chapter 3, an effective strategic approach will recognise the position and impact of the 'enemy'—competitors. Here the term 'competitors' refers to rival organisations providing either similar products and services or offering replacement or 'substitutable' products and services. For example, competitors of an indoor cricket centre may include not only other local indoor cricket centres but also any local centre that provides a com-

Table 8.4 Selecting a market research technique

Objective	Best approach	Sacrifice
Speed	Telemarketing questionnaire	Cost and depth
Detail	Interviews: focus groups or theoretical sampling	Breadth and time
Breadth	Detailed mailout questionnaire	Cost and time
Low cost	Suggestion boxes/complaint analysis/interviews	Time and breadth
Accuracy	Theoretical sampling combined with detailed mailout questionnaires	Time and cost
Versatility	Interviews: theoretical sampling or focus groups	Breadth and time
Low expertise requirement	Suggestion boxes and complaint analysis	Breadth and depth
Value for little or no monetary investment	Theoretical sampling	Breadth and time
Value for money	Telemarketing questionnaire	Cost and depth

parable indoor leisure activity, such as volleyball, tennis or bowling. While it is unlikely that all these indoor sports will be genuinely competing for the same individuals' leisure time, an appreciation of all alternative possibilities for consumers is critical in the selection of appropriate marketing strategies.

In most circumstances a properly constructed SWOT analysis (detailed in Chapter 3) will highlight any factors that influence the marketing approach to be taken. The SWOT analysis should consider the competition in terms of:

■ type and range of products and services provided
■ geographic location
■ demographics of customers
■ positioning strategy
■ approach to marketing mix (product, price, promotion and place strategies)

Analysing market opportunities

Information obtained via market research and competitor analysis should highlight market opportunities. A market opportunity is any situation where sales can be expanded by meeting unfulfilled needs. Because the nature of the market opportunity determines the composition of the target market, it is necessary to first establish whether the opportunity is worth capitalising

Table 8.5 Product-market expansion grid

	EXISTING PRODUCT	NEW PRODUCT
EXISTING MARKET	Market penetration	Product development
NEW MARKET	Market development	Diversification

upon. Once that is decided, the target market can be identified along with a solid idea of where the product or service can be placed within the market.

A useful tool for examining marketing opportunities is the product-market expansion grid. The grid is a matrix which combines existing and new products with existing and new markets to establish a neat summary of opportunities for 'selling' a particular product or service.[14] The product-market expansion grid is shown in Table 8.5.

Market penetration is the first possible type of market opportunity, and represents an attempt to increase 'sales' by attracting new customers without sacrificing the old. An example of a market penetration approach for the horseracing industry would be to attract still more males over the age of 50 to race meetings. It is therefore a 'more of the same' approach.

Market development is similar in that the product remains the same but in this case the target market is expanded. A market development approach would involve both the promotion of the product (or service) in existing markets and an attempt to attract a wider range of consumers. Examples include taking Australian Rules football to New South Wales and Queensland, or attracting young males and females to lawn bowls.

The third category, *product development*, involves bringing together the existing market and a new version of the product. This new (or modified) product is 'sold' to the same target market as the old product was—like limited-overs cricket in the 1980s and beach volleyball in the 1990s.

The final category departs from both the original product and the existing market, in an attempt to 'start over', and is termed *diversification*. Examples of diversification include indoor cricket, 'mixed' netball and Aussie football super-rules. In these cases a modified product is targeted at a new market.

Selecting target markets

There are three central approaches to defining the target market:

- mass marketing
- market segmentation
- multiple segmentation

Before any of these techniques can be applied, the base of potential consumers must be established. In other words, before any specific group of sports consumers can be targeted, the question *'Who are (potential) sports consumers?'* must be answered. This is achieved by creating a 'profile' or database of consumers, which includes statistical information concerning the

Table 8.6 Consumer segmentation criteria

Demographics	Psychographics	Lifestyle
Personal		
■ gender	■ cultural influences	■ social class
■ age	■ social forces	■ use of time
■ education	■ values and beliefs	■ hobbies/interests
■ geographic location	■ personality	■ brand loyalty
■ home ownership/rental	■ self-image	
■ marital status		
■ family size		
■ income		
■ ethnicity		
■ occupation		
■ mobility		
■ sexuality		
Geographical area		
■ population		
■ climate		
■ commerce		
■ media		

attributes of the population of sports consumers. This is obtained via market research.

Information about the people in the marketplace can be classified into four divisions:

■ demographics
■ psychographics
■ lifestyle
■ usage of products and services

Demographics is the distribution, density and vital statistics of a population. Psychographics relates to how the human characteristics of consumers affect their response to marketing efforts. Lifestyle is the manner in which consumers live. Usage reflects consumption behaviour, and is outlined later. Table 8.6 provides examples of these criteria.

Mass marketing

Once the population of existing and potential sports consumers is defined broadly, market selection can then proceed. The first approach listed above, mass marketing, is somewhat old-fashioned, despite the fact that it is still being used by many sporting organisations. With this method the total market is viewed as a single mass unit or entity. The approach does not recognise separate group needs or idiosyncratic individual preferences. Nor does it tend to acknowledge the potential to classify consumer groups according to specific characteristics.

Market segmentation

Market segmentation is an approach in which the marketing plan is targeted at one specific demographic component of consumers. This concentrated approach is popular because it identifies one sector of the market and pitches the marketing mix directly at it. Although relatively inexpensive, it is best used by organisations that have a defined 'niche', as market segmentation is a narrow method. Niche markets in the sporting world may include professional women, gay men, young suburban families and teenage boys.

Born of niche segmentation is the popular and effective technique of relationship marketing. This rests on developing a long-term relationship with the organisation's best customers.[15] It is a 'bottom-up' approach in which a small group of core customers' needs are met exclusively, with the objective of establishing responsive relationships together with brand loyalty. Examples of relationship marketing include prominent but 'exclusive' participatory sports such as indoor rock-climbing, in-line skating and mountain-biking. The needs of these 'new' sports consumers are met through specific and focused products ranging from distinctive equipment to magazines and videos.

Multiple segmentation

In the multiple segmentation approach the marketing plan is designed to appeal to more than one market segment; each segment, or specific group of consumers, is targeted in an individualised way. Multiple segmentation combines the 'shotgun' approach of mass marketing with the rifle 'sniper' approach of market segmentation. For most sporting organisations, multiple segmentation is the 'best' approach. It works particularly well where the objectives include expanding participation and membership by attracting new groups of customers. The organisers of the Australian Open Tennis Championship, for example, might aim its promotion at all middle age professional men, middle class women from Melbourne's eastern suburbs, adolescent girls in private schools, and suburban tennis club members.

Multiple segmentation combines effectively with database marketing, where detailed profiles of consumers are collected in order to enhance the precision of segmentation. Obviously, the more information an organisation possesses concerning its potential customers the more accurate it can be in meeting their collective and individual needs. Database marketing allows an enterprise to reduce market research costs and to handle customer inquiries and complaints more rapidly and expertly. The emphasis is on reaching customers more efficiently over the short term, and in contrast to niche marketing it can be conceptualised as a 'top-down', transaction-driven method.

Usage of products and services

We noted earlier four types of market information; the first three were demographics, psychographics and lifestyle. The fourth type, usage (or benefit), relates to the variety of consumer satisfactions that can arise from the use of a particular product or service. For the marketer, the aim is to deliver services in such a way as to meet the *variety* of consumer needs. Some golfers, for example, play in a competition every Sunday because they enjoy the social contact, while others play because they respond to a competitive environment. Another segment may simply get pleasure from being out in the open. Every marketed service requires an individual analysis, in which the different benefits or need satisfactions are revealed.

A further example of the multiple benefit approach lies in the different ways in which team-sports spectators find enjoyment from their experiences.

A classification of team-sports spectator behaviour

Before marketers diverted their attention to sports promotion, most studies of sports watching grouped all followers under the general heading of 'fans'. But it is clear that not all sports fans share the same characteristics or hold the same views about their favourite pastime. They have different motives for watching, different patterns of attendance, different levels of affiliation, different attitudes about the place of tradition, and so on.[16]

For some fans, identification with the team is so strong that attendance is habitual, while for others the only significant factor determining their attendance is the likelihood of their team winning. Moreover, some fans, while wanting to experience a high quality game, will see it not in terms of winning or losing but rather in terms of the game's entertainment value. In short, we can no longer talk about the 'average' sports fan, or notions of mass spectator appeal, since there exists a wide spectrum of customer needs and perceived benefits. As a result a number of spectator segments can be identified.

A survey of Australian football found that irregular attenders (those who attended fewer than ten games over a 22-week season) accounted for 60–70 per cent of total attenders.[17] It was also found that the irregular attenders had, over the previous three years, become ever more irregular in their attendance. On the other hand, the frequent attenders had, over the same three year period, been consistent in their attendance patterns. It was concluded that the key to increasing attendances was to concentrate on the 'irregulars' (or, as they were labelled, 'theatregoers').

Another distinction is that fans have different motives in attending games. Some fans go for no other reason than to see their favourite team contest the game. These *passionate partisans* are loyal to their team and get despondent when it loses and elated when it wins, and are prepared to suffer inconveniences such as a wet day in order to savour the fruits of success.

They form the hardcore support base of the competition, and their moods and identity are bound up with the successes and failures of their favourite team.[18] They are heavy purchasers of memorabilia and club merchandise and great defenders of their club's history and traditions. They have a significant personal investment in the club and its season-to-season performance.

There are also sports fans who are more interested in supporting a winning team than blindly following one team through thick and thin. These *champ followers* share some of the emotional highs and lows of the passionate partisans, but are more flighty and less fanatical. The champ follower's allegiance will change according to whatever team happens to be the top performer.[19] Alternatively, some champ followers may remain non-attenders until their favourite team starts winning a few games. Then they 'jump on the bandwagon' and become vocal and active supporters until such time as their team begins to lose again.

A third category is the *reclusive partisans,* whose interest in the 'game' and commitment to a team is strong but who attend infrequently. The reclusive partisan is opinionated, apparently loyal to his or her team, and would become a passionate partisan again if only the game could regain its 'old values', if only it wasn't ruled by the profiteers, if only it had the skills of earlier days, and so on. Reclusive partisans are susceptible to the influence of others, and may attend in response to friends' urgings or media coverage.

The common motive or need of the above categories of fans is the desire to see the team *win*.

There are other fans who, while notionally committed to a particular team, are more interested in the spectacle. They typically attend more frequently than the reclusive partisan but less frequently than the passionate partisan. They may be called *theatregoers.*[20] The theatregoer is motivated to seek entertainment but this involves more than 'pom-pom' girls, skydivers, giveaways and brass bands. It also includes comfortable and proximate viewing conditions, easy access, availability of complementary services and the partic-ipation of star performers. Theatregoers are attracted to comfort, excitement and uncertainty of outcome. Since their team and game loyalty is initially low, most theatregoers will attend less frequently than passionate partisans unless the likelihood of exciting and pleasurable contests continues throughout the season. At the same time, a few theatregoers will put such high value on their sporting experiences that they will become regular patrons. In other words, theatregoers may be described as either casual or *committed*.

Like the theatregoers, *aficionados* are attracted to games which are expected to be exciting and which contain star performers.[21] However, unlike most theatregoers, aficionados attend frequently because of their strong attachment to the structure of the game and its athletic practices. They will attend games that provide high skill levels, tactical complexity and aesthetic pleasure, even if the contests are likely to be one-sided or unexciting. They would call themselves purists, and will be at the match of the day, which may or may not include the top-performing teams. The aficionado will also be attracted to a quality venue since it will accentuate a quality performance. Both the aficionado and the theatregoer will show only moderate concern about who wins or loses. Their dominant concern is game performance or game quality, and not the likely success or failure of a particular team.

While each type of fan (i.e. each market segment) has an interest in the generic sports product, there are significant differences in the ways in which their interest is expressed. Different incentives and benefits will motivate different segments. A change to the structure or conduct of a competition that attracts more of one segment (e.g. theatregoers), may be resisted by another segment (e.g. passionate partisans). Of course, spectators can shift between categories, depending on the sport in question. Thus one individual may be a casual theatregoer when it comes to cricket but a passionate partisan in regard to volleyball.

Table 8.7 summarises the categories of spectators, their motivations and their typical behaviour.

Marketing implications

Marketers have the delicate task of ensuring, on the one hand, that a sporting competition provides good watching conditions, balanced competition and uncertain outcomes and, on the other hand, that the loyalty of partisan fans is maintained by ensuring the ongoing viability of teams in strategically positioned regions or districts (allowing fans to establish a sense of identity and community). While changes to the structure of a competition (like new recruiting laws, relocation of a team or the merger of clubs) are likely to weaken the loyalty of partisan supporters, this must be weighed against the attraction that such changes have for the other spectator categories, particularly the theatregoers. On balance, the future of spectator sport depends upon marketing and development programs that place emphasis on attracting the less committed spectator. The growing attendances at one-day international cricket matches, Australian open tennis championships, Australian Football League, National Soccer League and National Basketball League matches have demonstrated that a strategy of attracting theatregoers, and having them convert from casual to committed, or even from theatregoer to passionate partisan, can substantially enlarge the spectator base. Consequently, there are significant advantages in adopting a *multiple benefits* approach to sports marketing, in which different benefits are provided to a variety of market segments.

Market positioning

At the same time, sports products and services cannot be everything to everybody; none has a universal appeal. So even common services—health and fitness centres, for example—fight vigorously for 'brand' awareness and product specifity. Market positioning is the process of establishing brand

Table 8.7 Spectator categories, motivations and behaviour

Type of spectator	Motivation	Behaviour
Passionate partisan	Wants team to win	Loyal to team; in short term, loyalty undiminished by frequent losses; strongly identifies with and responds to team's success and failure.
Champ follower	Wants team to win	Short-term loyalty; loyalty a function of team success; expects team to dominate, otherwise supports another team or spends time elsewhere
Reclusive partisan	Wants team to win	Loyalty not always translated into attendance; strong identification but latent support only
Theatregoer (casual *or* committed)	Seeks entertainment, close contest	Only moderate loyalty to team; frequent losses create lack of interest in team; but may attend other games
Aficionado	Seeks quality performance	Loyal to 'game' rather than team, although may have a 'preferred' team; attends on regular basis; puts emphasis on aesthetic or skill dimension

identification. In other words, it is the technique marketers use to make their products and services 'unique' and therefore more easily identifiable.

Positioning involves a detailed examination of each target market segment as determined through market research and segmentation, and then developing a distinct position or strategy for each segment. The key, as we have noted, is to know precisely how products and services can be slanted to maximise their appeal to each segment—which should have been revealed by market research. For example, the generic services of a gymnasium can be skewed toward muscular development for young males and fat loss for middle-aged females. Similarly, a participation-orientated organisation could target the competitive and coaching aspects of its activities at junior members and the recreational and social aspects at adult members.

Table 8.8 lists the 'standard' range of positioning strategies.

Table 8.8 Generic positioning strategies

Strategy	Method	Example
Position on features	Concentrate on the unique features of the product or service	Most sports can do this effectively because they have a monopoly on the activity: e.g. soccer, cricket, tennis, netball
Position on benefits	Tell customers what they can get out of your product or service	Health, fitness
Position on specific use	Show customers what the product or service does in specific situations	'Drink Gatorade and play basketball like Michael Jordan'
Position on a user category	Show how the product or service can be used by others with whom the customers can relate	Tina Turner 'You're the best' Australian Rugby League promotion aimed at females
Position against competitor	Demonstrate how the product or service is better than the others available—in sport this can include the *actual* competitor	Positioning a team or individual as an underdog: Australian athletes in Olympics and Wimbledon Tennis Championships
Product class disassociation	Highlight how a product or service is revolutionary and therefore not comparable with others in its class	Sports supplements Training and playing equipment, such as sports shoes
Hybrid positioning	Incorporates various elements of several types of positioning	Nike: 'Just do it' AFL: 'I'd like to see that!'

The point of market positioning is to decide on a *general* strategy or theme for each market segment. In other words, the positioning strategy will steer the marketing mix so that the products or services, their price and how they will be promoted and distributed are consistent with overall goals, thereby maximising the potential for success.

The desired outcome of market positioning is formally known as product differentiation. Differentiation is the degree to which a product is different or perceived to be different from competing products. The classic example concerns athletic footwear, where many brands compete for the same segment's loyalty, fulfil essentially the same purpose, yet are differentiated with an almost unprecedented vigour. One shoe contains gel, another has air, while others possess 'torsion' bars. Naturally, each manufacturer claims its shoe is superior.

Differentiation is a sharp but double-edged sword. Because differentiation emphasises the characteristics that make each product unique, it can propel a product ahead of its rivals if these characteristics match the expectations of the target segment. However, if they do not, the differentiation process can destroy a product's demand with alarming rapidity.

Product or service life-cycle

Any marketing approach must recognise the mortality of its product or service. The process from inception to withdrawal from the market is known as the life-cycle. From a practical viewpoint, it is important to understand a product or service's life-cycle so that alterations can be made in accordance with the changing expectations of consumers: introducing additional products, modifying existing products or even withdrawing flagging products altogether. This concept of the life-cycle can assist in the positioning process. For example, the sport of lawn bowls is currently suffering because it fails to attract new young participants. Lawn bowls administrators need to reassess the positioning of their sport in light of the fact that it is dangerously near the end of its present life-cycle. Young people, it seems, have little interest in pursuing lawn bowls in its existing form. Perhaps the sport's only chance is to create a modified version, reflecting contemporary attitudes and interests, in order to attract the elusive youth demographic.

Tactics and activities

Market research and surveillance are a fundamental part of sports marketing. The following can help reveal market opportunities.

POSSIBLE TACTIC
Conduct market research to establish information concerning the market, the products provided and services delivered, and use marketing tools to analyse the results.

Possible activities
Use a product-market expansion grid to categorise and examine potential market opportunities.
Determine what products or services should be delivered and to whom (segmentation).
Develop a strategy for each target segment (market positioning), emphasising the unique characteristics of what is offered.

PRODUCTS AND SERVICES: THE SUPPLY SIDE

Now that we have looked at the 'demand' side of the marketing equation, it remains to examine the 'supply' side. There are four strategic factors to consider:

- the *product* (or service)
- the *price*
- the *place* (or way) in which the product is distributed or made available to customers
- the *promotion* of the product

These four factors constitute the 'marketing mix', and are colloquially known as the four Ps. As they are largely under the control of the seller, they play a pivotal role in the overall marketing strategy. A key marketing principle is that, if these factors are to be successful in stimulating customers to purchase, they must be consistent with and reflect customer needs. Always remember that customers might be able to afford a product, it might be readily available, it might be well designed and widely promoted, but they will purchase it only if it meets their needs and provides benefits.

The marketing mix

Product (or service)

The first action in developing the marketing mix is to take a hard look at what it is that the organisation provides (or could provide) to its members or customers.[22] The purpose in doing this is to ensure that the products or services provided—that is, their features—are compatible with the intended strategic positioning in the relevant market segments (and vice versa). Because most sporting organisations provide intangible services, rather than physical goods, it is not always immediately clear what the 'product' features are and how they can best be 'packaged' (or, in some cases, modified) so as to fit in with and support the desired marketing strategy.

It may help you in thinking about this problem to consider three types of 'product' features:

- *'Personal' features:* The psychological, social and other personal benefits offered (e.g. self-development, power, status, 'tribal' affiliation, social contact, fitness)[23]
- *'Physical' features:* The aspects of the product itself (e.g. a sporting fixture) that customers may find exciting, attractive, unpleasant, boring, etc.
- *Additional features:* The extra benefits that are available as a result of membership, attendance or participation.

Selecting and enhancing appropriate product features to fit in with the intended strategic positioning is not an easy task. Table 8.9 gives you a range

Table 8.9 Product features

'Personal' features

Choice 1	Choice 2
Social contact	Individual mastery
Vicarious thrill	Personal fitness
Escape	Intimacy
'Tribal' affiliation	Club membership
Elite status	Community identification
Risk and excitement	Security and safety

'Physical' features

Choice 1	Choice 2
Skill	Chance
Strategy	Intuition
Contact sport	Non-contact
Violent activity	Non-violent
Many players	Few players
Close to audience	Removed from audience
Large space	Small space
Many stoppages	Few stoppages
Frequent scoring	Limited scoring
Highly athletic	Little athleticism
High sensory stimulation	Low sensory stimulation
Routine	Uncertain
Attractive, sexually appealing players	Ugly, oafish, sexually unappealing players
Natural playing surface	Artificial playing surface
Indoor	Outdoor
High degree of fitness	Low degree of fitness

Additional features

Features checklist

Cheer squads and supporter groups
Childcare facilities
Food and drink
Heroes
Mascots, logos and icons
Medical and security services
Memorabilia and museum
Parking
Personalised customer service
Pre and mid game entertainment
Programs, souvenirs and merchandise
Public announcements
Transport to facility or venue
Video replays

of options to consider in relation to sports products, events or activities. The choices you make should always be framed within two axioms: first, will the choices add value to the sport product; and second, will they provide a competitive advantage?

Price

Price is a critical factor in determining the level of purchases, spectatorship or membership. There is a wide variety of pricing strategies which sporting organisations can employ successfully. These are set out in Table 8.10, together with comments on each. Discriminatory pricing is the most popular and commonly used, and involves charging different fees to different customer categories. For example, junior players may be charged less than adult players for a given activity. Like product features, pricing strategies need to be selected in accordance with the intended market positioning. Unless there are very good reasons to the contrary, pricing should also provide for a markup, or margin, that ensures the cost of delivering the sport can be recovered.

Place

The key to successful distribution of products and services is accessibility, location and the provision of quality facilities and venues. Sporting services, like many others, can generally be used only at a specific place. Customers therefore rank convenient location as an important factor in the decision to purchase services or to take up a membership. However, once an organisation chooses its location it is difficult and costly for it to move, making *place* the least flexible of the four Ps in the marketing mix. (See also Chapter 9.)

Promotion

The most versatile factor in the marketing mix is promotion. Organisations must ask:

- Which products or services will be promoted?
- What form will the promotion take?

There are four main approaches: advertising, sales promotion, personal selling, and publicity.[24] Each approach has particular methods and its own strengths and weaknesses, as illustrated in Table 8.11.

One of the sales promotion methods listed in the table is the 'selling' of heroes. Its power should not be underestimated. But, surprisingly, the energies that go into it at the organisational level pale in comparison with the efforts put into promoting sport through players' clinics and displays. Sporting heroes have in many respects been underutilised in promoting sport. Capturing the imagination of potential customers or players can best be

Table 8.10 Pricing strategies

Strategy	Method and best application	Variations	Advantages	Disadvantages
Break-even	Pricing products at 'cost' Useful for non-profit organisations		Simple and customer-friendly	Sets a precedent Little room to improve
Cost plus	Pricing calculated by adding the costs of delivering the product then adding a flat fee or percentage (e.g. cost + 10%) Useful when extra funds are needed to invest in a better quality product		Can ensure that consistent profits are made	Difficult to track during inflationary periods
Competition	Pricing copies or follows competitors Useful for profit-seeking organisations in highly competitive environments	'We won't be undersold'	Ensures competitors don't undercut you	A passive technique and reactionary
Market demand	Setting pricing according to market demand at the time, taking into account elasticity and growth/shrinkage rates 'Skim pricing' is useful for high demand events (such as grand finals) and new or unique products (such as advanced equipment) 'Price-lining' is useful to reach customers with varying levels of disposable income	*Skim pricing:* Setting a particular product at an inflated price when the product is held in monopoly (inelastic demand) *Price-lining:* Setting incremental prices for rising quality of products (e.g. full, medium and partial memberships); similar to discriminatory pricing	High profit potential Caters for all levels of income and service requirements	Chance of alienating customers by feelings of exploitation and attracts competition More variations of the product have to be generated

Table 8.10 Pricing strategies (cont.)

Strategy	Method and best application	Variations	Advantages	Disadvantages
Penetration	The opposite of 'skimming' is to introduce the product at such a low price that it will attract a large market share Useful for new products and organisations	*Buying market position:* Buying into the market with heavy subsidisation of products	Increases market share relatively quickly	Expensive: usually necessitates a loss
Discriminatory (differential)	Prices change according to categories of customers Useful for all organisations in generic markets (*not* niche markets)	*Customer type:* Students, disabled, aged, unemployed *Place:* Private box, serviced seat, premium seat, superior viewing, no smoking, no frills	'Fair' system, where products match price well	Tricky to keep everyone happy
Discount	Discount pricing involves the decrease in price of a service or product in special circumstances Useful for rapid increases in sales and special events	Long-term membership Frequent use Early payment Group concessions Family payments *Multiple unit:* Offering discounts for bulk purchases (e.g. two years membership)	Simple, effective and quick	Can only be used sparingly
Seasonal	Pricing according to seasonal demand Useful for overstocking or downturns due to the season (e.g. winter competitions)	Off season Pre season Early season Mid season Late season	Boosts sales during poor times, decreasing seasonal variation	Sometimes have to sell at a reduced profit or even below cost to maintain demand

Table 8.10 Pricing strategies (cont.)

Strategy	Method and best application	Variations	Advantages	Disadvantages
Off-peak	Pricing according to daily demand Useful for maintaining turnover during normally lower daily usage times		Makes use of resources when they would otherwise be wasted	Difficult to enforce
Psychological	Pricing where quality is more important than price because of 'special' circumstances Useful for any 'special' or essential services	Exclusive membership Special events Prestige seating Selective seating Celebrity seating Serviced seating 'Price is no object': Where the price of the product is irrelevant because it is so outstanding or essential	Capitalises on circumstances and necessary services	Appeals only to an exclusive market segment
Exchange	Used in reciprocal trade where exchanges are made: corporate boxes, signage, tickets to events and access to players and athletes in exchange for 'everyday' items including furniture and paper, as well as other necessities such as travel, accommodation and advertising Useful because exchange pricing is little more than bartering, allowing asset-rich, cash-poor sporting organisations to 'save' their liquid finances		Saves cash resources	Gains from 'bartering' must be declared as taxable income (not a means of avoiding tax)

Table 8.11 Promotional techniques

Approach	Methods
Advertising	
Strengths	press
Dramatic images	radio
Wide reach	television
Low exposure cost per unit	magazines
	ticketing agents
	direct mail
Weakness	scoreboard displays
High initial outlay	bus and taxi cards
	billboards
	posters
	brochures
	ticket stubs
	Internet
Sales promotion	
Strengths	in-store promotions
Attention grabbing	point-of-purchase sales
Informative	clinics
	exhibitions
	product give-aways (stickers, shirts, admission give-aways)
Weaknesses	two-for-one offers
Medium reach	free admission with purchase
Medium cost per exposure	prizes tied to tickets
	regular-attender price plans
	'selling' of heroes
Personal selling	
Strengths	telemarketing
Direct	door-to-door sales
Informative	endorsements/referrals
Weaknesses	party-plans
Narrow reach	sponsorship
Variable exposure per unit cost	
Publicity	
Strengths	press releases
Wide reach	results lists
Informative	photographs
Low exposure cost per unit	logos, slogans and 'brand' names
	commentary and reviews
Weakness	feature articles
Variable image	

achieved through the 'selling' of star players and their outstanding performances.

Creating the marketing plan on paper

Table 8.12 shows a simple method of documenting the marketing plan. When the market segmentation and strategic positioning have been completed, each element of the marketing mix can be finalised. Note that it is easier to deal with one product or service at a time. Each possesses a unique configuration of pricing, promotional and distributional arrangements. However, as overlap is common, it is reasonable in many cases to combine similarly priced, promoted and distributed items in the plan.

CORPORATE SPONSORSHIP

Although sponsorship could have been considered under the broad heading of promotion, it is such a significant part of contemporary sport that it deserves a section of its own. The marketing of spectator sport can be quite complex, since it involves two distinct but equally important sets of 'customers'. The first are the officials, players and spectators. These people are the foundation of any sporting organisation and are usually the justification for its existence. The second set are the *corporate supporters*, who are usually involved as sponsors. In the same way that individual members have to be convinced to join a club, so too do corporate customers have to be convinced that they will benefit from lending support to a club or association. The benefits that the corporate sector seeks are quite different, though, from the benefits sought by individual members.

Whereas members want immediate service in the form of competitions or social activities, the corporate sponsor will want to use the sports activity as a vehicle for promoting its own product to the market. The more a sporting organisation can attract an appropriate market (in terms of members, spectators or corporate clients) the greater its attractiveness to the sponsor. It should therefore aim in this case to promote, not so much its playing facilities or spectator services, as its 'commercial value' to the sponsor.

The benefits to sponsors

Sports sponsorship is usually defined as the support of a sporting organisation or individual competitor by a separate company (or person) for the benefit of both parties. It is obvious that the benefit to the sporting body will be additional funds (and occasionally other resources). It is not always so obvious what the benefits will be to the sponsor. For this reason the sporting body nearly always initiates the approach for a sponsorship. In doing

Table 8.12 Maryland Tennis Club: marketing activities

Segment/ target market	Service/ product	Positioning strategy	Price	Place	Promotion
Males/Females 8–17	Coaching	Skill acquisition and development	(Discriminatory) Reduced junior rate	Safe Qualified instruction	Promotion of heroes Publicity via schools
Males 18–35 Females 18–35	Coaching	Performance/skill Champion potential	(Market demand) Based on market rate and demand at time	Quality facilities Top coaches	Local newspaper Signage Exhibitions
Males 36–55	Coaching	Health and fitness	(Psychological) Exclusive attention and personalised tuition Standard rate	Convenient Good parking Easy access Quiet	Local paper Flyers Mail advertising
Females 36–55	Coaching	Social enjoyment	(Discount and off-peak) *Concessions:* Long term: 20% Frequent use: 10% Group: 15% Day use: 25% Standard rate: $X	Private Food and drink service Attractive Variety	Brochures Two-for-one offers Telemarketing

so, it must ask itself what it has to offer or 'sell' to a potential sponsor. The possibilities make an impressive list:

- naming rights
- image building (e.g. use of symbol or logo)
- goodwill (e.g. association with sporting heroes)
- political benefits
- direct advertising opportunities
- a new market
- additional sales (exclusive rights, special offers to members)
- demonstration of products (especially through use at events)
- media coverage/indirect advertising

Sponsorship targeting

Once an organisation has established what it has to sell to the corporate sector, it must identify potential sponsors. The following guidelines may assist in this.

- *Define the market:* Aim to attract sponsors who may be attracted to, or can tap into, your sporting market. If you are seeking a sponsor for a local league T-Ball team, it is unlikely that Carlton & United Breweries would be interested. However, a nearby clothing store or fast food shop looking for local customers might be.
- *Don't disregard an unlikely sponsor:* Don't overlook a sponsor that doesn't have an obvious relationship with your sport or organisation. An unusual sponsorship connection may draw publicity.
- *Assess the images associated with current advertisers:* National or local advertising presents numerous opportunities. Review the messages potential sponsors are aiming to get across. You might identify ways of putting together a proposal of mutual benefit.
- *Utilise the Yellow Pages, newspapers and the Internet:* Use these media to see which businesses are advertising locally and who their competitors are. By knowing the type and range of competitors you may well impress a potential sponsor.
- *Approach local professionals:* Self-employed professionals such as accountants, real estate agents and insurance salespeople are always seeking ways to get their name before the local public.

The formal proposal

The next step is to prepare a formal proposal. This needs to be undertaken in a thoroughly professional manner, and should be clear and detailed but not wordy. It should focus on the benefits that the sponsor will obtain, and your preparedness to service the sponsorship in order to help them maximise the benefits. The proposal should contain the following:

- a succinct description of your organisation and its activities, including membership profile, development and successes, affiliations and strategic outlook

- the likely financial and non-financial benefits to the sponsor, together with details of:
  - your market area—population size and profile
  - degree of exclusivity of the proposed sponsorship
  - expected media exposure
- a realistic assessment of the cost and value of the sponsorship required

Other points

Be candid about other sponsors' involvement, if any; but be careful and prudent in seeking multiple sources of support. Invite sponsors to meet your members and inspect your premises and facilities. If successful in obtaining a sponsor, seek to enter a term contract and encourage your sponsor to become involved with your organisation. Above all, don't ignore them once you've got their cheque. Finally, some form of evaluation should take place after the sponsorship cycle has been completed.

Detailed information on sponsorship proposals can be found in John Birkett's book, *Sports Sponsorship*,[25] and in Geldard and Sinclair's publication *The Sponsorship Manual*.[26]

PERFORMANCE MEASURES

Performance measures for marketing management provide a practical indication of how the systems approach to professional management practice works. Performance measures can be tied to sales or volume, and the sports equivalents would usually be membership, player participation, attendances, corporate support and merchandise sales. Performance can also be tied to the financial management of the organisation, and can involve either income analysis or cost analysis. Income analysis is conducted by examining the income from each product line and each market segment. By doing this, administrators can determine the percentage of their net income that is derived from each service and gain an insight into the effectiveness of their marketing for each target segment.

However, the weakness of this approach is that it fails to take into account the resources invested in each area. For example, service A may generate twice the income that service B does, but may cost four times as much. To combat this weakness, cost analysis may be undertaken, where the profit contribution of each service and market segment is measured instead of its total revenue.

SUMMARY

This chapter examined the techniques of marketing management and how they can be applied to sport. We showed that in the first instance successful marketing of sport requires a detailed appreciation of the sports market. This is achieved via market research, where existing and potential customers are studied with the objective of identifying possible target markets or customers. Once a target market has been pinpointed, a general positioning strategy may be created for each market segment. This positioning strategy is designed to match product or services features with consumers' expectations, creating a unique 'package' designed to add value, delight the customer and maximise income. The four Ps of the marketing mix, product, price, promotion and place, can then be applied to add further detail to the general positioning strategy. The chapter also provided instruction on the design, development and maintenance of sponsorship arrangements.

FURTHER READING

Mullin, J., Hardy, S. & Sutton, W. (1993) *Sport Marketing*, Human Kinetics, Champaign, Ill.

Pitts, B. & Stotlar, D. (1996) *Fundamentals of Sport Marketing*, Fitness Information Technology, Morgantown, W.Va.

Schaaf, P. (1995) *Sports Marketing: It's Not Just a Game Anymore*, Prometheus Books, Amherst, Mass.

Shilbury, D., Quick, S. & Westerbeek, H. (1998) *Strategic Sport Marketing*, Allen & Unwin, Sydney.

9 Facility management

After reading this chapter you should understand the general process of managing a sporting facility to the benefit of members, players, clients and spectators.
   More specifically, you should be able to:

- outline the main components of facility management
- give an account of performance measures in the administration of a facility

INTRODUCTION

Facility management involves the co-ordination of the physical setting and associated services with the users' needs. It ranges from the management of world standard sports stadiums, like the Sydney Cricket Ground or the Brisbane Entertainment Centre, to community, club or private facilities such as scout halls, netball courts and indoor rock-climbing centres. In some cases, like a privately owned gymnasium, the facility itself is the service, while for other organisations, such as a rowing club with a boat house, the facility is a 'shell' that accommodates the delivery of the service.

Facility management should not be confused with facility planning and design, which concentrates on the architectural and engineering side. The planning and design of sports stadiums is in itself a major industry. Journals like *Panstadia International* provide outstanding surveys of major developments, while *Athletic Business* focuses on trends in planning and design for community sport and fitness facilities.

This brief chapter looks at real estate and its location and touches on equipment, maintenance, safety and auxiliary services (see Figure 9.1). But it should be noted that all the chapters in this book are relevant to the task of managing a sporting facility.

MAIN COMPONENTS OF FACILITY MANAGEMENT

Real estate and its location

Selecting the 'right' real estate for a sporting facility is critical to its success. An obvious factor to consider is the number and proximity of prospective users.

Figure 9.1 Main components of facility management

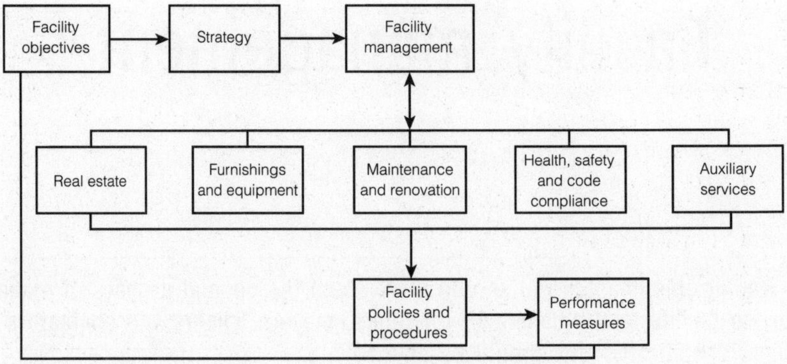

But the selection of a suitable place requires more than a cursory glance at an Australian Bureau of Statistics printout on local government demographics. Other considerations include:

- direct costs such as rent, utilities and insurance
- physical suitability of the building
- proximity to staff and suppliers
- transport availability
- site restrictions and other complications such as environmental factors or heritage requirements

Considerations of these kinds are just as important for existing facilities as they are for new facilities. Tables 9.1–9.3 list a variety of factors to be

Table 9.1 Typical cost considerations

Insurance:
- property damage
- theft
- product and general liability
- disability
- worker's compensation
- business interruption
- health and medical

Rent

Maintenance

Operating expenses

Rates

Taxes

Telephone

Electricity

Gas

Water

Table 9.2 Site-related considerations

Appropriateness of building
Safety of structure
Attractiveness/aesthetics
Design features
Development potential
Availability of staff
Customer proximity
Supplier proximity
Density of competitors
Parking proximity
Public transport proximity
Utility restrictions

Table 9.3 External considerations

Historical value, heritage issues
Native title legislation
Environmental issues
Meteorological conditions
Planning restrictions, zoning regulations
Pollution and contamination
Road use impact
Social impact

taken into account; in fact they form the basis for a feasibility study of a building or development proposal.[1] (The factors are not listed in order of importance.)

Operational features of real estate management

The day-to-day management of a sporting facility requires a flexible personality and a variety of skills that can cope with the routine of an office system and the changing circumstances of a multipurpose operation. Figure 9.2 shows three segments of administration in the context of real estate management.

Office facilities

Office facilities are no different in their management practice requirements; administrators must pay the rent and see to the maintenance. As office staff are often the 'face' of the organisation, particular attention must be given to the selection and training of reception officers, who must be courteous, knowledgeable and sensitive to customer needs. This issue is examined in more detail in Chapters 8 and 10.

Figure 9.2 Real estate management

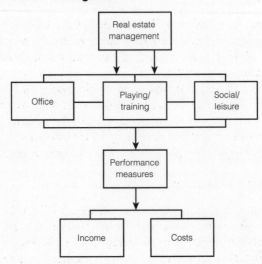

Playing/training facilities

The playing and training facilities can vary widely, even for clubs in national league competitions or for elite athletes and teams. Also, the ownership of the facility can impact upon its management. Large, privately owned facilities are normally managed independently, and sports administrators in these cases do not often have to concern themselves with logistical management within venues. On the other hand, some sporting organisations lease (or own) their facilities and run all their events at the central location. These organisations, and clubs in smaller competitions, use these facilities as both playing and training venues, and therefore may be required to set up an appropriate facility management system for their sporting activity.

The dominant concern for administrators whose organisations lease training facilities is finding an appropriate venue and negotiating its use. For administrators managing training facilities, the dominant interest should be in continued maintenance of the venue, with safety and appropriateness the key issues. Athletes and players must be able to train in safety, in an environment that mirrors actual competition conditions as closely as possible. Furthermore, players and athletes must have access to appropriate pre- and post-training equipment and amenities (e.g. weights and showers/changing rooms, respectively). Maintaining these areas necessitates finding staff who can undertake a number of activities, including cleaning, grounds-keeping, equipment maintenance, and who can operate essential facility systems, such as lighting, plumbing and power. We discuss the staffing issue in more detail in Chapter 10.

Social/leisure facilities

Social and leisure facilities may be divided into three areas: corporate; gaming; and members. Corporate social facilities are those services provided to companies at playing venues, such as special seating, boxes and dining areas. Gaming facilities, if available (and usually limited to clubs), should be located at an organisation's headquarters, which normally houses both the office and the training facility. Thirdly, members can be provided with special access to social facilities such as dining areas. As we indicated in Chapter 8, these social and leisure facilities are an important part of the marketing mix, and should be reviewed through customer surveys on a regular basis.

Furnishings and equipment

These fall into two categories: specific and general. The type of facility and the nature of the services offered determine the specific equipment needs. The range is too wide to discuss here, but maintaining a satisfactory inventory of equipment is clearly vital in facility management. General furnishings and equipment are typically the same as used in a comparable non-sporting organisation.

Maintenance and renovation

A crucial element in the overall operation and success of a facility is careful maintenance and continuing renovation. A discussion of detailed requirements in this area is beyond the scope of this book, but interested readers are referred to John and Sheard (1997).

Health, safety and code compliance

Health, safety and code compliance are essential features of sound facility management, and must be controlled tightly to minimise risk of injury and any resulting litigation. Negligence and liability are issues to be continually addressed in order to avoid legal action against the facility or organisation. It is also important to put in place and closely monitor policies that help prevent breaches of standards and safety codes, which may attract a penalty. This issue is covered in more detail in Chapter 11. An excellent overview of safety and health matters is provided in John Mathew's book,[2] which covers topics ranging from ergonomics to ultraviolet radiation. Interested readers should also consult the appropriate Acts and government publications applying to sport and related fields of activity.[3]

Auxiliary services

Auxiliary services include specialist food outlets, other shops, 'outsourced' programs such as nutritional education, and groups that hire rooms in the facility in order to present, for example, martial arts or yoga classes. Like the other components of facility management, auxiliary services must be planned and administered with users' needs clearly in mind.

PERFORMANCE MEASURES

Performance measures for facility management are derived from financial management and customer service outcomes. The 'systems' approach we advocate presupposes that organisational objectives will translate into key performance indicators. Here the indicators are based on two financial measures: income and costs, as we saw in Chapter 7.

In using performance measures in larger facilities it is often helpful to identify cost centres. This enables you to isolate the profitability of specific 'paying' services (e.g. the swimming pool, indoor sports hall or conference room) and thus to exercise greater administrative and financial control.

While costs can be measured for training and office facilities, they typically create no reciprocal income, and evaluating their performance is a more difficult task. In such instances you can use comparative costing, where operating costs are contrasted with previous years (allowing for inflation). Player/athlete complaints and coaches' feedback are further measures of performance, although these can be difficult to quantify.

Other performance indicators may cover external factors that focus on facility usage levels.[4] They include:

■ membership levels
■ facility usage levels
■ equipment usage levels
■ merchandise sales
■ special events held
■ income from facility and equipment hire
■ attendance levels
■ participation of special or minority groups

These indicators can be refined by creating 'rates' of usage and participation. For example, you may wish to measure the utilisation level of a sports hall as a percentage of its total availability. A 50 per cent rate would normally be poor, while a 90 per cent rate would be excellent.

SUMMARY

This chapter introduced the reader to the basics of effective facility and venue management. We highlighted the need to be well organised and to focus on those everyday activities that directly impact upon the customer, member and fan. We demonstrated that the design of the facility was a pivotal factor in attracting members, users and fans. Five complementary dimensions of effective facility management were examined. They were the physical location, furnishings and equipment, maintenance, safety and code compliance, and auxilary services. We also pointed out that performance indicators were an essential part of the facility management process. In this context, the proper maintenance of a facility became a critical success factor, since poorly maintained and unsafe structures and venues will quickly turn off customers.

FURTHER READING

Farmer, P., Mulrooney, A. & Ammon, R. (1996) *Sport Facility Planning and Management*, Fitness Information Technology, Morgantown, W.Va.

Frosdick, S. & Walley, L. (eds) (1997) *Sport and Safety Management*, Butterworth Heinemann, Oxford.

John, G. & Sheard, R. (1997) *Stadia: A Design and Development Guide*, 4th edn, Architectural Press, Oxford.

Torkildsen, G. (1992) *Leisure and Recreation Management*, 3rd edn, E. & FN. Spon, London.

10 Human resource management

After reading this chapter you should have a broad understanding of the main components of human resources management and their application in a sports setting.

More specifically, you should be familiar with key principles in:

- assessing an organisation's needs for staff
- completing a job analysis and job description
- recruitment and selection processes
- compensation systems
- performance appraisal
- staff training and development

INTRODUCTION

One of the great mysteries of Australian sports management is that, while it has always relied on the efforts of thousands of volunteer workers in sustaining its programs, it has generally ignored their need for training. Likewise, there has been little in the way of proper recruitment, clear duty statements or appropriate recognition or reward. This is bad enough, but in too many organisations the same applies in relation to paid staff.

The purpose of this chapter is to set out a system of human resource management that incorporates these and other functions. The system is illustrated in Figure 10.1. With certain exceptions, our discussion will encompass both volunteer and paid personnel, while reflecting the growing professionalisation of sports management. Toward the end of the chapter, we will have a little more to say on the situation of volunteers.

Human resource management (HRM) is concerned with the overall management of people and the development of their professional skills and abilities so that they can contribute fully to the organisation's mission. Raymond Stone defines HRM as the 'productive utilisation of people in achieving the organisation's objectives and the satisfaction of individual employee needs'.[1] In other words, HRM is a pivotal component of any

Figure 10.1 Components of human resource management

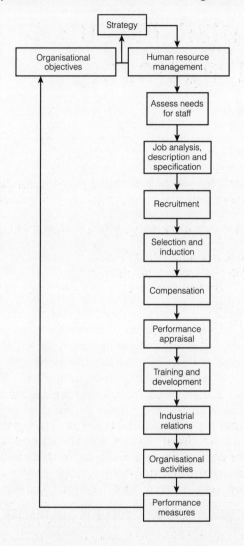

organisation's planning system and should be aligned with the corporate mission and vision. It should also involve anticipatory and forward thinking, and be concerned with continually improving the quality of staff performance.[2] It therefore fits neatly within a philosophy that embraces strategic thinking and total quality management, which were examined in detail in Chapters 3 and 4 respectively.

Good HRM is both person-centred and goal-directed. The best HRM program provides for employee support, welfare and counselling assistance, and personal growth and development (the soft side) *and* the design of efficient work practices, precise work standards, clear performance benchmarks, and

Table 10.1 Purposes of an HRM system

Purpose	Score
Effective staff induction	
Identification of low performance areas	
Cost containment through proper work procedures	
Improved customer service through extensive training schedules	
Rewards and incentives to stimulate greater staff effort	
Thorough description and promotion of safety program	
Staff education on anti-discrimination legislation and policies	
Processes for the organisation's evaluation of staff	
Processes for staff evaluation of the 'organisation'	
Monitoring of absenteeism and sick leave	
Planning to avoid skill shortages	
Planning to enhance staff competencies	
Staff education on the principles and practice of enterprise bargaining	
Advising staff on new federal Industrial Relations legislation	

productivity-enhancing training activities (the hard side).[3] Moreover, it seeks out as much employee involvement as possible and is more collaborative than directive.[4] Human resource management is not the same as 'personnel management'.[5] The latter has its antecedents in the payroll and staff record keeping functions, and is now essentially a mechanistic activity that requires a good eye for detail, but not much imagination or strategic thinking.

Table 10.1 lists the purposes that a comprehensive HRM system can encompass. You may wish to reflect upon the fourteen items, and rate your sporting organisation for each item on a scale of 1 (weak or ordinary) to 5 (excellent). A total score of 14–28 would indicate a very poor and unorganised HRM system, while a score of 56–70 would indicate a well-structured and operational HRM system.

THE CHANGING HUMAN RESOURCES SCENE IN AUSTRALIAN SPORT

Australian sporting clubs have traditionally been managed on an honorary basis. They have relied on volunteers freely giving their services and taking on positions of responsibility. However, the increasing commercialisation of sport at both the elite and the local or community level means (i) that there is a growing need to employ *trained* people, on a full or part time basis, and (ii) that the future growth and development of sporting enterprises demands the application of professional management practices. There is a financial cost in responding to these trends, of course, but if a club or association can attract more members, sponsorship, or match attendances, then it will be better off. Indeed, there are many winners: the sport will provide employment opportunities, its facilities and services will be deployed in a competent manner, volunteer officials will be able to operate with better support, and members will receive a wider spread of benefits.

The reliance on volunteer officials, no matter how committed or enthusiastic they may be, is totally inconsistent with the complex and sophisticated commercial environment in which most prominent sporting organisations now operate. The negotiation of a lucrative television contract, the design of a merchandising program, the establishment of workable and equitable disciplinary tribunals and dispute resolution boards and the creation of detailed planning systems all require skilled staff. The days of appointing people because they happen to be 'free', available, an old player or a good friend are gone. A proper HRM system is not just a good idea; it is now *vital* for successful sports management.

The appointment of just any person to undertake specific duties is unlikely to provide a long-term benefit or to generate sufficient new funds to cover the costs of the position. The scarce funds of the club or association will realise comprehensive benefits only if the recruitment process is undertaken properly. It is sometimes suggested that it is just a matter of hiring a 'competent person'. This view is too narrow. The better approach, of course, is to hire someone who can perform the required tasks at a *high* level and can also develop their professional skills over their time with the enterprise.

This can only be achieved by having in place a well-structured and properly administered HRM system, to which we now turn.

STAFFING REQUIREMENTS AND JOB ANALYSIS

Assessing the needs for staff

The first step in any HRM program is to review your current staffing establishment (the structure of existing jobs) in the light of your organisation's likely future requirements. A useful way to commence this process is to ask yourself a few questions—for example:

- Can the visualised future workload be carried out by existing staff?
- Will more or fewer people be needed?
- Can any jobs be eliminated to free people for other work?
- Are there seasonal patterns of demand associated with particular events and programs, and if so can they be levelled out or must they be accommodated?
- Are turnover rates consistent and predictable, or is there no pattern?
- What balances of full and part time, paid and unpaid, permanent and temporary, salaried and hourly staff currently exist, and should (or can) these balances be continued?
- What specific skills will be required in the future? Do the skills lie in,

say, event management, finance, computer applications, sports development, recruitment or coaching?

- Will any new jobs be easy to fill?
- Can they be filled internally?
- To what extent will existing staff need to be retrained?

Forecasting the demand for staff

In forecasting the demand for staff, it is necessary to look at previous trends and project them into the future. For example, if in the past an additional State Table Tennis Association promotions officer has been required for every five new regional developments, this simple relationship can be used to estimate the staff needed to expand the program. Of course, the projections may need to be modified later due to unforeseen circumstances.

Other questions must also be taken into account—for example:

- Is the membership or participation base changing and how much growth, if any, is expected?
- Do members need additional services?
- Do existing member services need to be rationed or rationalised?
- Do additional events or programs need to be put in place?
- Is there is a need for new offices or program technologies?
- What are the likely staff turnover rates?

Examining the supply of staff

In examining the labour supply, you should determine, at least in broad terms, the availability of suitably qualified people elsewhere in the working population. This may be done by consulting government agencies or employment firms. The suitability of new university and TAFE graduates may also be a relevant consideration.

Another step is to identify those of your existing staff who have the skills and experience to take on a new role, if required. This involves making a detailed review of every staff member in order to create a skills inventory for the organisation. The skills inventory should desirably contain, for each job, a full job history, including (for example):

- educational qualifications
- specific accreditations
- previous and current duties
- technical, managerial and interpersonal skills
- major projects undertaken
- training programs undertaken
- career aspirations

Skills inventories not only provide a ready review of who might be able to move into new positions but also reveal the training needs of employees—to their ultimate benefit as well as the organisation's.

Job analysis: formulating a job

Implicit in our discussion of HRM is the notion that many sporting organisations must become more 'professional' in their structure, personnel and mode of operation. For reasons other than simple growth in an organisation's activities, therefore, new or different jobs will need to be created from time to time. Where this means additional, or higher paid jobs, the funds needed to pay for them must be available.

Once it has been agreed that a new function should be carried out, and that the position to be created can be funded, the next task is to undertake a job analysis. Job analysis (or, as it is sometimes called, job formulation) is the process leading ultimately to a definition of the duties involved in the position. It has three components: job content, job requirements, and job context. A typical job analysis will examine the new function in terms of:

- content
  - primary tasks
  - other implied tasks
  - indicators of successful performance
- requirements
  - skills and competencies needed: physical, psychomotor, personal, intellectual
  - cognitive demands: routine and repetitive versus problem-solving and creative
  - qualifications needed
  - experience needed
- context
  - supervision and reporting relationship
  - job characteristics, including location, travel, work times, physical setting
  - equipment to be used

A further technique in job analysis is to look at the function in terms of three types of activity: data-based, people-based and 'things'-based. If this is done, functions can be studied (and compared) on the basis of the degree of complexity of each type of activity.[6] They can be examined using the following variables, which move from most complex to least complex.

- data
  - co-ordinating and analysing
  - compiling and computing
  - copying and comparing
- people
  - 'mentoring'
  - negotiating
  - instructing and supervising
  - directing and persuading

- – speaking and serving
- – helping
■ 'things'
- – setting up
- – precision work
- – controlling and operating
- – driving and manipulating
- – tending
- – handling

On this basis it is possible to grade proposed jobs in terms of their complexity or difficulty, assign to them appropriate levels of authority and create appropriate levels of remuneration. By highlighting the skills and competencies required for each position, job analysis also indicates the training that may be necessary.

The job description

You are now in a position to prepare a job description, covering the *job content* and *job context* outlined above. This document indicates the job title, what the job involves, how it is to be performed and under what conditions it is to be performed. To give an example, the job description for the director of the Southern Districts Orienteering Association might include the following items:

■ seeks avenues of sponsorship
■ implements development plans
■ prepares annual operating budgets
■ supervises the activities of paid support staff
■ consults with State government authorities
■ travels interstate as required
■ has frequent weekend work

The job specification

The job description should be followed up with a job specification, which is effectively an extension of the *job requirements* listed above. The job specification does *not* list the tasks to be done but rather identifies the skills, knowledge, personal qualities, qualifications and experience required to competently perform the job. Some of the job specification items for the Orienteering Association position referred to above might be:

■ basic financial management skills
■ proven ability to negotiate sponsorship and merchandising arrangements with the corporate sector
■ ability to prepare publicity and media material
■ highly developed report writing skills

- well-developed interpersonal skills
- tertiary qualifications in business or sports management
- prior experience with a State sporting body

To this should be added a personal specification (i.e. the personal attributes required to do the job properly). It might include:

- a sporting background
- availability for interstate travel at regular intervals

With the completion of the job specification, an employment contract for the position can be drafted to reflect the various responsibilities and conditions of employment.

AUSTRALIAN FOOTBALL CLUB: JOB DESCRIPTION AND JOB SPECIFICATION EXAMPLES

These examples, taken from an Australian football club, set out the duties, skills and responsibilities of two different jobs. See if you can distinguish between the job description items (both content and context) and the job specification items (requirements).

MANAGER: FOOTBALL DEPARTMENT

Job identification
Manager: Football Department

Job statement
The Football Department Manager is responsible for the efficient operation of the day-to-day activities, and overall performance of the Football Department of the Club, with particular attention to the contractual arrangements, welfare and professional development of staff and players. The Football Department Manager should also represent the Football Department in its dealings with external bodies.

Duties and responsibilities
- Attend to all matters affecting the proper conduct of the Football Department's administrative systems.
- Oversee and supervise the purchasing, control of use and maintenance of all football materials, uniforms, playing aids, video equipment and medical supplies.
- In consultation with the General Manager, undertake all player contract negotiations.
- Attend to all necessary applications for permits and registration of players as required by league rules.

- Acquire a detailed working knowledge of player rules, draft rules and other league rules.
- Organise pre-season practice matches.
- Co-ordinate match day arrangements at both home and away venues. (It is the Match Day Manager's role to oversee team requirements on the actual match day.)
- Maintain close liaison with key officers of the league and other league clubs.
- Oversee the supervision, maintenance and upkeep of all equipment, including medical and gymnasium facilities.
- Impose fines on players for breaches of Club rules as advised by Match Committee or Senior Coach.
- Arrange for players' representation at Tribunal hearings or personally represent players.
- Arrange special functions for players and their partners.
- Attend to all medical claims and loss of wages claims that are made by Senior List Players within the set Club policy on these matters.
- Ensure all part-time staff are optimally deployed through their respective supervisors, so that players are serviced in a professional manner and optimal returns from all players are ensured.
- Provide comprehensive support and welfare provisions to players.
- Ensure an induction program is in place for players and staff and be accountable for ensuring the effective introduction of new players and football staff into the Club.
- Organise and chair meetings with the players' social committee and monitor the organisation and booking of venues.
- Oversee and monitor players' time at the Club and give feedback to coaching staff to allow players to maintain a balanced and healthy lifestyle.
- Ensure the partners of players/staff have the opportunity to be involved in after-match functions.
- Ensure all players have appropriate transport to/from training and matches.
- Ensure all staff understand their job requirements and the organisational structure within the football operations division.
- Ensure all staff have a comprehensive induction program on arrival.
- Ensure all staff understand the Club 'code of conduct' regarding non-coaching versus coaching roles, negative versus positive attitudes, conflict resolutions, and confidentiality (e.g. injuries).

Key selection criteria

- Tertiary qualifications and/or relevant experience in management or business.
- Demonstrated ability to manage people and establish a 'professional' administrative climate.
- Experience in 'event' and leisure management activities.
- Sound knowledge of employment and contract law.

Other relevant skills and knowledge

- Professional training in the human resource management field.
- Ability to negotiate players' contracts.
- Ability to design and manage a budget.

Job conditions

- The Football Department Manager is responsible for submitting monthly reports to the General Manager.
- The Football Department Manager is expected to attend committee meetings on a regular basis.
- The Football Department Manager must be an individual who can gain the trust and respect of both players and staff and maintain confidentiality.

Reporting requirements

- The Football Department Manager reports to the General Manager.
- The Football Department Manager is responsible for directing and leading all professional staff employed by the Football Department— namely the Head Coach, Recruiting Manager, Assistant Coaches, Fitness Co-ordinator, Information Technology Manager, Chief Medical Officer, physiotherapists, as well as the Match Day Manager.

HEAD COACH: FOOTBALL DEPARTMENT

Job identification
Head Coach: Football Department

Job statement

The Head Coach is responsible for ensuring the optimum performance of the club's league football teams by developing an environment of excellence and innovation in which both players and the coaching and support staff can develop their professional competencies.

Duties and responsibilities

- Where appropriate, represent the club in its public relations activities.
- Introduce and manage training programs by which players and coaching staff can develop their skills and abilities.

- In consultation with the Assistant Coaches, design and manage training sessions for players during the pre, in and post season periods.
- Co-ordinate the activities of the coaching and player support staff throughout the year.
- In consultation with the Recruiting Manager, formulate and implement strategies for recruiting players to the club.
- With the co-operation of the medical and para-medical staff and Fitness Co-ordinator, identify injured players, prescribe remedial programs, and monitor their progress.
- In consultation with the selection committee, select teams for matches relating to practice games, the summer knockout competition, and the winter league competition.
- Ensure players are physically, psychologically and emotionally prepared for match day competitions.
- Formulate and implement match day strategies and tactics for league matches, and motivate and encourage players during the game.
- Assist the Marketing Manager in planning promotion and public relations activities, and attend appropriate promotional and marketing functions.

Key selection criteria
- Extensive experience in coaching at the league level.
- Demonstrated ability to manage support coaching staff.
- Demonstrated ability to communicate with players and senior management.
- Previous playing experience at league level.

Other relevant skills and knowledge
- Understanding of general principles of sports psychology.
- Understanding of theory of skill acquisition in Australian football.

Job conditions
- The Head Coach is required to attend committee meetings on a regular basis.
- The Head Coach is required to submit written monthly team reports to the General Manager.
- The Head Coach is provided with ongoing professional training in both the management and coaching areas.

Reporting requirements
- The Head Coach reports to the Football Development Manager.
- The Head Coach liaises with the Recruiting Manager and the Chief Medical Officer.
- The Head Coach is responsible for leading the Assistant Coach (Planning and Strategy), the Assistant Coach (Player Development), the Fitness Co-ordinator, and the Information Technology Officer.

THE STAFFING PROCESS

Recruitment

The club or association executive is now in a position to seek applicants for the job. While there are a number of important steps to be taken, primary attention should be given to the legislative and cultural framework in which the recruiting and selection must take place. The Commonwealth *Racial Discrimination Act 1975* and *Sex Discrimination Act 1985* make it unlawful for an Australian employer to discriminate on the basis of race, colour, national or ethnic origin, sex, marital status or pregnancy. Moreover, some State legislation also makes it unlawful to deny employment on the basis of physical or intellectual impairment, religious affiliation, sexual preference or age. This is discussed in more detail in Chapter 11. Meanwhile, be sure *not* to ask the following kinds of questions when sending out employment documents or interviewing prospective staff:

- How old are you?
- Do you have a problem working with younger people?
- Are you married?
- Do you have any children?
- How will you care for your children when at work?
- How long have you been a single parent?
- Do you intend to have any more children?
- Where do you attend church?
- Do you have a Christian background?
- What are your views on taking prohibited drugs?
- Please send a recent photo with your application form.
- What are you going to do about your weight problem?
- Do you have a communicable disease?
- What clubs do you belong to?
- Do you belong to a trade union or professional association?
- Tell us about your political affiliations.
- Have you undertaken any military service?

The job advertisement and the application form

At this stage the position should be ready to advertise. This will involve the preparation of a clear and concise advertisement, which provides enough information to attract suitable applicants. You should then choose an appropriate advertising medium and style of advertisement. Remember that staff can be selected from either internal or external sources, and that existing staff must see the advertisement.

The next step is the production of an application form based on the job description and job specification. Once it has been checked and approved by the responsible manager, it can be sent to those responding to the advertisement. Note that the application form can be used as a preliminary screening device and should be designed with that in mind.

The interview

If the advertisement is placed in the appropriate media, is attractively laid out and succinctly highlights the key features of the job, then it is likely that a number of suitably qualified people will apply. In most cases there will be more applicants than can feasibly be interviewed; there are also likely to be some who need not be interviewed. A team of at least two should determine the people you wish to interview and then organise the interview procedures:

■ shortlist the applicants and notify them of their forthcoming interviews
■ establish the interview panel and other arrangements
■ brief the panel members on suitable interview techniques

Table 10.2 can help you determine the strengths and weaknesses of your interview process. If a majority of the items get a 'no' answer, it indicates a poorly structured and inefficient interview procedure which will yield unsatisfactory selection outcomes.

Selection and induction

It is now possible to make a decision about the appointment. It is usually best to get the interview panel to recommend one candidate for appointment, rather than referring two or three alternatives to the management committee or, worse still, leaving it all to the chief executive officer or a volunteer official. At the same time, it is useful to rank the two or three next best interviewees, since, if the first preference rejects the job offer, the second preferred person may be quickly offered the position. A brief interview report in support of the decision should be written. Once this has been completed, the successful applicant can be notified.

Conditions of employment

A contract of employment should include the following items:

■ salary and allowances
■ leave and other entitlements
■ duties, responsibilities and obligations
■ lines of authority and reporting relationships
■ the period of employment
■ an escape clause for termination of employment that is suitable to both parties and consistent with any industrial relations legislation covering dismissal procedures

Table 10.2 Interview techniques checklist

- The interview schedules were clearly identified and adhered to.
- An interview panel convenor was nominated.
- Panel members reviewed the job description before the interview.
- Panel members agreed on the key selection criteria.
- The convenor introduced the candidate to panel members.
- The convenor made the candidate feel at ease.
- The candidate was given a clear and accurate picture of the club or association's vision and core objectives
- The candidate was given time to answer questions in appropriate detail.
- Panel members did not harangue, preach or talk too much.
- Panel members listened carefully and took concise notes.
- The candidate was given the opportunity to ask panel members questions.
- The candidate was made aware of how and when the new appointment would be made.

Induction and orientation

An induction process is essential. While the precise activities will vary from organisation to organisation, induction should include introduction of the new recruit to other staff members and perhaps committee members, special briefings on the organisation, and the provision of a staff handbook. The handbook need not be a large volume but it should contain, among other things, a statement of the mission and vision, core policies and procedures, and a summary of staff entitlements. A well-produced handbook can reinforce the organisation's culture, or at least improve the way work gets done. It can also save staff an enormous amount of time if it includes information on major policies and principles of the club or association.

FURTHER COMPONENTS OF HUMAN RESOURCE MANAGEMENT

Compensation

The compensation issue is central not only to the HRM function but also to the financial viability of a sporting club or association, since wages, salaries and allowances usually form at least 70 per cent of the total operational costs. This should not mean, though, that the 'professional' sports administrator should always be aiming to keep wage and salary costs to a bare minimum, resisting any claim for a pay rise or an increased expense allowance. In the main, a sporting organisation that wants to obtain high performing staff must be prepared to pay at least the 'market rate'. Traditional awards and the provisions of enterprise agreements also need to be taken into account.

As far as setting specific compensation levels is concerned, sporting organisations should aim to avoid payment solely on the basis of seniority and past performance or merit, and instead use a skills-based system. Such a system pays staff for their demonstrated skills and knowledge and their ability to undertake a variety of tasks at some benchmark level. For example, a staff member responsible for tournament planning and administration may undertake a training program in computerised project management and subsequently use those skills to design a customised event-planning model. The improvement in productivity that results can then be used to provide a pay rise. Thus the remuneration has been directly linked to performance and more efficient time management. A skills-based system also has the bonus of creating a culture of learning and personal development, which in the long run enables all staff to provide quality customer service and 'professional best practice'.

Compensation often involves more than just the weekly or monthly pay. Fringe benefits are an increasingly important part of the compensation package. Salary packaging can get quite complex and requires advice from experienced financial consultants, particularly when superannuation is involved. Other elements are bonuses and incentives. Bonuses are usually paid after the successful completion of a project, and are not quantified in advance. Incentives, on the other hand, are built into the task, and are directly related to a performance standard or benchmark.

Performance appraisal

It is an axiom of the learning process that 'knowledge of results' is essential if individuals or groups are to improve their performance and maintain their commitment to the organisation. In the sporting world athletes are appraised continually, but managers and administrators are rarely subject to the same discipline of performance standards.

The performance appraisal process must be thought through carefully since it is not always obvious what dimensions of performance need to be appraised. (See accompanying box.)

PERFORMANCE APPRAISAL: SELECTING THE RIGHT DIMENSIONS

Take the case of a national promotions officer (NPO) with the Australian Bocce Federation. The expectation may be that the NPO will put together a marketing plan for elite competition, develop close links with the Australian Sports Commission, consolidate the Federation's affiliation with the international governing body, establish a broad profile for the sport which highlights its skill, multicultural milieu and adaptability to different participant needs, and, finally, design a national strategy for junior development. However, this general statement of what needs to be done must be expanded to include a set of clear dimensions against which the NPO's work output and handling of the tasks can be appraised.

As an exercise you may wish, using what you have learned about the technique so far, to develop a set of performance indicators for the NPO job.

Performance appraisal has a strong underlying logic, but should be implemented cautiously and with prior consultation. It will only work effectively if it is seen as a collaborative process in which the essential purpose is to create a climate or culture of innovation and risk taking, continual learning, improvement of customer service, and individual employee development.[7] If performance appraisal is seen primarily as a tool to discipline and regulate staff, then it will be doomed to failure.

Training and development

It has become fashionable to measure the likely success of organisations in terms of their ability to learn,[8] and to adapt to changing external conditions by developing appropriate competencies.[9] This is equally important here since sport trades within a high technology service industry. Moreover, sport must compete in the cutthroat competitive leisure industry, in which the 'customer' is no longer prepared to support a recreational activity on the basis of some traditional or customary belief. Likewise sports administrators who use traditional and habitual management practices to sell their sport to the public are destined for redundancy. Basketball in Australia is an excellent example of how imaginative management and innovative planning have been used to capture the youth of the nation. A combination of American cultural and sporting icons and local development clinics and schools produced enormous public interest. When this was complemented by strategically appropriate promotional programs and events, success followed. However, new skills had to be learned and implemented.

There is no doubt that ongoing training and staff development are essential to the growth of any sport. Unfortunately, Australian industry has a poor training history, and it was only the introduction of the federal *Training Guarantee Act* in 1990, which required employers to spend a minimum 1 per cent of gross payroll on training that provided the stimulus for them to take the issue of employee training seriously. Sport was even more blasé than the general business sector—it was generally believed that a quick tour of the premises or facility, a convoluted description of the task to be done and some rough trial and error was sufficient training to ensure a good standard of performance. Sports administrators who continue to be neglectful of their training responsibilities now do so at their own peril.

Training can take many forms. One must distinguish between off-the-job and on-the-job training. The former might include:

■ class room lectures and exercises
■ role playing
■ case studies
■ 'critical incident' reviews
■ administrative experience programs
■ adventure training

On-the-job training might include, for example:

■ job rotation
■ secondments
■ coaching and mentoring

While on-the-job training is usually the least costly, it cannot on its own provide the depth of training now required for the successful operation of an innovative and entrepreneurial sporting organisation. Off-the-job training may be more time consuming and inconvenient, but if it is organised efficiently and run by well-qualified instructors it can produce sizeable rewards. It will not only expose staff to different and often better ways of doing things, but also stimulate them to develop significant improvements in internal processes and customer service. Ongoing training and staff development form an essential component of TQM, which we examined in detail in Chapter 4.

Industrial relations and negotiated agreements

The rapid commercialisation of sport means that sporting organisations are now subject to a plethora of employee awards, enterprise agreements and legislated health and safety regulations. As a result, sports administrators must be able to sensitively and decisively deal with grievances and disputes, and also negotiate enterprise agreements.

In Australia the industrial relations system has always been highly centralised for most of its long history. At the federal level, the Industrial Relations Commission (IRC) or its forerunners had enormous power in setting basic conditions of employment for much of the Australian workforce. As the arbiter for industrial disputes covering more than one State, the IRC was able to set 'awards' that covered whole occupations—traversing many firms and industries.

However, the recent trend is toward greater individual industry, enterprise and workplace negotiation. In the field of professional sport, a number of important industry and workplace agreements have been signed, all of which have important implications for future relationships between employer and employee. In both the Australian Football League and the National Soccer League, collective bargaining agreements have been negotiated and, together with standard playing contracts, set minimum conditions for all players who have been put on a club's contract list. The employment conditions agreed to include, for example:

- minimum annual base salary
- minimum senior match payments
- hospital and medical benefit payments
- relocation expenses
- termination payments
- grievance processes
- consent to promotional and merchandising activities

In addition, in January 1997 the Commonwealth Government introduced the *Workplace Relations Act*, which has two important provisions. First, it allows employees to negotiate individual employment agreements, which override existing awards and collective agreements. Second, the Act allows a group of workers to negotiate a 'non-union' employment contract, which again overrides the industrial award. These agreements are called Australian Workplace Agreements, or AWAs. The legislation focuses on bargaining at the enterprise level, which in many sports means the association, league or club. The legislation also substantially modifies the earlier 'unfair dismissal' provisions, making it easier for employers to 'downsize' their staff.

Disciplinary procedures

It may at times be necessary to take corrective action if an employee's performance or behaviour is unsatisfactory. In the first instance some form of counselling or further training should be considered. It may be revealed, for example, that the workload is excessive, that a skill deficiency exists or that others in the organisation are not providing reliable support. In such cases the problem might be remedied by constructive assistance from the CEO or executive committee. If, on the other hand, there is a suggestion of continual disobedience, negligence, absenteeism or 'personal' misbehaviour, then a warning should be given. It is prudent to document the occurrence and the management action taken. If the offence occurs a second time, the warning should be given in front of a witness or even recorded. Counselling should be offered. In addition, advice should be given at this point that makes it clear that the next instance of inappropriate behaviour will result in dismissal.

The following are examples of specific offences that can reasonably lead to an employee being severely reprimanded or, if necessary, dismissed:

- stealing, or knowingly obtaining stolen property
- vandalism that results in significant damage to association or club property
- constantly failing to observe safety regulations

- being drunk or affected by drugs while on duty
- deliberately falsifying documents and records
- grossly indecent conduct
- consistent failure to follow reasonable work-related instructions
- failing to maintain staff, player, client or member confidentiality

THE SITUATION OF VOLUNTEER PERSONNEL

The recruitment and selection of volunteers and honorary officials need not be as formal or as detailed as for paid staff. There are, however, certain principles that apply to volunteers as much as they do to other people. Volunteers should be seen as responsible individuals who have the capacity to work without constant supervision, who have the need to seek responsibility and who want recognition. They need to work in a secure environment where their physical or mental health will not be at risk. And they have a right to expect a clear description of their tasks and duties, the level of authority and responsibility involved, and their formal relationship with staff members.

The relationship between volunteers and paid staff may not always be a happy one. Volunteers can feel threatened and rejected, while paid workers may feel that the volunteers are conspiring to undermine their authority. These feelings can be minimised by counselling all parties and by ensuring that their respective duties and responsibilities are clearly defined. At the same time, volunteers working closely with paid colleagues should as far as possible be given jobs that maintain some level of authority and influence.

PERFORMANCE MEASURES

Performance measures for human resource management centre on the contribution made by officials, employees, members and players to the success of the club or association. A high performing human resource management function will produce job satisfaction, low resignation and turnover rates, and high productivity. Qualitative indicators include staff morale and committment; quantitative indicators include absenteeism levels, rate of position turnover, and gender and race equity.

SUMMARY

This chapter discussed the ever-increasing importance of human resource management for sporting clubs and associations. Traditionally sporting clubs have relied on the enthusiasm and dedication of volunteers and so human resource management systems have not been put in place. In today's highly competitive and commercial sport industry it is absolutely essential to implement a soundly designed and people-friendly staffing policy and program. We have provided the reader with a comprehensive staff plan in which the first steps are to identify staff needs and undertake detailed job analyses. From this beginning, it is then possible to design job descriptions, job specifications, and selection processes.

We also noted that staff morale and high levels of performance can only be sustained through the design of appropriate staff appraisal, staff support and training programs. The chapter concluded with a review of the place of volunteers in the management of sporting clubs and associations. We emphasised that volunteers are valuable resources who must be nurtured and not taken for granted, and they must be given clear guidelines and performance standards which establish a clear set of expectations. At the same time, they must be rewarded for their contributions, and this should be done through visible encouragement and concrete incentives.

FURTHER READING

Critten, P. (1994) *Human Resource Management in the Leisure Industry*, Longman, Harlow, Essex.

Marquardt, M. (1996) *Building the Learning Organisation*, McGraw-Hill, New York.

O'Neill, G. & Kramer, R. (1995) *Australian Human Resource Management*, Pitman, Melbourne.

Nankervis, A., Compton, R. & McCarthy, T. (1996) *Strategic Human Resource Management*, 2nd edn, Thomas Nelson, Melbourne.

Stone, R. (1995) *Human Resource Management*, John Wiley and Sons, Brisbane.

11 Legal management

After reading this chapter you should have an understanding of a number of legal principles and arrangements that affect the way in which sports administrators manage their organisations.

More specifically, you should be able to outline the essentials of:

- an organisation's constitution
- incorporation as a legal entity
- duty of care issues
- equal opportunity requirements
- contracts
- disciplinary tribunals
- other issues: health and safety, restraint of trade, defamation

INTRODUCTION

It is clear that dynamic sporting organisations can no longer be administered from a kitchen table or managed as if they were merely a social club. Nor is it possible to assume that sporting organisations are entirely special—that they can operate as if the laws governing the profit-based commercial sector are not relevant to the world of sport. All that has changed. Sport now employs many thousands of permanent, casual and contract staff, and has developed significant commercial relationships with venue managers, with radio and television, with merchandisers and corporate sponsors.

Just a few years ago, questions of duty of care, liability of officials, insurance and incorporation were the dominant issues that sports administrators addressed. However, during the last ten years the list of legal matters impacting on sport has expanded to include criminal assault, tax deductions for professional athletes, discrimination, vicarious liability, broadcasting legislation, defamation, misleading advertising, and intellectual property rights. The impact has been so significant that a number of specialist books and journals on Australian sport and the law have been published.[1] The *ANZLA*

216

Newsletter, published by the Australian and New Zealand Sports Law Association, has become a popular and valuable source of cases and commentary on sports law issues.

The law continues to make itself felt in the world of sport, and administrators must become familiar with the major legal influences on their organisation and its activities and on competitions. The knowledge required has gone beyond a basic understanding of legal structures, duty of care, liability and insurance cover. It now includes a good working knowledge of anti-discrimination legislation, contract negotiation and design, health and safety laws, rules and conventions governing disciplinary tribunals, restraint of trade and similar issues, and aspects of defamation. A sound legal framework is now essential for an organisation wishing to pursue best practice management in sport.

In this chapter we outline a legal framework within which sports administrators can manage their organisations. As the law can vary considerably from country to country, we limit ourselves to a discussion of Australian legislation. At the same time, the issues we examine should have broad relevance to sporting organisations outside Australia.

The process involved in setting up policies to meet legal requirements is represented in Figure 11.1.

Figure 11.1 Components of legal management

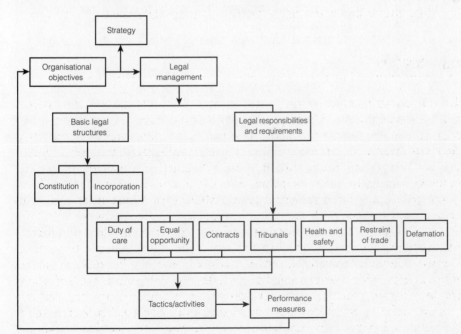

ISSUES ARISING FROM THE COMMERCIALISATION OF SPORT

The growing commercialisation of sport has not only enabled players to get more money but also transformed many sporting organisations into multi-million dollar enterprises. The Melbourne Cricket Club has an annual turnover of more than $40 million, while the major professional sporting clubs generate season incomes ranging from $2 million in the case of National Basketball League clubs to $15 million in the case of the wealthier Australian Football League clubs. A number of soccer clubs in Europe, like Manchester United and Newcastle United, have been listed as public companies on the stock exchange with a market value of hundreds of millions of dollars. The commercialisation of sport has also enabled clubs and associations to expand and improve their facilities and services. In turn, sports administrators have had to consider and deal with the many legal issues that have arisen. The accompanying box lists twenty questions frequently asked by contemporary sports administrators.

TWENTY LEGAL ISSUES FACING SPORTS ADMINISTRATORS

- Is my club incorporated, and if not, is it worthwhile incorporating it?
- Is my organisation protected if a player wins a claim for negligence against our coach or trainer?
- Can my club be sued for damages as a result of one of our players assaulting an opponent?
- Do player recruitment laws unnecessarily restrict the rights of our players?
- Are contracts with players 'reasonable' and enforceable?
- To what extent can teams in our league withdraw and enter a rival one without our league's permission?
- How can I protect our sporting name and logo and the reputation of our athletes? What action can be taken against commercial interests that use our insignia, or players' names without permission?
- What action can be taken to prevent unauthorised use of an athlete's 'personality' as a promotional vehicle?
- What has to be done to obtain permission to sell liquor at games and at the social club?
- What do I need to do to gain a gaming licence and to install and run gaming machines?
- Does equal opportunity and anti-discrimination legislation apply to our sport, or is it exempt because it is conducted in a private club setting?
- Is it legal to allow tobacco advertising on our buildings or grounds?
- Is having a sponsorship arrangement with a tobacco company illegal?

- What actions can be taken to preserve the 'good name' of our officials and players?
- Do our disciplinary tribunals provide a fair and equitable hearing to the participants?
- Should aggrieved players be given the opportunity of appealing against a disciplinary tribunal decision?
- Are our drug testing and enforcement rules consistent with the Australian Sports Commission policy?
- Is ambush marketing illegal?
- Is trade practices and competition policy applicable to sporting organisations, and to what extent can we engage in cartel-like behaviour with other clubs or associations?
- Are collective bargaining and enterprise agreements appropriate to our sport?

Some of these issues are, of course, of no direct concern to small amateur clubs. Others can be so complex that professional legal advice is essential.[2] But there are many basic matters that are both easily understood and relevant to most clubs or associations. We look at these now. (For the sake of simplicity, when we refer to clubs we are also referring to associations and similar bodies. Certain parts of the discussion also concern purely commercial enterprises.)

BASIC LEGAL STRUCTURES

Traditionally, most sporting clubs have been organised around a committee system. The policy-making function is carried out by the general committee or board of management, while the more specialised and week-to-week activities are delegated to sub-committees. The basic rules and guidelines governing the club's operation are contained in its constitution.[3]

What is a constitution?

A constitution identifies how the club will operate, informs members of their rights and obligations, helps to prevent abuses of power on the part of the board or committee, and generally saves time that might be spent in argument or negotiation over issues of policy or administration. A workable constitution should aim to cover a number of standard matters plus any issues that may be peculiar to the club. It should also aim to strike a balance between a lot of detail (which can make for inflexibility) and vague statements of principle (which can lead to ambiguity and confusion). A club's consitution does not have the force of law.

A constitution should contain the following items, among others:

- mission or purpose of the club
- election of office bearers
- appointment of chairperson
- holding of meetings
- voting
- quorum for each type of meeting
- amendments to constitution
- by-laws
- membership provisions
- committee arrangements
- finance
- suspension or expulsion of members
- dissolution of club

Each item should contain details which clearly indicate the rules that apply. As examples, the membership provisions and committee arrangements might be as follows:

Club membership

Membership shall be open to any member of the community who possesses an interest in the game of _____.

There shall be the following categories:

- Ordinary Member
- Associate Member
- Junior Member
- Honorary Life Member
- Honorary Member

The ordinary members and honorary life members shall be the general body of members of the club with the right to elect the committee and vote at general meetings.

The annual membership subscriptions for all categories shall be determined at each annual general meeting.

The Secretary shall forward a statement to all members for the subscription due. Membership shall cease automatically when the subscription is two months in arrears.

Members, having paid their annual subscription, shall be deemed financial until the succeeding year's subscription is due.

Committee arrangements

The business and affairs of the club shall be under the management of a general committee consisting of a president, two vice-presidents, honorary secretary, honorary treasurer and four members, all of whom shall be elected by the financial members present at each annual general meeting of the club.

The general committee shall, subject to decisions made at general meetings, exercise all powers of the club and do all such acts and deeds as may be necessary or expedient to carry out the objects of the club.

Any financial member may be nominated, and such nomination shall be made in writing and shall be proposed and seconded by two financial members of the club and acknowledged by the nominee. Such nomination is to be in the hands of the secretary no later than seven days prior to the meeting.

Any committee member who has absented himself or herself from three consecutive committee meetings without forwarding a satisfactory written explanation shall be deemed to have vacated the office.

Incorporation

A club that has both a formal structure and a properly drafted constitution is well on the way to having a sound administrative system. But there is the question—an increasingly important one—of whether or not to become incorporated; that is, to become a legal corporation, or company. For most of Australia's sporting history, clubs have been unincorporated.

The fundamental feature of the unincorporated club is that it is not a legal entity in its own right—it does not have a separate legal 'personality'. Rather, its personality is defined by its members, and changes with a change in membership. Contrast this with the following judicial comment on an incorporated body:

> . . . a corporation has perpetual succession: It maintains its identity and its personality notwithstanding changes in its membership, which may occur from day to day. Its property does not belong to its members; but the property of [an *unincorporated* body] does belong to its members from time to time, and that property may be owned by entirely different persons at different dates. (Williams v. Hursey (1959) CLR, p. 54)

There is no legal requirement that a sporting club whose primary role is service to members must become incorporated. Being unincorporated does mean, though, that the club may not contract, sue or be sued in its own name or take part in any legal proceedings on its own behalf. From the members' viewpoint, the weakness of non-incorporation is that, if legal proceedings are successfully initiated against the club, it is the members or the elected committee who will be held liable—and may have to pay compensation out of their own pockets.

With the establishment of Association Incorporation Acts by State governments, the benefits of incorporation have become available at low cost (at present $500 or so) to clubs that are not run for profit.

Incorporation, then, provides that a club:

- exists as a separate legal entity, regardless of changes in its membership
- may enter into contracts and make formal submissions and representations before tribunals
- may own land and other property in its own name
- can sue and be sued, with no member being personally liable
- is legally liable for its actions unless the rules of the club state otherwise

How does a club become incorporated?

Clubs are eligible for incorporation under the abovementioned Acts as long as they were established for purposes other than making a profit; if there are *incidental* profits, they must not be distributed to members in the form of dividends. To obtain incorporation, a meeting of the members must be convened. At this meeting, a majority of the members must:

■ Authorise an adult person who is a resident of the State concerned, to incorporate the club pursuant to the Act. This person will become the first 'public officer' of the club.

■ Approve, or consent to, a 'Statement of Purposes' for the proposed incorporated club, which must be added to the constitution if it is not already included.

The application, including a declaration of authority to act, a copy of the club's constitution, the name of the public officer and the appropriate fee, is then lodged with the State's 'Corporate Affairs Office' (the name will vary). Once the club has become incorporated it may use the term 'Inc.' after its name.

It should be remembered that, because incorporation legislation is State-based, it is not suitable for an organisation that wishes to be recognised outside its State of incorporation. In these cases it should seek registration under the federal Corporations Law, and lodge the appropriate documents with the Australian Securities Commission.[4]

Incorporation of commercial enterprises

A sporting organisation whose *aim* is to generate income from commercial sources and make a profit generally has to be incorporated under the Corporations Law. However, any such organisation consisting of *members* will normally have a different legal structure from that of a business with *shareholders*. Where there are shareholders, creditors are able to claim the shareholders' contributions only if the business is wound up—hence the term 'limited liability' to describe this type of structure. A sporting organisation (and its members) can obtain similar protection by registering as a 'company limited by guarantee', which means that if it is wound up the members are only liable for an amount specified in the organisation's Memorandum of Association (an official document prepared for purposes of incorporation).

LEGAL RESPONSIBILITIES AND REQUIREMENTS

Duty of care, negligence and liability

Sport is an inherently risky activity, a source of injuries, some of which can seriously impact on future life opportunities. While most participants in sport are aware of the risk of injury, clubs have a legal responsibility to exercise a 'duty of care'. In practice this means that they must design sensible rules, provide for their enforcement, provide a safe playing environment, and construct facilities which allow spectators to watch games in a secure and safe setting. If clubs fail to exercise a duty of care, they risk being sued for the act of negligence and being required to pay compensation to the injured party.

For a claim of negligence to be successful, four conditions need to exist:

■ A legal duty of care must be owed. This duty of care can extend to members, players, volunteer officials, coaches, referees and spectators.
■ The person who has the duty of care must exercise it at a standard appropriate to his or her professional training, skill level and status. The standard of care for a doctor would be higher than it would be for a Level I sports trainer.
■ Some real or tangible injury must be suffered that can be verified.
■ There must be a direct relationship between the injury and the behaviour of the person exercising the duty of care. In other words the act, or failure to act, by the person having the duty of care must be a significant contributory factor in the injury.

In order to reduce the risk of litigation against a club, it is recommended that a number of precautions be attended to prior to a game or other activity. Table 11.1 provides a checklist of what might be considered the minimum precautions. Remember that those having a duty of care obligation include not just the club's administration but also the instructor or supervisor, the coach, the umpire or referee, the facility manager, and even the players or other participants.

Table 11.1 Risk management checklist

■ Is all equipment properly serviced and maintained, and in good working order?
■ Has the facility been inspected prior to the activity?
■ Is the facility safe, free from hazardous protrusions and unnecessary obstacles, and suitable for the activity?
■ Will there be an appropriate level of supervision, particularly where the participants are inexperienced or young?
■ Are the instructors or coaches appropriately trained and accredited?
■ Have the participants been clearly warned of the inherent risks in the activity?
■ Are medical or injury facilities available that are consistent with the risks of the activity?
■ Are there documented rules that set proper standards of behaviour to be followed during the activity and in the venue as a whole?
■ Have all participants been made aware of these rules?
■ Are there appropriate signs that highlight the basic rules and regulations?

Protection against litigation

Having a formal constitution and being incorporated are recommended for a club whose members want protection against internal complaints and external litigation. However, the club itself also needs protection against claims by other parties, no matter how well organised it is or how good its safety record has been. It is therefore important that the club should put in place a portfolio of insurance cover. It is usually the responsibility of the club secretary to ensure appropriate cover for both the members (in their roles of officials or players) and the physical assets of the club. The following types of insurance need to be considered. An insurance agent or broker can give further details.

Professional indemnity insurance

It is recommended that clubs take out professional indemnity insurance to cover their medical officers, coaches, trainers and any other persons giving professional advice or imparting skills. This insurance protects such persons for claims made against them for negligent acts, advice or instructions during their work. For instance, a medical officer could be liable for failing to treat an injury correctly, or for advising a player to continue in a game after receiving a serious injury. In some cases, coaches who are accredited under the National Coaching Accreditation Scheme may be covered by a policy taken out by their State or national association.

Public liability insurance

Public liability insurance is an important form of insurance for a club since it protects both the employees and the members of the organisation. This insurance aims at providing indemnity to the club against its legal liability to pay damages arising from accidental injury (including death) and accidental damage to property. This covers claims arising from negligence of the club or one of its employees, or from the condition of the premises. It also provides for payment of legal costs related to such claims. The policy must be written specifically for the club concerned. It is prudent to define the insured as all the members of the club. It may also be extended to provide cover for goods supplied to customers, and for any claims by one member against another.

Player accident insurance

Insurance for sports participants is now recognised as a priority issue. There is both a moral and an administrative obligation to provide protection against injury arising out of participation, which may include training and travel to and from functions. There are different types of covers, on which a broker can advise you.

WorkCare compensation

Any organisation, partnership or individual who employs somebody to work for them is required by law to take out a WorkCare policy. This type of policy covers costs relating to accidents occurring at the workplace or while travelling to and from work. WorkCare insurance covers expenses incurred as a result of loss of wages, and medical bills. It does not cover injuries resulting from sporting activities—in these cases, personal accident insurance cover is needed. Nor does WorkCare cover volunteers, since they are not classified as employees.

Voluntary workers' insurance

A club can take out separate policies for its voluntary workers (known as voluntary workers' personal accident policies). These policies are designed to cover voluntary workers in the case of injury occurring while undertaking their honorary work or travelling to and from it.

Property insurance

The preceding insurance plans are designed to protect a club and its members against liability claims. However, insurance should also be taken out to cover the club's assets. Examples include Fire, Consequential Loss, Burglary, Money, Cash in Transit, Motor Vehicle, Rain (cancellation of events).

Equal opportunity

Sport has a history of segregation and discrimination, particularly involving males and females. Until recent years, in many clubs, only men were allowed to take out full membership. Women were only eligible for limited or associate membership. This meant that men had priority over certain playing times, particularly Saturday afternoons. Men and women were also often segregated as spectators. The best and most public example involved the members of the Melbourne Cricket Club. Until the 1980s women were not allowed to sit in the main pavilion, which was reserved for men. Sport, because of these traditions, is therefore vulnerable to legislation in the area of equal opportunity.

Anti-discrimination and equal opportunity legislation has been passed at both State and federal levels. One of the first pieces of anti-discrimination legislation was the federal *Racial Discrimination Act 1975*, which makes it illegal to exclude people from access to places, products and employment on the basis of race, colour or national or ethnic origin.

In 1984 the federal government enacted the *Sex Discrimination Act*, which made it unlawful to discriminate against a person on the grounds of sex, marital status or pregnancy. This Act and the *Racial Discrimination Act* are both administered by the Human Rights Commission. If the Commission finds a complaint proven, it can order the offender to stop the behaviour, to redress any loss or damage caused by the conduct or, if appropriate, require that the aggrieved person be employed or re-employed. A particularly relevant part of the Act so far as sport is concerned is section 25, which includes the following provisions:

■ a club may not, on the grounds of sex, discriminate among applicants, or in the terms and conditions offered to applicants for membership
■ a club may not, on the grounds of sex, discriminate among members in respect of terms or conditions of membership, classes of membership made available, or access to benefits provided by the club

The second provision was invoked in a landmark 1985 case involving female members of the Keppera Golf Club in Queensland. It was claimed that female or associate members were discriminated against on the grounds that they were severely restricted from playing on Saturdays. The rules allowed only two associate foursomes to play. The Commission, in declaring that this contravened the Act, ruled that women or associate members be allowed equal access to Saturday play.

Another relevant piece of federal legislation is the *Disability Discrimination Act 1992*, which makes it unlawful to discriminate against people in employment on the basis of some disability which has no impact on their performance of the job.

A number of Australian States have also passed legislation that makes discrimination in the workplace illegal. Let's take Victoria as an example. The Victorian *Equal Opportunity Act 1995* makes it unlawful for an employer or supplier of a good or service to engage in discriminatory behaviour. Both the employer and the individual employee may be liable, and a complaint may be lodged against either or both of them. Furthermore, discrimination is unlawful for all stages of the employment process, which includes the offer of employment, the terms of employment, access to training, promotion or transfer, and dismissal. It is unlawful to discriminate either in favour of or against a number of personal characteristics, for example:

■ age
■ physical features
■ disability
■ marital status
■ pregnancy
■ sexual orientation
■ political or religious belief or activity
■ race
■ sex or gender

While, in general, sporting clubs are covered by this legislation, there are some special clauses which need to be discussed. Section 65 states that a person cannot refuse or fail to select a person in a sporting team on any of the grounds listed above (and some others). At the same time, section 66, in line with federal government legislation, allows for single sex sport. That is, athletes from one sex can be excluded from an activity in which strength, stamina or physique is a relevant factor. However, this exclusion clause is only available for competitions, and does not cover umpiring, coaching or managing. The exclusion clause enables women to play against women, and men to play against men, which can be beneficial. It is also open to abuse, since it may be used to justify single sex competitions in community sport where many women are superior to many men. Similarly, it may be used to maintain a gender difference in player payments in professional sport. In other words, this section may lead to segregation when it is neither necessary nor fair.

The Act makes it clear that any club that occupies or uses Crown land, or receives State or local government grants, must comply with the Act. It also indicates that private, single sex clubs need not be illegal. For example, section 78 allows for certain exemptions for private clubs (including sporting clubs) whose purpose and membership provisions explicitly centre on the provision of services to a special group. However, some of these clubs—if they have more than thirty members, maintain their facilities from their own funds and have a liquor licence—are required to comply with the federal *Sex Discrimination Act*.

Victoria's Equal Opportunity Act also makes it unlawful to sexually harass another person. In view of the fact that most sporting organisations have a mix of men and women, where traditionally men have been in positions of power, this aspect of the legislation needs to be clearly understood. Sexual harassment occurs when one person makes an unwelcome sexual advance, makes a request for sexual favours, or engages in some related and unwelcome form of conduct of a sexual nature. The following behaviour may be judged to be unlawful:

■ comments about someone's sex life
■ suggestive behaviour like ogling or leering
■ offensive sexual jokes
■ sexual propositioning
■ unwelcome fondling and touching
■ offensive telephone calls

The sexual harassment can be physical, written or spoken. It can be 'transmitted' by letter, phone, fax, video or e-mail. Many people in sporting organisations value the social networks that exist in them, and as a result close interpersonal relationships will naturally emerge. At the same time, club members need to made aware of both the protocol that should be followed in order to avoid a complaint and, where one occurs, the mediation process that can follow.

Contracts

In sport, as elsewhere, there must be fair, transparent and legal contracts. Mere goodwill—a nod, a wink or a handshake—does not make a contract. Indeed, even a simple agreement between people does not constitute a contract. An informal arrangement whereby a group of club members agree to meet every Sunday afternoon for social tennis is not a contract. A contract is a special form of agreement and must contain a number of elements. It must include an *intention*, an *offer*, a *consideration* and an *acceptance*. For example, a sporting footwear manufacturer may decide to approach an athlete to seek her endorsement of one of its lines of sporting shoes. In return for a payment of $100 000. This constitutes the *intention*. The offer is the exchange of an 'endorsement' for money, while the consideration is $100 000. If the athlete subsequently *accepts* the offer and its rights and obligations, then a contract is a made. Consequently it becomes a legally enforceable agreement.

While a contract need not be in writing, there are significant advantages in having it in written form. It is much easier to prove that the contract exists, and what its contents are.

A contract has legal status only if the parties to it have the capacity to enter into an agreement. In Australia, any person under 18 years of age used to lack the capacity to enter into a contract. At the moment the general rule at common law is that a contract made with a person under 18 years of age is binding unless the under-age party decides otherwise.

A contract must also involve identifiable parties. This may not appear to be a problem, in that it is usually obvious who the parties are. However, if an unincorporated club enters into a contract and subsequently its membership changes significantly, the other party will have difficulty in enforcing the contract, since the original signatories may no longer be in the club. This problem emerged in a dispute in Victoria between the Fitzroy Football Club and the Carlton Football Club in 1970 when Fitzroy broke a tenancy agreement. When Carlton tried to enforce the agreement the court held that the contract could not be enforced, because the Fitzroy entity that existed when the agreement was made was not the same entity when it was broken.

Breaches of contract

A breach of the terms of contract may lead one or other of the parties to turn to the courts to enforce it, or to seek other remedies. Depending on the particular circumstances, the possible remedies include:

■ an order that the 'offending' party carry out its part of the agreement
■ a declaration that the contract is at an end, with damages being awarded to the aggrieved party
■ a declaration that the contract is still operative, with damages awarded to the party who is not getting what was originally agreed upon

The employment relationship

While paid staff have always been employees in a legal sense, the employment relationship is becoming increasingly relevant to players and athletes also. In the past, when sport was less commercially orientated, players were viewed in legal terms as independent contractors. This distinction between 'employee' and 'independent contractor' is an important one, since the existence of an *employment* relationship imposes some important obligations on the employer. At common law, a master or employer is vicariously liable for the acts or omissions of his servant or employee. 'Vicariously' means that the employer is liable for the behaviour of the employee, regardless of whether the employer has been involved or is at fault. The employer is therefore liable for, for example, personal injury suffered by an employee where there has been a breach of a statutory duty.

The courts have traditionally had difficulty in deciding whether a worker (in this instance, a player or athlete) is an employee or an independent contractor. The main criterion commonly applied is whether or not the employer has the ability to control or regulate the activities of the worker. For example, a cricketer who signs with a club and agrees to attend training, receives regular match payments, plays in all matches for one or more seasons and makes himself available for promotional activities on behalf of the club would in all probability be held to be an employee. On the other hand, a person who merely agrees to play in a particular event would probably be seen as an independent contractor. An example might be a tennis player who reaches an agreement with Tennis Australia to play in the Australian Open, and gets prize money on the basis of her wins.

Whereas the cricketer's training regime would be controlled by the club coach, with facilities and equipment made available on a regular basis, the tennis player would have her own coach and have access to the facilities only for the duration of the tournament.

Player contracts

Any paid professional player who agrees to play exclusively for one club and is committed to play for a number of years would be deemed to have entered a contract of employment. A contract of this type usually contains a number of specific provisions:

■ method of payment (e.g. fixed salary, match payments, bonus payments, or a mix)
■ service obligations (e.g. participation in all training sessions, sportsman-like behaviour)
■ injury and health provisions (e.g. medical and insurance cover)
■ fines and suspensions
■ termination clauses

In some instances, a player contract may be supported by a collective bargaining agreement between the governing body for the sport, or the central administration, and the player's professional association. At the moment, such agreements have been established for players in the Australian Football League, the NBL and the National Soccer League.

Other types of contracts

Other types of contract the sports administrator is likely to encounter include those concerned with equipment purchase, facility construction, event sponsorship, officiating at events, advertising, transportation and rentals. Most commercial vendors have standardised contracts that are used in the normal conduct of their business. These contracts should be reviewed carefully so all conditions are fully known prior to entry. When an administrator enters into a contract with another party as a representative of his or her organisation, the organisation becomes legally obligated to fulfil the terms of the agreement. This administrative duty should not be taken lightly.

Disciplinary boards and tribunals

In some ways, sport is an artificial construct. It must have a body of rules and regulations governing its conduct or it would be chaotic and inconclusive. Rules cover the way a game is played, the way clubs and associations are managed, the behaviour of officials and players, the recruitment and transfer of players, and the conduct of special events and tournaments.

In most sports there is a need to have some form of independent board or tribunal to administer and enforce the rules. With the growing commercialisation of many sports and larger payments to players, a decision taken by a tribunal to disqualify someone from competing will place a significant financial burden on them, as well as affecting their reputation. It is therefore necessary that a tribunal should be properly constituted and conducted, and that its decisions and penalties be seen to be fair and equitable.

A number of procedures should be followed in the setting up and running of a disciplinary tribunal. These procedures arise from the principle of 'natural justice'. It is a general legal principle that decisions affecting the rights of citizens must be reached only after a fair hearing. The principle applies in all courts and also in 'domestic tribunals', of which those in sport are a good example. The notion of natural justice gives the 'accused' person protection in the following ways:

■ the person accused of misconduct must know the nature of the accusation made
■ the person must be given an opportunity to state his or her case
■ the tribunal must act in good faith

The enforcement of the rules of natural justice is not as strict in a domestic tribunal as it is in the courts. This is because the parties involved have agreed on the tribunal's involvement, or have chosen to abide by association rules that guide its operation.

In the day-to-day practice of disciplinary tribunals, the following principles should apply:

- the accused has the right to a proper hearing: adequate notice of the hearing should be given; details of the incident and the charges laid should be provided; evidence from both sides should be presented
- the accused has the right to representation
- the tribunal procedure should allow for cross-examination (further questioning of witnesses, etc.)
- decisions should be made on the evidence before the tribunal and not on hearsay, biased assumptions or idle gossip
- the penalty should be commensurate with the offence (penalties should be flexible)
- the members of the tribunal must be seen to be independent

In general, the more onerous the penalty that is likely to be involved the greater the care that should be taken by the tribunal.

Assault

For many years there was a general belief in sport that the rough and tumble of body-contact games was an attractive feature that should not be discouraged. In particular, there was tacit agreement that even violent episodes should be dealt with by the sport itself, through its disciplinary tribunals, and not taken to the courts. However, a number of recent cases have made it clear that actions taken by players or spectators that cause serious injury or trauma to an opponent may be treated as criminal assault and judged accordingly. Cases in New South Wales and Western Australia resulted in football players being found guilty of grievous bodily harm. In each case the offending player received a jail sentence. There are also numerous cases where victims of assault on a sporting field have obtained damages for injuries caused by the assault. The moral here is clear. It can no longer be assumed that players can break the rules of the game, and maybe someone else's jaw, and expect to get away with it by arguing that it is a 'man's game'. This is the 1990s, not the 1950s.

Health and safety

We have seen that a strong disciplinary structure can signal the need to provide a safe social context for sports participation. It is also important to provide a safe physical setting, and again the law plays a part in securing this. There is now a raft of State and federal health and safety legislation in Australia that must be taken into account in the management systems and policy documents of sporting organisations. A number of books have recently been published that look at issues like risk management, the culture of safety, crowd management, safety in design and safety certification.[5] As we demonstrate in Chapters 9 and 13, a number of policies and programs can be introduced that create a safe playing and watching environment. Once, for many sporting organisations, the provision of an on-site first-aid officer was the major contribution to safety. It is now the bare minimum requirement.

Restraint of trade

With the growth of professional sports leagues in Australia, the question of restraint of trade has become an important management concern. One of the most entrenched conventional wisdoms in sport is that, for team competitions, a high degree of regulation is necessary to ensure stable, balanced and fair competition. The standard argument is that new players or 'recruits' should not be free to play with any team they choose, but rather should be directed to one or another team on the basis of the team's 'need' or the player's place of residence. Zoning, drafting and player-retention schemes have been used in allocating players to teams and keeping them there. The primary aim is to distribute the best players as equitably as possible between competing teams, so that any one team has its share of highly skilled players and a reasonable chance of winning matches.

However, a number of legal judgments (the Tutty rugby league case of 1971, the Foschini Australian football case of 1983 and the Adamson rugby league case of 1992) have made it clear that any rule that severely restricts a player's ability to optimise his or her income, or to move freely between competing clubs, is an unreasonable restraint of trade and therefore illegal. Indeed, the current arrangements for the Australian Football League are legally brittle, and it is only the support given to them by the Players Association that keeps them in place. Administrators should therefore be careful, when preparing player transfer rules, to obtain sound advice on their legality.

Restrictive trade practices and anti-competitive behaviour

The *Trade Practices Act 1974* (TPA) has been employed a number of times in the sporting world to challenge management decisions and sporting structures. The TPA is a key means by which the Commonwealth Government pursues its National Competition Policy, which was set up under the *Competition Policy Reform Act 1995*. The primary goal of the TPA is to 'enhance the welfare of Australians through the promotion of competition and fair trading', and it aims to prohibit any conduct that is anti-competitive, restrictive, collusive or unconscionable.

One of the most relevant sections of the Act for sporting organisations is section 45, which prohibits anti-competitive agreements and exclusionary provisions, including arrangements and understandings that have the purpose or effect of market sharing, fixing prices or excluding or limiting dealings with suppliers or customers. The other important section is section 46, which prohibits the misuse of market power, which for example could involve damaging a competitor or deterring entry of a potential rival into the market.

Both sections 45 and 46 were invoked by News Limited in 1996 when it challenged the Commitment and Loyalty Agreements that the Australian Rugby League (ARL) entered into with its 20 league clubs. These agreements effectively bound the clubs to the ARL until 2000, and therefore aimed to prevent News Limited from signing up the teams to play with the newly designed, independent 'Super League' competition. At the same time, News Limited had contracted a number of rebel clubs, and the ARL responded by claiming breach of contract. News Limited argued that the ARL loyalty agreements contained exclusionary provisions which substantially lessened competition (section 45), and furthermore that the ARL had, by entering into these agreements, misused its market power (section 46).

While the initial decision in the Federal Court by Justice Burchett found against News Limited, the appeal hearing by the Full Court found in favour of News Limited. The Full Court concluded that the ARL–clubs arrangements were clearly exclusionary for two reasons. First, the clubs had already begun to negotiate with News Limited, and the agreement prevented any further negotiation. Second, a substantial purpose of the agreement was to restrict the supply of players and teams to a rival competition, and this was anti-competitive. The Full Court rejected Burchett's finding that the ARL–clubs relationship had created a set of 'reciprocal fiduciary obligations' involving mutual trust and confidence, and that these obligations had been breached when the clubs signed with News Limited. Instead, the Full Court found that, in practice, the ARL clubs and the ARL administration had many conflicting commercial interests, particularly in respect of sponsorship and merchandising. Also, the ARL had the power to exclude any team that wanted to enter the competition, and clubs could withdraw at any time. Each of these features was seen to be inconsistent with 'fiduciary obligations and duties'. In other words, the interdependency and mutual trust that was supposed to characterise the ARL and its clubs was more myth than fact.

The decision makes it clear that non-profit sporting organisations are subject to the competition provisions of the TPA. It is also clear that they cannot maintain their monopoly position on the grounds that they are the custodians of the game or that a rival competition or league would, in their view, 'not be good for the game'. That is, sports leagues, like any other service enterprises, cannot engage in anti-competitive or cartel-like behaviour without the threat of legal action against them. The traditional belief that sport was different from business and therefore could get away with collusive behaviour has been well and truly destroyed in recent years. As we suggested in Chapter 2, sport now has as much in common with the world of commerce as it does with the world of community recreation.

Section 52 of the TPA is also relevant to sport, since it prohibits a 'corporation from engaging in conduct which is misleading or is likely to mislead or deceive'. A number of cases have arisen where a business has used an athlete's name or personality to promote a product without his or her permission. Names and photographs of athletes have been displayed with company products or logos—causing consumers to believe that the products had official endorsement, when in fact there was no such endorsement by the athletes.[6]

Defamation

Thousands of words every week are written about sport and its participants. A lot of it is complimentary, but a lot of it is critical. Players are harangued over losing games, coaches are criticised for tactical stupidity, and administrators are maligned for making offensive statements on the state of the sport—and on just about anything in the case of a few prominent officials. In such an environment there is a high risk that statements will be made that are likely to injure someone's reputation or subject them to ridicule.

While the laws covering defamation vary from State to State, there are three core tests that are usually applied to decide whether or not a statement (or its direct implication) is defamatory. They are:

- Does it bring the person into hatred, ridicule or contempt?
- Is the person's reputation or estimation lowered?
- Does it lead to the person being shunned or avoided?

It would not be defamatory to criticise a player for being slow and overweight, or playing below their potential. However, the case for defamation would be strong if it was also stated that the player was incompetent, unfit to play at the elite level, stupid and generally unattractive to most people. It might even be defamatory to suggest that someone is a 'poor sport' or an unreliable employee. So it is important to err on the side of caution when making public comments about the performance of players and officials.[7]

PERFORMANCE MEASURES

Performance measures for legal management centre on the capacity of clubs or associations to deliver their services in a safe environment and avoid serious litigation. Indicators of high performance include ongoing review of risk management policies, constant monitoring of legal developments, and low levels of claims for damages and compensation.

SUMMARY

This chapter discussed the increasing array of legal issues that sport managers have to deal with. We pointed out that the ever-escalating commercialisation of sport means that the laws and regulations which shape the behaviour of business firms are now relevant to sporting clubs and associations. The basic legal issues that govern the structure of sporting organisations were discussed, together with the pivotal place of an organisation's constitution and articles of association. We also discussed duty of care, liability and negligence, and the need for appropriate insurance to cover the risk of injury, accident, theft, fire and bad luck.

There are a myriad of additional legal issues that sports managers must understand. We reviewed the influence of equal opportunity and anti-discrimination legislation on sporting club management. We also highlighted the need to understand the obligations that arise out of establishing employment contracts, and the sensitivity required when disciplining or dismissing staff. Finally, we examined the relevance of the Trade Practices Act for the sports manager, in particular misleading advertising, passing off and anti-competitive behaviour.

FURTHER READING

Fewell, M. (ed.) (1995) *Sports Law: A Practical Guide*, Law Book Company, Sydney.

Healey, D. (1996) *Sport and the Law*, 2nd edn, University of New South Wales Press, Sydney.

Kelly, M. (1987) *Sport and the Law*, Law Book Company, Sydney.

McGregor-Lowndes, M., Fletcher, K. & Sievers, A. (eds) (1996) *Legal Issues for Non-Profit Associations*, Law Book Company, Sydney.

12 Structure management

After reading this chapter you should have a good grasp of the major issues involved in developing an effective organisational structure.
More specifically, you should be able to:

■ identify key structural elements in an organisation
■ outline the use of organisational charts
■ discuss alternative organisational models
■ discuss the use of project teams
■ explain the process of delegation

INTRODUCTION

The term 'organisational structure' refers to the *pattern* of roles and functions within an organisation. In principle, at least, the roles and functions concerned are essential if the organisation is to fulfil its purpose, but the way in which they are patterned or structured is to some extent a matter of choice. In many organisations, the roles are called jobs and the functions are called departments, divisions, etc. In a large number of sporting organisations, the roles include honorary positions and the functions may be run under the control of part-time committees. Small details aside, though, the same general principles of organisational structure and development apply.

The conservative traditions of many sporting bodies are manifested in their organisational structure and supporting operations. Most local clubs and indeed many of the larger associations are organised around the conventional roles of president, secretary and treasurer, supported by committees which implement the 'executive' decisions. However, such a structure is essentially second best, and the now constantly changing and highly competitive sporting environment demands a more flexible form of organisation.

Two key themes run though this chapter. The first is that there is no one best way to structure a sporting organisation, although it is important to ensure efficiency, adaptability and flexibility.[1] The second is that in effective

Figure 12.1 Components of organisational structure management

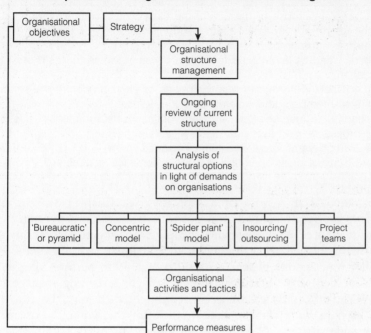

organisations there are two broad categories of personnel: the 'steerers', whose primary concern is to set the policy framework and strategic direction (traditionally 'the management committee' or 'executive'); and the 'rowers', whose primary concern is to deliver the service to the customer or client. The rowers traditionally are the sub-committee members who take responsibility for creating a fixture, putting on an event or organising a fund-raising activity. They aim to ensure that things actually happen at the right time and place, and that the event or activity offers value and entertainment. (See also Chapter 13.)

Figure 12.1 illustrates the process involved in developing a flexible and decentralised structure.

STRUCTURAL ELEMENTS

Sporting clubs and associations, like all other organisations, must have some sort of structure if their programs are to be carried out with any degree of efficiency and rationality. While no two organisations are structured in exactly the same way, there are a few points that apply to all organisations.[2]

The first point is that a club or association has some mission or common

Table 12.1 Organisational structure checklist

- Is the general purpose or mission of the club or association well understood?
- Can the central management team be identified?
- Are the roles of this team known to everybody?
- Are there clearly differentiated functional divisions within the club or association?
- Can the essential tasks and responsibilities of each division be described?
- Do all staff members know clearly who they report to?
- Does each staff member have a clearly defined set of responsibilities?
- Do all project teams have clear terms of reference?
- Do all project teams know who they report to?
- Is there a set of clear operating guidelines for each committee?

purpose, even if it is not stated explicitly (see Chapter 3). The mission determines the roles and functions needed within the organisation.

The second point is that when people work together they can achieve things that would be impossible if left to individuals working alone. Putting it another way, no one person is likely to be able to perform the full range of tasks needed—e.g. secretary, treasurer, coach, recruiting manager, junior development officer, fitness adviser. Accordingly, there must be a division of labour, even in quite small organisations.[3] But the larger the organisation, and the wider its activity base, the greater the necessity to divide up tasks and responsibilities and allocate them to different individuals and groups. (See the sections in Chapter 10 on job analysis and job descriptions.)

The third point is that all organisations have a hierarchy of authority. There are people at the top of the hierarchy who have a fair amount of authority; those at the bottom have less authority. Those with less authority receive guidance or instructions from above on what should be done and perhaps how. For example, a management committee, acting through the secretary or manager, will indicate to staff what procedures are to be followed with respect to the season's competitive activities, their scheduling, and the preparation of the ground or facility, and so on. A hierarchy of authority also involves official communication channels by which instructions or messages are sent, received and responded to. (There are informal communication channels as well, which may be very different from the established lines of authority.)

Table 12.1 will help you to judge how well structured your club or association is and what might need to be done to improve it.[4]

ORGANISATIONAL CHARTS

An organisational structure (or some part of it) can be visually represented in the form of an organisational chart. Figure 12.2 shows the structure of the football department of an elite Australian football club.

Figure 12.2 Organisational chart for a club's football department

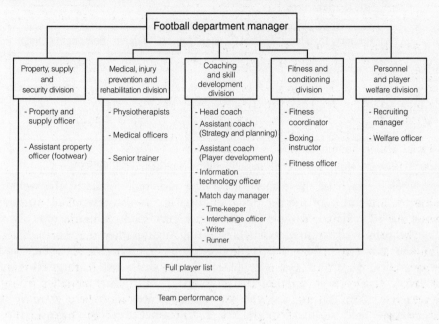

The chart reflects the *traditional* elements of organisational design:

■ hierarchy of tasks or jobs
■ strictly vertical chain of command
■ specialisation of tasks and jobs based around specific functions
■ standard procedures for each task and job
■ clear and singular reporting relations, or unity of command
■ emphasis on co-ordination and control.[5]

This football department is organised on the basis of five different and identifiable *functions*. However, 'functional specialisation' is not the only basis for organising activities. They can be grouped, for example, on the basis of '*product*', which in the case of a sporting club might mean separate divisions for the various teams—the under 18 team, the men's team, the women's team and so on. This approach has the benefit of giving each team a high degree of autonomy and responsibility, but also creates a large amount of duplication. Each team may end up with its own masseur, medical officer, fitness adviser and property officer, thus increasing the cost of managing the organisation as a whole.

The problems associated with the functional basis (it can be very hierarchical and rigid) and the product basis (it can cause excessive duplication) can be reduced by the creation of a *matrix* model. In this approach, each staff member effectively belongs to two areas: the core function or specialist activity; and the product, or team, affiliation. For example, the

Figure 12.3 A matrix model, showing 'two-way' responsibilities of individual staff members

	Property Division	Medical Division	Fitness Division	Personnel Division
Team 1	Property Officer A	Doctor B	Instructor C	Welfare Officer D
Team 2	Property Officer A	Doctor B	Instructor C	Welfare Officer D
Team 3	Property Officer A	Doctor B	Instructor C	Welfare Officer D

medical officer 'belongs' to the medical and rehabilitation division but is also *responsible* to each of the teams for services required. Similarly, the welfare officer is a member of the personnel division but is also responsible to each team. An abbreviated example is shown in Figure 12.3. A matrix model can apply equally well to other types of sporting organisation.

The strength of the matrix model lies in its inherent flexibility and adaptability. As teams (or, say, projects) are disbanded, reorganised or replaced, the vertical scale of the columns in the chart is extended or contracted according to the changes taking place. Likewise, it may be necessary to add another column for a functional area like 'membership'. This can be done without serious disruption to the other organisational arrangements.

How useful is an organisational chart?

The organisational chart shows the tasks or responsibilities that need to be undertaken, the authority relationships between those performing the tasks, and the channels of communication. This 'bare bones' structure can be given more administrative flesh by adding details about the functional responsibilities of each area. The number of people reporting directly to a given manager or supervisor constitutes that individual's 'span of control'. For example, the head coach in the football department (Figure 12.2 above) is responsible for supervising the activities of two assistant coaches, the IT officer and the match day manager—a span of control of four. The fitness coordinator, on the other hand, has a span of control of two. There is no ideal span of control. Some people say that it should lie between three and seven. However, it all depends upon the jobs being done and how much responsibility has been given to each job.

Organisational charts, of course, do not tell the whole story. They tell us little or nothing about, say, the informal arrangements that exist between officials and members, or the ways in which influence and communication really work at staff level. It often happens that some people, because of their experience, personality or political 'clout', become the focal point for communication and decision making. The football department manager, while in principle the most powerful member of staff, might defer on a management matter to the head coach as a result of the coach's influence in the club. Alternatively, the manager might challenge the coach in the latter's area of responsibility, thus setting up a chronic source of conflict and disputation.

Despite all this, an organisational chart indicates the basic structure and people's place in it. It also highlights the fact that structure is important; a structure that leads to effective co-ordination, good communication, staff involvement and successful organisational performance is essential.

Committee arrangements

Some management boards or committees may have between five and ten members; others may have up to twenty members. While the larger membership may allow greater member involvement at the highest decision-making level, it may prove unwieldy and time consuming. The smaller committee may be more efficient in making decisions on contentious issues, even if it is less representative of members' interests.

As far as day-to-day decision making is concerned, most clubs use an executive committee comprising the president, secretary, treasurer and another senior official. The role of the executive committee and its powers are usually established by the management board. A third tier of committees also usually exists. Commonly called sub-committees, these units are given specific functions involving administrative tasks and/or advisory roles. Sub-committees might include Finance, Social, Coaching, Selection, Junior Development, and Facilities.

Such arrangements can also be displayed on an organisational chart. This chart is usually constructed in the form of a pyramid, with the board of management at the top and the sub-committees at the bottom. The units are joined by vertical lines, indicating the formal lines of communication.

ALTERNATIVE WAYS OF STRUCTURING ORGANISATIONS

There is a growing body of literature that demonstrates that traditional ways of organising sporting activities are no longer able to achieve optimal results, particularly where there is a growing commercial dimension involving extensive event management, marketing, fundraising and sponsorship. The old ways are frequently unable to adapt to rapidly changing circumstances like changing customer tastes and new communication and computer technologies. Tom Peters, the prominent American management consultant, believes that business has now entered the age of 'unstructure'. He argues that the traditional concept of an organisation is no longer useful to managers, and that it is now dysfunctional to think of an organisation 'as a single entity standing on its own'.[6] Peters cites the production and sale of ice hockey equipment as an example of how the final result is achieved through a network of loosely connected but interdependent arrangements. The equipment is designed in Scandinavia, engineered in the United States to meet the demands of a massive North American market, manufactured in Korea, and distributed through a multinational market network with initial distribution from Japan. In this and many other cases, according to Peters, there is no single organisation 'with design, engineering, manufacturing and sales under the one corporate roof'. Instead, temporary manufacturing teams, workgroups, design groups and sales forces are brought together quickly and efficiently to create the final 'product event'.

Gifford and Elizabeth Pinchot, writing in *The End of Bureaucracy and the Rise of the Intelligent Organisation*, develop a similar theme. They conclude that bureaucratic structures no longer work, and should be replaced by an underlying operational philosophy, that emphasises 'freedom and community'. In other words, the rigid hierarchy referred to earlier will be replaced by a network of semi-autonomous work groups (or, as they are alternatively called by the Pinchots, liberated teams) which provide the customer service, and make things happen.[7]

The concept of the flexible organisation is also developed by Osborne and Gaebler in *Reinventing Government*, where they stress the distinction between (i) the core policy and decision-making processes and (ii) the operational or service delivery area. They make two important points. First, they say that policy and strategy formulation—that is, the steering function—is integral to the organisational purpose and must be directly resourced and internally controlled. But, second, the service to the customer can be organised in a number of ways—it can be delivered by permanent internal staff or by casual employees or by subcontractors. The service deliverers are the rowers.[8]

Pinchot and Pinchot talk about the same thing when they distinguish between 'insourcing' and 'outsourcing'. They give the example of Nike which, in its outsourcing, effectively subcontracts 100 per cent of its athletic shoes manufacture to production partners—while it concentrates on research, design, marketing and sales (insourcing).[9] A good way of determining what should be insourced and what should be outsourced is to ask what your core competencies are. What you are very good at, and particularly what you are better at than your competitors, you should retain, not outsource. Those things that you do only fairly well or not well at all *should* be outsourced, to someone who can do them very well.

It is already the case that many sporting organisations have become flexible providers of services. For example, associations frequently contract a special events organiser to manage an event or tournament or to design a schedule of fixtures. They are therefore well positioned to use the insourcing/outsourcing approach when they restructure themselves. This point should be kept in mind when we come to Chapter 13 on event management.

Figure 12.4 A concentric organisational structure

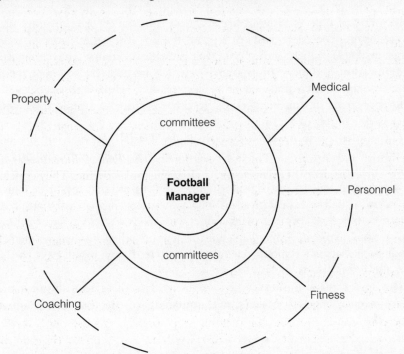

The concentric model

These thoughts lead to the idea of a concentric structure instead of the familiar pyramid or the matrix. It involves a central circle surrounded by one or more outer circles and is joined up in such a way as to look a bit like a bicycle wheel. The hub comprises central management and the executive committees, the spokes are communication channels between the centre and the rim and at the rim are the functional divisions, sub-committees or project groups. The concentric model is represented in Figure 12.4.

The concentric model is intended to create a different set of organisational relationships; in particular, to spread the decision making among the outer committees and work groups and to encourage these groups to communicate with each other as well as with the centre. (While this can and does happen in the pyramid model, the nature of that structure all too often *discourages* communication between groups in the organisation. In the concentric model, each group has a greater degree of autonomy. Most of the interaction is between the groups—making for better co-ordination 'on the ground'—rather than between each group and the central administration.

The 'spider plant' model

Another way of representing an organisation is in the form of a spider plant. This interesting species consists of a plant in a pot (the central administration in this analogy) which sends out long threadlike stems (the channels of communication and flow of resources), which in turn create small replicas of the primary plant (divisions or project teams), which subsequently send out further stems or 'umbilical cords' to other entities. A simple spider plant model is illustrated in Figure 12.5.

The spider plant model was devised by Gareth Morgan in his book *Imaginization: The Art of Creative Management*.[10] It offers useful insights into the management process, including whether an organisation is structured in such a way as to ensure good performance, and if not what might be causing it to perform below expectations. While your own club or association may well not be based on a spider plant model with its 'pot' and various offshoots, the questions listed in Table 12.2 will be helpful when applied to elements of your organisation's structure or operating style. But you will have to think about the implications of your answers.

The spider plant model highlights the variety of relationships that can exist between the policy makers and strategists, on the one hand, and the

Figure 12.5 A 'spider-plant' organisational structure

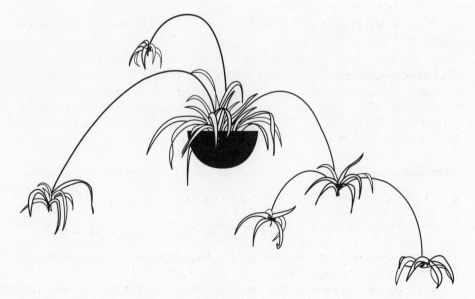

Source: Adapted from Morgan, G. (1993) *Imaginization: The Art of Creative Management*, Sage, London, p. 73.

Table 12.2 'Spider plant' analogy: questions about organisational health

- The offshoots are thriving but not the pot?
- The pot is growing in size but the offshoots are withering?
- The offshoots have been staked fast to the pot?
- The pot is not being fed?
- The offshoots are dangling without any clear direction?
- The stems are thickening but the offshoots fail to grow?
- Both the pot and the offshoots are thriving?
- Some of the stems have been severed?
- The stems are thick but the offshoots are wilting?

operational staff or service providers, on the other. It also gives another slant on the steerer/rower distinction and on the question of insourcing and outsourcing. As well, it offers a basis for thinking about the process of delegation, which we address in a later section.

USE OF PROJECT TEAMS IN A FLEXIBLE STRUCTURE

Before we look at a key aspect of the 'flexible' organisation—the use of project teams—we must get the context clear. Two main issues arise. First, what are the core management tasks (the steering activities) and what are the operational or service delivery tasks (the rowing activities)? Second, how are the tasks to be carried out?

We can address the first issue by asking the following questions about each major task or activity:

Core management area

- Does the activity involve a policy issue?
- Does it involve setting a strategic direction?
- Do associated decisions have club-wide implications?

Operational area

- Does the activity involve direct customer or community contact?
- Does it have operating guidelines?
- Can it be undertaken without constant referral back to management?

A 'yes' answer to the questions under one of the two headings indicates that the activity concerned falls within that area.

We must now address the second issue—the 'how'. Again we may ask a number of questions about each major activity, under headings relating to the approach that might be taken:

Team arrangement

■ Does the activity require a broad range of professional skills?
■ Is it complex and time absorbing?

Individual arrangement

■ Does the activity require base level skills?
■ Is it a routine activity?

Insourcing

■ Are we really good at this activity?
■ Are the resources available within the club?
■ Are there aspects of the activity that we do not want our competitors to know about?

Outsourcing job

■ Do we lack the necessary skills for the activity?
■ Is it in some other way one of our 'weak spots'?

The answers to these questions will help decide how each activity should be carried out. The exercise applies equally to both core management and operational activities. In other words, for most operational activities, decisions will have to be made about whether to create a project team, individualise it, keep it in-house or contract it out.

An example of the need for a technique of this kind might be the South Australian Bocce Association's decision to run an international event in 2000. This is an operational activity that will have direct community involvement. The Association recognises that it has little experience in running such an event, and acknowledges that specialist personnel are needed to make a success of it. On this basis, the task has to be outsourced, and it is highly likely to be handled by a project team.

Sporting clubs in particular can make good use of project teams because of the common need to conduct special events with a combination of paid and volunteer personnel. A project team has a fixed life and involves delegation, which makes it particularly useful in the case of one-off functions at either the local level or the more complex international level. If a local club decides to organise a fun run, for example, it may establish a special project team to conduct the event. The secretary may be appointed to head the team, and have one representative from each of the publicity, junior development, finance and players sub-committees. The project team will operate as long as it takes to organise, conduct and review the event, at which time it will disband.

Not all project teams will automatically produce high quality outcomes or provide outstanding customer service. But the chances of a project team fulfilling its potential will be dramatically enhanced if it possesses all or most of the following features:

- a shared purpose that energises everyone
- realistic and concrete goals that are agreed upon by the team
- a common understanding on the 'path' to be taken
- a guaranteed and appropriate 'life span' for the team
- agreement that the rewards for successful completion will be shared
- unimpeded flow of communication, both within the team and with the 'steerers'
- a good working relationship with related teams

DELEGATION

Delegation is what occurs when a manager gives a subordinate the authority to carry out a range of tasks falling within the manager's area of responsibility. The authority given may be ongoing (as in the case of a typical individual job) or it may be for a specified period. In a flexible organisational structure, we may speak of delegation of authority to a project team rather than an individual. Along with the authority to make decisions and to act upon them, the person or group given the delegation is held accountable for the outcome of the decisions or actions—although the ultimate responsibility remains with the manager.

Delegation requires skill and care if staff and volunteer personnel are to find it challenging or stimulating but not an onerous burden causing undue stress. The process will be enhanced where senior officials are:

- willing to let go of tasks
- willing to let others make mistakes
- willing to trust subordinates
- receptive to their ideas

On the other hand, subordinates may show resistance to delegation. This may result from:

- fear of criticism over possible mistakes; lack of confidence
- finding it easier to ask a senior official for instructions
- inadequate personal resources to do the job
- inadequate incentive
- being already overworked

If these concerns can be allayed and if the controlling officials have confidence in subordinates, then delegation is workable.

Delegation is not just a way of involving more people, it is a way of tapping into staff or volunteer skills and abilities and getting the most from those who want to contribute. Effective delegation makes for greater clarity in what needs to be done since the delegation process requires a clear statement of the tasks and responsibilities involved. It is also likely to make for faster decisions since those actually involved in the activity no longer need to seek approval for their actions. Delegation thus allows the rowers to act quickly and responsively when dealing with clients or the community.

PERFORMANCE MEASURES

Performance measures for structure management centre on the ability of the club or association to operate efficiently and adjust its work processes to fit changing circumstances. High performing sport organisational structures combine clearly defined lines of authority and responsibility with flexible ways of solving problems and managing standard services, special projects and major events. Indicators of high performance include the appropriate delegation of authority, the appropriate use of project teams and the prudent use of outsourcing where internal expertise is weak or where resources are limited.

SUMMARY

This chapter examined the various ways in which sporting organisations can be structured. Structure is essential in every sporting organisation, no matter how small or narrowly focused. A club or association must have a mission or common purpose, a way of dividing the labour of its staff and a hierarchy of authority. We showed how an organisation chart can be used to clearly identify the main areas of functional responsibility, the tasks and duties to be performed and the expected reporting relations. Traditionally, sport was organised around a Committee of Management, which appointed mainly volunteer staff to carry out a variety of tasks and duties. With the growing professionalisation of sport, a more sophisticated approach to organisation structure is needed. We used a number of cases to show that delegation, project teaming and outsourcing can be used to provide flexible responses to changing needs.

FURTHER READING

Bridges, F. & Roquemore, L. (1996) *Management for Athletic/Sport Administration: Theory and Practice*, 2nd edn, ESM Books, Decatur, Ill.

Morgan, G. (1993) *Imaginization: The Art of Creative Management*, Sage, London.

Pinchot, G. & Pinchot, E. (1993) *The End of Bureaucracy and the Rise of the Intelligent Organisation*, Beret Koeller, San Francisco.

Slack, T. (1997) *Understanding Sport Organizations: The Application of Organization Theory*, Human Kinetics, Champaign, Ill.

13 Event management

After reading this chapter you should be able to design a working template through which to deliver an event on schedule and within budget and that provides the customer with a quality sporting experience.

More specifically, you should be able to:

- identify the special parameters for different types of sports events
- appreciate the factors impacting upon the feasibility of an event
- understand the steps involved in planning an event
- apply time management and quality management tools to sports events
- identify and apply key criteria for evaluating an event

INTRODUCTION

While operational efficiency is an important part of event management, successful event delivery also has a lot to do with careful preparation. A central ingredient is therefore planning. Event management in sport is typically associated with a limited resource base, fluctuating personnel numbers, unpredictable environmental factors (such as poor weather), the use of outsourced services (such as facilities and catering), and a strong risk management policy. These features make thorough planning and preparation doubly important.

While the inherent flexibility of sporting events make them troublesome to manage well, the underlying event management principles remain much the same, and the difficulties encountered are similar to those associated with the delivery of any sporting service. First and foremost, event management is an exercise in logistics and may be described as the single co-ordination of the process of planning, organising and delivering a single sporting experience or collection of sporting episodes. This chapter concentrates on the management tools that can be employed to set up and deliver quality sports event outcomes.

Sports events vary enormously in style, scope and size, ranging from the Olympic Games to, say, a special exhibition of a local cricket club's memorabilia. Some are single, one-off events; others are continuing events that occur on weekly, monthly or annual cycles. Events can be further distinguished according to whether they are participant based or spectator based.

249

Participant events are those organised for the benefit of the players, and tend to emphasise player facilities, the pleasure of direct participation and quality equipment.

Spectator events, on the other hand, are held primarily for the benefit of the audience. Organisers of major spectator events will always pay particular attention to viewing facilities, amenities and 'peripheral' services such as ambience, pre-game and half-time entertainment, food and drink outlets, seating, parking, signage and so on. These things are important from a commercial perspective, as the ticket price for an event is often less than half the total amount a patron will spend. This issue is examined in detail in Chapter 8.

Community sporting bodies, meanwhile, tend to pay less attention to the variety of customer needs that go beyond the game itself—we have all experienced the homely informality of a suburban football club. This sort of experience sometimes has its own special, traditional quality, and might be seen as an attractive, unpretentious sideline to the on-field contest. In other words, the patrons' expectations of the event are important.

EVENT PLANNING

A sporting event is only as good as the planning that goes into it. The stages of event planning are illustrated in Figure 13.1. As you can see this event planning chart is based on the strategic planning model that we designed in Chapter 3, and shows the need to systematically address basic issues like the purpose of the event and its feasibility. To refresh your memory of the importance of strategy and planning, it may be worthwhile to re-read Chapter 3.

The principles of planning are always the same, and it is only the context that varies[1]. As for any organisation providing a product or service, the first step in event planning in sport is to identify the strategic direction of the event being considered. We recommend that event mission and vision statements are created, accompanied by specific event objectives and key performance indicators.

Once the strategic direction of the event has been carefully documented it is prudent to undertake a preliminary feasibility check before investing any additional time and effort. You should be reasonably certain that the event can not only be designed and conducted in the designated time frame, but that it can also be managed within budget. The list of questions set out in Table 13.1 is adapted from *Special Event Management*, produced by the consulting firm, Ernst and Young.[2] A decision on whether to proceed should be based on the answers to these questions. The more 'yes' answers the better. You should be wary of staging an event that cannot generate broad public interest, is unable to provide a budget surplus, and attracts little interest from the media or from sponsors. A particular event might be a 'good idea', but the implementation of a 'good idea' without a firm administrative foundation generally leads to failure. If, on the other hand, you have conceived an event that is likely to capture the public imagination

Figure 13.1 Event planning

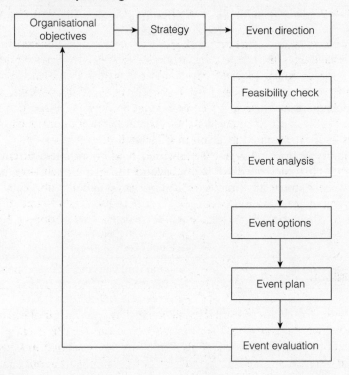

and produce an operating surplus, then you are ready to proceed to the next stage. This involves performing a comprehensive strategic event analysis.

An event analysis first necessitates the identification of competing events or activities that may affect the successful operation of your event. Next, a SWOT analysis must be undertaken to highlight the existing or anticipated strengths and weaknesses of your event, as well as potential environmental opportunities and threats. We have nominated some SWOT criteria to consider in Table 13.2.

Table 13.1 Preliminary feasibility check

- Has the event worked well before?
- Do we have the necessary resources (human, financial etc.)?
- Do we have access to people with the appropriate skills?
- Can we secure an appropriate venue?
- Does the event have a specific 'hook' that will bring people in?
- Is it likely that we will get media support?
- Is it likely that we will get sponsors?
- Will the event impact on the community positively?
- Will we have sufficient resources to advertise?

Table 13.2 SWOT criteria for events

Management areas and services delivered	Strengths/Weaknesses/Opportunities/ Threats
Player management	■ impact of facilities on players ■ quality of playing surface and equipment ■ celebrity (big name) participants
Financial management	■ budget ■ accounting methods ■ likelihood of making a loss
Marketing management	■ sponsorship ■ sales ■ merchandising ■ prospecting ■ promotions (advertising) ■ media involvement ■ community interest
Facility management	■ venue quality and appropriateness ■ admissions ■ amenities (toilets, food) ■ design ■ comfort ■ seating ■ hospitality
Human resource management	■ recruiting ■ training ■ supervising ■ motivation of staff ■ use of volunteers ■ conflicts between staff
Legal management	■ insurance costs ■ risk (liability and negligence) ■ potential for violence and crime ■ potential for strikes ■ likelihood of bad weather and other uncontrollable occurrences
Structure management	■ communication systems ■ structure and function of committees
Culture and change management	■ employee commitment and involvement
Quality management	■ realistic quality specifications ■ quality infrastructure
The sport itself	■ entertainment value (promotions) ■ historical value of event ■ tourist interest ■ government support

Next, event strategic options are considered with the use of a gap analysis. Benchmarking also may be used to nominate standards of performance, or to provide options from other events worth duplicating. Event strategies emerge out of the list of options and, consistent with the planning process described in Chapter 3, operational tactics and activities should also be constructed. These activities become the actions that successfully deliver the event.

A thorough event plan typically takes into account players, financials, marketing, facilities, human resources, legals and service quality.[3] Each of these areas has been addressed in detail in other chapters of this book. Rather than reiterating these details, we have constructed simple question tables for each area that highlight the specific issues that event managers should focus on (Table 13.3). However, we strongly advise that these tables be used as a supplement to the material covered earlier in this book, rather than as the primary event management tools.

Table 13.3 Event planning checklist

Player management
- How many participants/athletes need to be catered for?
- How much time and expertise is involved in the construction and maintenance of specific equipment and facilities?
- Do the athletes have any special needs (e.g. ramps for equipment, food, accommodation)?
- Has transportation been organised for athletes/participants?
- Have amenities been considered for athletes (e.g. portable toilets)?
- Has the appropriate hospitality and protocol been organised for coaches and guests associated with the team?
- Has the type of venue and facilities been considered with respect to the training and pre-event warm-up needs of athletes?

Financial and marketing management
- Has a specific budget been created, taking into account all the expenses to be incurred?
- Does the purpose of the event include making a profit, or is breaking even sufficient?
- How will the total cost of the event impact on the price of admission?
- Has cash flow been considered (in the form of a cash-flow projection statement), as well as income and expenditure?
- Has sufficient market research been conducted to determine the viability of the event and the interest it may generate in each demographic area?
- Has the marketplace been segmented?
- How will the event service each different market segment?
- Has the event been positioned specifically for each market segment?
- Is there an overriding marketing strategy or 'hook' driving the event (e.g. international rivalry)?
- Has a marketing mix been established for the event?
  - price—admissions
  - place—venue

- promotions—public relations, advertising
- product—event itself

- How may the media best be used to promote the event?
- Has an event sponsor or sponsors been secured?
- Has the possibility of government support been considered?
- Are advertising and public relations efforts congruent with the overall marketing strategy for the event?
- Has the merchandising potential of the event been addressed (e.g. T-shirts, memorabilia)?
- Have all avenues for sales been considered?
  - direct sales
  - merchandise
  - ticketing

Facility management
Have the following criteria been considered?
- access to and quality of food and beverages
- amenities (toilets, food and drink)
- appropriate size
- change rooms: lockers, showers, warm-up area
- cleanliness
- comfort
- convenience/accessibility (compliance to standard regulations for safety, and access for the elderly and disabled)
- emergency exits
- equipment
- fire hazards
- hat and coat checkpoints
- information booths
- lighting
- phones: number, quality and access
- power
- proximity to hospital
- proximity to social and auxiliary facilities (e.g. restaurants, hotels)
- quality of playing area or surface
- safe and adequate parking
- seating
- shade
- sound
- spectator areas
- stages
- temperature
- ticketing
- ventilation
- water fountains

Human resource management
- Are there sufficient human resources to run the event?
- Are there sufficient volunteers to help?
- Has it been considered that 15–20 per cent of volunteers won't turn up to the event?

- How many employees are needed and which skills do they require?
- Have precautions been taken to ensure people with personality conflicts are not working together?
- Are there communications systems through which organisers can contact each other?
- Have supervisors and troubleshooters been appointed?
- Do organisers have authority to act without approval, or is a more centralised approach being used?
- What are the needs of staff and volunteers in terms of amenities, dress, food and drink, rest and remuneration?
- Are the organisation's policies well known, understood and practised by vounteers (e.g. customer focus)?
- Is the necessary equipment available to organisers (e.g. radios, mobile phones, schedules, contingency plans)?
- Have officials with the appropriate credentials been employed?
  - building supervisor
  - caterers
  - communications officer (scoreboard, public address, public phones)
  - doctors
  - drivers
  - entertainers/celebrities
  - entertainment co-ordinator
  - marketing manager
  - media liaison officer
  - local council officials
  - parking director
  - police liaison officer
  - referees
  - safety officers (fire, natural emergencies)
  - security
  - sponsorship liaison officer
  - sports trainers
  - supervisors
  - technicians (computer, power, lighting, heating, cooling)
  - ticketing and admissions personnel
  - trainers
  - ushers
  - visitor information officers
  - volunteer co-ordinator

Legal management
- Have all the appropriate permits been acquired?
  - selling food and beverages
  - operating gaming machines
  - council regulations and permits for noise, lighting and power
- Do you have insurance?
  - participant/athletes
  - staff/volunteers
  - facility/venue
  - negligence

■ Are there legally enforceable contracts with the venue and other suppliers, including clear and precise quality specifications?

Service quality

■ Has the provision of the following auxiliary services been considered?
 – catering
 – child-minding
 – information
 – lost property
 – ushers
■ Is it clear exactly how the auxiliary services will be delivered?
■ Are there clearly defined quality specifications that are measurable?

Source: Graham, S., Goldblatt, J.J. & Delby, L. (1995) *The Ultimate Guide to Special Event Management and Marketing*, Irwin Professional Publishing, Chicago, Ill.

EVENT SCHEDULING

Scheduling (examined in detail in Chapter 6) is pivotal to the success of an event. Scheduling is the planning of non-repetitive projects, and is used to ensure the most efficient utilisation of resources. Scheduling is also used to evaluate the progress of a project or event's completion, and can focus attention on problems or hurdles. The following section explains how to apply two scheduling tools: Gantt charts and PERT diagrams.[4]

Gantt charts

A Gantt chart is simply a bar chart featuring time on the horizontal axis and the steps in preparing an event on the vertical axis. The activities that must be completed are represented by lines or bars across the chart, and these lines or bars clearly illustrate the sequence of procedures as well as their expected duration. The great strength of Gantt charts is their ability to highlight the required timing of concurrently undertaken, but independent steps. Figure 13.2 shows an example Gantt chart.

Pert diagrams

The second tool is known as the Program Evaluation and Review Technique (PERT), and is a more sophisticated method of illustrating components in an event, particularly because it reveals interconnected and interactive steps quite simply. Like the Gantt chart, PERT diagrams are depicted on a time scale, and look a bit like total quality management flowcharts, with circles representing steps, and arrows showing the duration of the activity and how they link to other steps. The power of the PERT diagram is its ability to pinpoint the event's critical path, which identifies not only the essential procedures to follow, but also the pivotal, most lengthy or difficult point in preparation. For example, a critical path in a major event may 'hinge' on the acquisition of sponsorship funds, or on the timely construction of a specific facility. Figure 13.3 shows an example PERT diagram.

Figure 13.2 Example Gantt chart

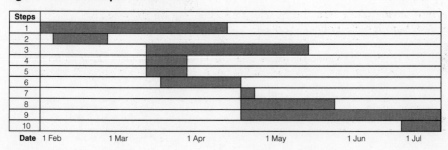

Steps
1. Seek and secure sponsors
2. Construct committees for each management area
3. Book venue and begin construction of mobile stage
4. Apply for council permits
5. Apply for food and beverage sale permits
6. Conduct market research
7. Book caterers
8. Contact volunteers to be involved as officials
9. Segment market/decide positioning
10. Move stage to venue

EVENT MANAGEMENT AND TQM

The physical delivery of a sports event is similar in character to the delivery of any sports organisation's service. That is, facilities and people are combined to produce a leisure service that gives the customer a pleasurable experience. As a result, the techniques used to manage an event do no differ from those explained in Chapter 4, which covers total quality management. For example, organisers of a three-day netball tournament may, after the first day of competition, use a Pareto chart to determine the chief areas of complaint, providing an insight into the best application of resources for corrective action. Alternatively, organisers of a gymnastics club championship may ask the doorkeepers to tally on a simple chart the number of children under three years old who enter, to determine whether an additional supervisor needs to be sent to the makeshift creche.

Figure 13.3 Example PERT diagram

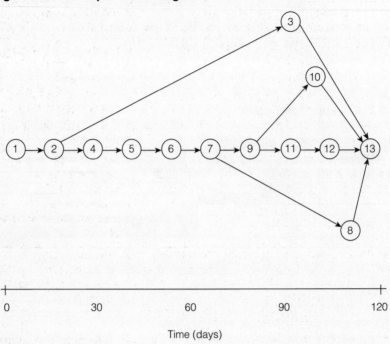

Time (days)

Steps
1. Form event committee
2. Complete planning
3. Seek sponsorship
4. Evaluate alternatives and book venue
5. Apply for permits
6. Arrange insurance
7. Arrange entertainment
8. Begin marketing and promotional campaign
9. Organise volunteers
10. Start taking ticket bookings
11. Finish and distribute contingency charts

Contingency charts

Contingency charts can be invaluable in the management of events. Circulated to all organisers and staff involved in the delivery of the event, contingency charts provide a formal but succinct outline of alternative actions to undertake in circumstances where the original plan is thwarted. A good contingency chart thoroughly identifies all possible permutations and combinations of situations that may go wrong, and can also establish responsibility for corrective action. For example, in the event that the computers fail in a pentathlon competition, a back-up plan must exist to

Table 13.4 Example contingency chart: Day/night cricket match

Area	What can go wrong?	How will we know?	What do we do about it?
Actual game	Inclement weather	It will be wet	■ initiate wicket covering ■ play video on scoreboard ■ officials to calculate new length of match
	Lights fail	It will be dark suddenly	■ initiate emergency generator
Human resources	Employee calls in sick at the last minute or doesn't show up	Section supervisors keep track of all employees	■ section supervisors call someone on standby list ■ supervisor covers until employee shows up
Customer supplies	Running low on beer	In-house retailers will contact central supervisor	■ extra beer on standby to be transported to retail outlets

allow the competition to continue, as well as to provide any cumulative data. See Table 13.4 above for an example of a contingency chart.

EVENT EVALUATION

An event manager's job does not finish at the conclusion of an event. The event must be evaluated at two levels: on a macro scale, using key performance indicators (discussed in the early part of this chapter); and on a micro scale, by completing an event evaluation chart, which can be used in combination with the data acquired through total quality management processes. A sample event evaluation chart follows in Table 13.5.

Operations manual

An event operations manual should be produced once the event has been comprehensively evaluated. The operations manual comprises the original event plan, modified to contain the improvements highlighted during the evaluation, a complete schedule and contingency charts, all culminating in a document that details every activity undertaken in staging the event. The event operations manual should be sufficiently detailed so that an outsider can be instructed how to run the event, with information on all procedures, steps, interrelated activities and critical paths.

Table 13.5 Event evaluation chart

- Was the event organisation completed on schedule?
- If it wasn't, what went wrong and how can it be fixed?
- What were the critical paths in completing the event organisation?
- How will these critical paths be dealt with differently next time?
- How close to budget was the event?
- If it was substantially over or under budget, what were the causes?
- How can these causes/problems be remedied in future events?
- Was the event of sufficient and appropriate quality?
- In what areas did it exceed quality expectations and why?
- In what areas did it under-perform compared to quality expectations and why?
- How did our customers judge our event, based on qualitative feedback (applause, atmosphere, riots)?
- How did our customers judge our event based on quantitative feedback (complaints)?
- What can we learn from our customer's feedback to improve the quality of the event in the future?
- What can we learn about staffing arrangements that can improve the event in the future?
- What can we learn about our marketing approach that can improve the event in the future?
- What can we learn about the auxiliary services we provided that can improve the event in the future?
- What can we learn as a result of dealing with service organisations and outside vendors?
- What can we learn about the type and quality of facility the event requires?
- What can we learn from the legal support in place for the event, to improve safety in future
- What can we learn from the support provided to the participants and athletes that can improve the event in the future?
- What can we learn about the contingency plans that were in place in order to improve the event in the future?
- Is it worth running the event again?

SUMMARY

This chapter discussed the practice of successful sports event management. We pointed out that while sports events have their own special features, they should be underpinned by sound project management principles. We showed that the most important process for ensuring a successful event is the design of a detailed plan that covers both the lead up to the event, and the management of the event itself. In other words, a properly organised event demands a well-constructed schedule and a transparent budget that lists the anticipated revenues, expenses and cash flow movements. We paid particular attention to Gantt charts and PERT diagrams, which are excellent tools for co-ordinating a variety of linked tasks and procedures that must be completed within strict time limits. Once a schedule is in place, the specific organisational processes can be implemented. The final task is to undertake a broad-based event evaluation to determine how successful the event was and whether it is worth running the event in the future.

FURTHER READING

American Sport Education Program (1996) *Event Management for Sport Directors*, Human Kinetics, Champaign, Ill.

Catherwood, D.W. & Van Kirk, R.L. (1992) *The Complete Guide to Special Event Management*, John Wiley and Sons, New York.

Graham, S., Goldblatt, J. & Delby, L. (1995) *The Ultimate Guide to Special Event Management and Marketing*, Irwin Professional Publishing, Chicago, Ill.

Haynes, M.E. (1989) *Project Management: From Ideas to Implementation*, Crisp Publications, Menlo Park, Ca.

■ Conclusion

We trust you have found this manual a valuable tool for improving your sports management practices. As you may have noticed, there are a number of core management principles that underpin quality sports management. When implemented, they will engender a culture of strategic thinking, continual improvement and customer focus. We have designed a simple and uncluttered approach by creating a management template that concentrates on a model of professional best practice management or PBPM. As part of PBPM we spent some time discussing how sport is a special cultural practice which requires a blend of hard-nosed business acumen and an understanding of the strong emotional ties that people make with their favourite sporting pastimes.

As we explained in the early chapters, the core management principles are strategic planning, total quality management, and culture and change management. Strategic planning in particular is so fundamental to successful sports management that we have given it primary attention. As we showed in Chapter 3, designing a strategic direction and setting strategic plans is a time-consuming activity, but if done properly will deliver programs and events that build membership, improve the standard of athletic performance, and generally enhance the image and reputation of your sport. Total quality management, which we addressed in Chapter 4, highlighted the need to continually improve the service delivery process, and not to rest on the laurels of previous successes. Also, as we examined in Chapter 5, an understanding of a sporting organisation's culture is essential, since it influences the behaviour and work output of staff, members and players alike. But, as we demonstrated, many cultures can be dysfunctional and impede future successes. It is therefore important to create cultures that place high value on quality service delivery and continual improvements in the ways things get done.

The core management principles therefore underpin every decision made and service delivered. In chapters 6–13 we discussed the eight functions that all sporting organisations must perform in order to provide a minimum level of service to fans, members, clients and players: player, financial, marketing, facility, human resource, legal, structure and event management. These functions should be integrated with the core management principles in order to achieve best results. In other words, if sports administrators are serious about achieving good outcomes for their customers, they must ensure that each function is managed according to the core management principles. Each function should be placed within a strategic framework, continually evaluated and improved, and driven by a culture that focuses on innovation and customer service.

In this book we have also explained the special features of sport that make it especially exciting if sometimes confusing and contradictory domain to manage. We highlighted the role that passion and tradition play in the administration of sport, but also warned that attempts to separate sporting practice from its commercial context is fraught with danger. For all its special features, sport still has a commercial base which must be addressed and developed. It is no surprise to find that popular sports like Australian football, basketball, tennis and rugby have a history of applying best practice marketing, finance and legal policy to ensure their future viability. Luck can only explain a very small part of any sport's success.

Professional best practice management in sport therefore requires a holistic approach, where the interdependencies between processes are recognised and where, for example, a change in marketing programs may require a strategic rethink, a budget review, a staffing analysis and a change in organisational structure. We suggested that readers should take the 'big picture' approach, and recognise that the role of the good sport administrator involves not just the ability to seize opportunities, but to also convert them into realisable programs that fit the resource base and parameters of their sporting body. At the same time, a large amount of writing on management is faddish and convoluted. This can often obscure the basics that constitute quality management practice. We distilled a variety of models, theories and prescriptions into a set of guidelines that will provide a sound strategic direction for any sporting enterprise and enable it to seize the windows of opportunity that the leisure industry presents.

We also expressed our concern about the view that all that is needed to manage a sporting organisation successfully is common sense. We reject this view with the same force that we reject the claim that a work process should not be changed if it is functioning adequately at the moment. Our observations and research tell us that the best performing sporting enterprises are those that are continually seeking out ways of doing things better, whether it is running a major sport event, or managing the office arrangements of a state sports governing body. Common sense is not enough to ensure a prosperous future. Common sense may enable a club official to conduct a meeting in a moderately efficient manner. However, it does not replace an effective strategic plan, a systematic human resource management program or safety management procedures. The recommendations and prescriptions in this book move beyond common sense. We believe in the power of applied intelligence and grounded model building, where theories, experience and best practice processes are transformed into workable solutions to changing circumstances. Sport can no longer be managed as if it was something set apart from the commercial world, where all that matters is preserving a few old traditions and sporting artifacts, organising a few tough disciplinary committees and enforcing anachronistic dress codes.

Finally, we want to acknowledge this book's limitations. It has not paid much attention to the behavioural aspects of sporting organisations like morale and motivation, interpersonal communication, networking, lobbying, group dynamics, leadership and conflict management. It is not that these issues are unimportant, but rather that we have focused on the foundation management practices that set the performance agenda. All the interpersonal and people skills in the world will fail if they are not underpinned by best practice tools and techniques.

Endnotes

Introduction

1 McGilvray, A. (1985) *The Game is Not the Same*, ABC Books, Sydney, p. 10.
2 *Sport Business*, which calls itself the 'magazine for the international business of sport', is published out of London. It is a full colour magazine, and contains features and brief reports on every commercial aspect of sport around the world. It is published monthly. The Internet address is www.sportbusiness.com

Chapter 1 Professionalism and the management of sport

1 See Drucker, P. (1993) *Post Capitalist Society*, HarperCollins, New York, pp.1–47. If you want to look further into the features of postcapitalist and postmodern society, we recommend the following texts: Bell, D. (1978) *The Cultural Contradictions of Capitalism*, Basic Books, New York; Crook, S., Pakulski, J. & Waters, M. (1992) *Postmodernisation: Change in Advanced Society*, Sage, London; Drucker, P. (1989) *The New Realities*, Harper & Row, New York, pp. 3–4; Jameson, F. (1991) *Postmodernism: The Cultural Logic of Late Capitalism*, Verso, London; Harvey, D. (1989) *The Condition of Postmodernity*, Blackwell, Oxford; Irat, A.F., Dholakia, N. & Vinkatesh, A. (1995) 'Marketing in a postmodern world', *European Journal of Marketing*, 2(5), 40–56.
2 A succinct review of the changing face of business is provided in Kiernan, M. (1996) *The Eleven Commandments of 21st Century Management*, Prentice Hall, Englewood Cliffs, pp. 1–33.
3 An excellent review of Australian management and the need to reform it is contained in: Industry Task Force on Leadership and Management Skills (1995) *Enterprising Nation*, Commonwealth of Australia, Canberra. It is also known as the Karpin Report, after the name of its chairperson.
4 See, for example, Peters, J. (1993) *Liberation Management*, Pan Books, New York.
5 Mautz, R.K. (1988) 'Public accounting: which kind of professionalism?', *Accounting Horizons*, 2(3), 75–77.
6 Arkin, Anat (1992) 'Professional updating of the employer's role', *Personnel Management,* April, 36–38; Auld, C. (1993) 'The professionalisation of Australian sports administrators: some implications', in *Proceedings, ANZALS Conference* (eds Boag, A., Lammond, C. & Sun, E.), Brisbane; Box, R.C. (1991) 'Resistance to professional managers in American local government', *American Review of Public Administration*, 23(4), 403–18; Davis, J. (1994) 'Reputation of

quality and professionalism helps keep U.S. equities in the forefront', *National Real Estate Investor*, February, 17–19; Parkhouse, B. (1981) *Sport and Fitness Management: Career Strategies and Professional Content*, Mosby Year Book, MO; Reed, M. & Anthony, P. (1992) 'Professionalizing management and managing professionalization: British management in the 1980s, *Journal of Management*, 29(5), 591–611; Thibault, L., Slack, T. & Hinings, B. (1990) 'Professionalism, structures, and systems: the impact of professional staff on voluntary organisations', *International Review for the Sociology of Sport*, 26(2), 22; Zanger, Beverly & Parks, Janet (1990) 'Professional style', in Zanger and Parks (eds) *Sport and Fitness Management: Career Strategies and Professional Content*, Human Kinetics Books, Champaign, Ill; Zeigler, Earle (1983) *Management Competency Development in Sport and Physical Education*, Lea & Febiger, Philadelphia.

7 James, David (1995) 'Perth's Eagles fly high on a TQM philosophy', *Business Review Weekly*, 13 March, 66; Mills, R. (1994) 'The professionalisation of Australian sport: practice and discussion', *Leisure Options*, 4(2), 43–48; Stewart, R. (1990) 'Sport as big business'. in Lawrence, G. and Rowe, D. (eds) *Powerplay: The Commercialisation of Australian Sport*, Hale & Iremonger, Sydney, 56–68; Westerbeek, H., Shilbury, D., & Deane, J. (1995) 'The Australian sport system: its history and an organisational overview', *European Journal of Sport Management*, 2(1), 42–58.

8 Aris, S. (1990) *Sportsbiz: Inside the Sports Business*, Hutchinson, London; Wilson, N. (1988) *The Sports Business*, Pitkus Press, London.

9 For an extensive analysis of the conduct approach to professionalism see Maister, D. (1997) *True Professionalism: The Courage to Care About Your People, Your Clients, and Your Career*, The Free Press, New York.

10 Massey, M. (1996) 'The business of sport: playing for keeps', *Business Review Weekly*, 1 April, 75–78.

11 Aris, S. (1990) *Sportsbiz: Inside the Sports Business*, Hutchinson, London.

12 See Wilson, B. (1990) 'Pumping up the footy: the commercial expansion of professional football in Australia', in Rowe, D. & Lawrence, G. (eds) *Sport and Leisure: Trends in Australian Popular Culture*, Harcourt Brace & Jovanovich, Sydney.

13 See Slack, T. (1995) 'From the locker room to the boardroom: changing the domain of sport management', *Journal of Sport Management*, 10, 97–105.

14 Graham, P.J. (1994) *Sport Business: Operational and Theoretical Aspects*, WCB Brown and Benchmark, Madison; Gorman, J. & Calhoun, K. (1994) *The Name of the Game: The Business of Sports*, John Wiley, New York; Quirk, J. & Fort, R. (1992) *Pay Dirt: The Business of Professional Team Sports*, Princeton University Press, Princeton.

15 Kimball, D.S. & Kimball, D.S. Jr. (1947) *Principles of Industrial Organisation*, McGraw-Hill, New York.

16 Terry, G.R. (1960) *Principles of Management*, Irwin, Illinois.

17 Mason, J.G. & Paul, J. (1988) *Modern Sports Administration*, Prentice Hall, New Jersey.

18 Mason & Paul, p. 19.

19 Mason & Paul, p. 3.

20 Hogg, D. (1989) 'Professional development needs of sports administrators in Australia', Biennial Conference in Management and Sport, Canberra, in Buchanan, J., & Schneider, S., (eds), *Management and Sport Conference Proceedings*, Vol. 1, University of Canberra, Centre for Sports Studies.

21 Arthur Andersen Consulting, Internet address: http://www.arthurandersen.com/bus_info/services/gbp/define.htm

22 Reder, A. (1996) *75 Best Business Practices for Socially Responsible Companies*, Putnam Books, Canada.

23 Watt, L. (1992) 'Sports management: the pros take over', *Management*, 38(8), 56–62.

24 Love, M. (1993) 'Turning pro by degrees', *Management*, 39(8), 56.

25 Maloy, B.P. (1994) 'Beyond the balance sheet', *Athletic Business*, 16(1), 29–32.

26 Moore, D. (1993) 'The professionalisation of sports management—15 years on', *Sportsnetwork*, Winter, 8–9.

27 Moore, p. 18.

Chapter 2 The special features of sport

1 Auld, C. (1993) 'The professionalisation of Australian sports administrators: some implications', *Proceedings, ANZALS Conference*, Brisbane; Mills, R. (1994) 'The professionalisation of Australian sport: practice and discussion', *Leisure Options*, 4(2), 14–22; Moore, D. (1993) 'The professionalisation of sports management—15 years on', *Sportsnetwork*, Winter, 8–9; Watt, L. (1992) 'Sports management: the pros take over', *Management*, 38(8), 56–62; Whitson, D. (1988) 'The professionalisation of Canadian amateur sport: questions of power and purpose', *Arena Review*, 12(2), 18.

2 Frisby, W. (1988) 'A conceptual framework for measuring the organisational structure and context of voluntary leisure service organisations', *Society and Leisure*, 8(2), 61–74; Kikulis, L., Slack, T., Hinings, B. & Zimmerman, A. (1989) 'A structural taxonomy of amateur sport organisations', *Journal of Sport Management*, 6, 129–50.

3 Stewart, B. (1990) 'Sport as big business', in *Powerplay: The Commercialisation of Australian Sport*, Hale & Iremonger, Sydney.

4 Auld, C. (1993); Hogg, D. (1989) 'Professional development needs of sports administrators in Australia', Biennial Conference in Management and Sport, Canberra; Thibault, L., Slack, T. & Hinings, B. (1990) 'Professionalism, structures, and systems: the impact of professional staff on voluntary organisations', *International Review for the Sociology of Sport*, 26(2), 22.

5 Peters, T. (1993) *Liberation Management*, Pan Books, New York.

6 Wilson, B. (1990) 'Pumping up the footy: the commercial expansion of professional football in Australia', in Rowe, D. and Lawrence, G. (eds) *Sport and Leisure: Trends in Australian Popular Culture*, Harcourt Brace & Jovanovich, Sydney.

7 Brohm, J. (1978) *Sport: A Prison of Measured Time*, Inks Links, London; Rigauer, B. (1981) *Sport and Work*, Columbia University Press, New York; Stewart, R. (1989) 'The nature of sport under capitalism and its relation to the capitalist labour process', *Sporting Traditions*, 6(1).

8 James, D. (1995) 'Perth's Eagles fly high on a TQM philosophy', *Business Review Weekly*, 13 March, 66.

9 Gorman, J. & Calhoun, K. (1994) *The Name of the Game: The Business of Sport*, John Wiley, New York.

10 Morely & Wilson (1984) *The Demand for Australian Rules Football*, Faculty of Business Staff Paper, No.8401, Footscray Institute of Technology, Victoria.

11 Dabscheck, B. (1975) 'Sporting equality: labour market v. product market control', *Journal of Industrial Relations*, July, 174–90; Sloan, P.J. (1971) 'The

economics of professional football: the football club as utility maximiser', *Scottish Journal of Political Economy*, June, 121–46.

12 Vamplew, W. (1988) *Pay Up and Play the Game: Professional Sport in Britain, 1875–1914*, Cambridge University Press, Cambridge, p. 77.

13 Quirk, J. & Fort, R. (1992) *Pay Dirt: The Business of Professional Team Sports*, Princeton University Press, Princeton.

14 Demmert, H. (1973) *The Economics of Professional Team Sports*, Lexington Books, Lexington, Ma.

15 Quirk, J. & Fort, R. (1992).

16 Morely & Wilson (1984).

17 Quirk, J. & Fort, R. (1992).

18 Dabscheck, B. (1975).

19 Cairns, J., Jennett, N. & Sloane, P.J. (1986) 'The economics of professional team sports: a survey of theory and evidence', *Journal of Economic Studies*, 13(1), 56–64.

20 Vamplew, W. (1988).

21 Arnold, A. & Stewart, G. (eds) (1986) *Financing and Management in the Football Industry*, Barmarick Press, London.

22 Morely & Wilson (1984).

23 Arnold, A. & Stewart, G. (eds) (1986).

24 Wilson, J. (1994) *Playing By the Rules*, Wayne State University, Detroit.

25 Gorman, J. & Calhoun, K. (1994).

26 Gorman, J. & Calhoun, K. (1994).

27 Staudohar, P. & Mangan, J. (1991) *The Business of Professional Sports*, University of Illinois Press, Illinois, p. 15.

28 Stewart, R. (1995) *The Commercial Development of Australian First Class Cricket*, unpublished PhD thesis, Latrobe University.

29 Staudohar, P. & Mangan, J. (1991).

30 Gorman, J. & Calhoun, K. (1994), p. 47.

Chapter 3 Strategic plannning

1 The grandfather of corporate strategy and planning is Henry Mintzberg. An excellent introduction to his writings is contained in Mintzberg, H. (1994) *The Rise and Fall of Strategic Planning*, Prentice Hall, New York. Another good introduction to strategy, particularly for service organisations, is Bryson, J. (1995) *Strategic Planning for Public and Nonprofit Organisations*, revised edition, Jossey Bass, San Francisco.

2 There are a number of textbooks that cover the strategy process in full detail, but they are 'business' based and not geared to the world of sport. They are nevertheless worth reading. See, for example, Higgins, J. & Vincze, J. (1995) *Strategic Management: Texts and Cases*, 5th edn, The Dryden Press, Fort Worth; Hill, C. & Jones, G. (1995) *Strategic Management: An Integrated Approach*, 3rd edn, Houghton Mifflen, Boston; Thompson, A. & Strickland, A. (1996) *Strategic Management: Concepts and Cases*, 9th edn, Irwin, Chicago; Wheelen T. & Hunger, J. (1995) *Strategic Management and Business Policy*, Addison-Wesley, Reading.

3 An outstanding collection of corporate vision statements is provided in Jones, P. & Kahaner, L. (1995) *Say It and Live It: The 50 Corporate Mission Statements That Hit the Mark*, Currency Doubleday, New York.

4 Drucker, P. (1990) *Managing the Non-profit Organisation*, Butterworth-Heinemann, Oxford.

5 Jones, P. & Kahaner, L. (1995).

6 Handy, C. (1988) *Understanding Voluntary Organisations*, Penguin Group, London.

7 Argenti, J. (1992) *Practical Corporate Planning*, Routledge, New York.

8 See references in Notes 9–19.

9 Clemmer, J. (1996) 'What you see is what you get', *CMA Magazine*, 70, 8.

10 Haskell, L. (1995) 'Acute vision helps distinguish opportunities', *Indianapolis Business Journal*, 16, 12B.

11 Collins, J.C. & Porras, J.I. (1991) 'Organisation visioning organisations', *California Management Review*, Fall, 30–50; Senge, P.M. (1990) *The Fifth Discipline: The Art and Practice of the Learning Organisation*, Doubleday Currency, New York.

12 Kuhn, T. (1995) 'Seeing where you want to go', *Electric Perspectives*, 20, 22; Weller, D. (1994) 'Principles and TQM: developing vision', *Clearing House*, 67, 298.

13 Kuhn, T. (1995); Massengale, J. (1995) 'Visionary leadership and the physical educator', *Physical Educator*, 52, 219; Nanus, B. (1996) 'Leading the vision team', *Futurist*, 30, 20.

14 Nanus, B. (1996); Nelson, B. (1995) 'Ways to foster team spirit', *HR Magazine*, 40, 47.

15 Fackelmann, K.A. (1991) 'The vision thing', *The Economist*, 321, 81; Fishman, A. (1995) 'Business strategic plan should be ongoing process', *Inside Tucson Business*, 5, 16; Haskell, L. (1995); Jones, B. (1996) 'Strategic planning in government', *Program Manager*, 25, 12; Mintzberg, H. (1994) *The Rise and Fall of Strategic Planning*, Prentice Hall, UK.

16 Argenti, J. (1992) *Practical Corporate Planning*, Routledge, New York; Weller, D. (1994).

17 Blanchard, K. (1993) 'The power of a clear vision', 27, 25; Collins, J.C. & Porras, J.I. (1996) 'Building your company's vision', *Harvard Business Review*, September–October, 65–77.

18 Blanchard, K. (1993); Drucker, P. (1974) *Management: Tasks, Practices, Responsibilities*, Harper & Row, New York; Kuhn, T. (1995); Neave, H.R. (1990) *The Deming Dimension*, SPC Press, Knoxville, Tenn.

19 Brown, A. (1995) *Organisational Culture*, Pitman Publishing, London, pp. 165–78.

20 Collins, J.C. & Porras, J.I. (1996).

21 Argenti, J. (1992) *Practical Corporate Planning*, Routledge, New York.

22 Evans, A. (1994) *Benchmarking*, The Business Library, New York.

23 Ernst & Young (1992) *Best Practices Report: An Analysis of Management Practices that Impact on Performance*, American Quality Foundation.

24 Morgan, G. (1993) *Imaginization*, Sage, London.

25 Mintzberg, H. (1994) *The Rise and Fall of Strategic Planning*, Prentice Hall, UK.

26 Hamel, G. (1996) 'Strategy as revolution', *Harvard Business Review*, 74(4), 69–82.

27 Mintzberg, H. (1994).

28 Mintzberg, H. (1989) *Mintzberg on Management*, Macmillan, London.

29 McInnes, N. (1996) *Bidding to win—A System*, Corporate Management Systems Pty Ltd, Hawthorn, Victoria.

30 Loehle, C. (1996) *Thinking Strategically*, Cambridge University Press, Cambridge.

Chapter 4 Total quality management

1 Bocka, B. & Bocka, M. (1992) *Quality Management: Implementing the Best Ideas of the Masters*, Business One Irwin, Homewood, p. 6 (Bocka & Bocka provide a succinct introduction to TQM in Chapter 1).

2 Jablonski, J.R. (1992) *Implementing TQM*, Pfeiffer & Company, San Diego, Ca.

3 Imai, M. (1986) *Kaizen, the Key to Japan's Competitive Success*, Random House Business Division, New York.
4 Walton, M. (1989) *The Deming Management Method*, Mercury Books, London.
5 See, for example, Hill, T.J. (1992) *The Quality Manual*, John Wiley, New York; Oakland, J.S. (1994) *Total Quality Management: The Route to Improving Performance*, Butterworth, Oxford.
6 Reichheld, F.F. & Sasser, W.E. (1995) 'Zero defections: quality comes to services', in Van Matre, J.G. (ed.) *Foundations of TQM: A Readings Book*, The Dryden Press, Harcourt Brace College Publishers, Fort Worth, pp. 27–38.
7 McConnell, J. (1986) *The Seven Tools of TQC*, Delaware Books, NSW.
8 For more information regarding the sequential incident technique, see Stauss, B. & Weinlach, B. (1997) 'Process oriented measurement of service quality', *European Journal of Marketing*, 31(1), 33–55.
9 Ishikawa, K. (1982) *Guide to Quality Control*, Asian Productivity Organisation, Tokyo.
10 See Blakemore, J. (1989) *The Quality Solution*, The Business Library, NSW.
11 Cohen, P. & van Ewyk, O. (1994) 'How to think up a storm', HCI Consulting, Sydney
12 Blakemore, J. (1989).
13 Dewar, D.L. (1980) *Team Leader Manual*, Horst Blanch Pty Ltd, Quality Circle Institute of Australia, Victoria; Dewar, D.L. (1980) *The Quality Circle Handbook*, Horst Blanch Pty Ltd, Quality Circle Institute of Australia, Victoria.
14 Scholtes, P.R. (1989) *The Team Handbook*, Joiner, USA.
15 Martin, W.B. (1993) *Quality Customer Service*, Crisp Publications, Ca.
16 Deming, W.E. (1982) *Out of the Crises*, MIT, Cambridge, Mass.
17 Jablonski, J.R. (1992) *Implementing TQM*, Pfeiffer & Company, San Diego, Ca.
18 Fox, R. (1991) *Making Quality Happen*, McGraw-Hill Book Company, Sydney.
19 Adapted from Longman Group UK Ltd (1992) *Quality First: Quality Management in the Leisure Industry*, Longman, UK.
20 Tribus, M. (1988) *The Tribus Lectures on Total Quality Management*, Melbourne.
21 United States General Accounting Office (1992) *Management Practices: US Companies Improve Performance Through Quality Efforts*, Report to US House of Representatives.
22 Example adapted from Scholtes, P.R. (1989) *The Team Handbook*, Joiner, USA.
23 Hammer, M. & Champy, J. (1993) *Reengineering the Corporation*, Nicholas Brealey Publishing, London.

Chapter 5 Organisational culture and change management

1 Barley, S.R. (1985) 'Semiotics and the study of occupational and organisational culture', *Administrative Science Quarterly*, 28(3), 393–413; Schawtz, H. & Davis, S.M. (1981) 'Matching corporate culture and business strategy', *Organisational Dynamics*, 33, 30–48.
2 Ott, J.S. (1989) *The Organisational Culture Perspective*, Brookes-Cole, Pacific Grove, Ca.
3 For more information concerning culture's link with strategy, see Mintzberg, H. & Quinn, J.B. (1991) *The Strategy Process: Concepts, Contexts and Cases* (Chapter 7), Prentice Hall, Englewood Cliffs, NJ.
4 Peters, T. & Waterman, R. (1982) *In Search of Excellence*, Harper & Row, New York, pp. 74–79, 318–21.
5 Cooke, R.A. & Szumal, J.L. (1993) 'Measuring normative beliefs and shared

behavioural expectations in organisations: the reliability and validity of the organisational culture inventory', *Psychological Reports*, 72, 1290–1330; Wilkins & Ouchi (1983) 'Efficient cultures: exploring the relationship between culture and organisational performance', *Administrative Science Quarterly*, 28(3), 468–81.

6 Schein, E. (1985) *Organisational Culture and Leadership*, Jossey-Bass, San Francisco, pp. 45–56.

7 Chapman, P. (1988) 'Changing the corporate culture of Rank Xerox', *Long Range Planning*, 21, 23–28.

8 Scholz, C. (1987) 'Corporate culture and strategy—the problem of strategic fit', *Long Range Planning*, 20, 78–87.

9 Pettigrew, A. (1979) 'On studying organisational cultures', *Administrative Science Quarterly*, 24, 570–581; Gordon, G.G. & DiTomaso, N. (1992) 'Predicting corporate performance from organisational culture', *Journal of Management Studies*, 29(6), 782–95.

10 Schneider, B. & Rentsch, A. (1988) 'On the aetiology of climates', *Personnel Psychology*, 28, 447–79.

11 Adapted from Robbins, S. & Mukerji, D. (1994) *Managing Organisations*, Prentice Hall, Sydney.

12 Smith, A.C.T. & Stewart, R. (1995) 'Sporting club cultures: an exploratory case study', *Australian Leisure*, December, 31–37.

13 For additional cultural models, see: Deal, T. & Kennedy, A. (1982) *Corporate Cultures: The Rites and Rituals of Corporate Life*, Addison Wesley, USA; Hrebiniak, L.G. & Joyce, W.F. (1985) 'Organisational adaptation: strategic choice and environmental determinism', *Administrative Science Quarterly*, 30, 336–49; Johnson, C. (1987) *Strategic Change and the Management Process*, Basil Blackwell, London; Kabanoff, B. (1992) 'Identifying organisational distributive culture using content analysis', University of New South Wales Working Paper Series; Mondy, W.R. (1990) *Management and Organisational Behaviour*, Allyn & Bacon, USA.

14 Adapted from Beyer, J. and Trice, H. (1984) 'Studying organisational cultures through rites and ceremonies', *Academy of Management Review*, October.

15 Huber, G.P. & Glick, W.H. (1993) *Organisational Change and Redesign*, Oxford University Press, New York.

16 Menkus, B. (1988) 'Five facts about change', *Journal of Systems Management*, April, 5.

17 Greenberg, J. & Baron, R.A. (1995) *Behaviour in Organisations*, Prentice Hall, Englewood Cliffs, NJ.

18 For a detailed review of planned change and organisational renewal, see Harvey, D. & Brown, D.R. (1996) *An Experiential Approach to Organisational Development*, Prentice Hall, NJ.

19 Conner, D. (1995) *Managing at the Speed of Change*, Villard Books, New York.

20 For more information, see Kotter, J.P. (1995) 'Leading change: why transformation efforts fail', *Harvard Business Review*, March–April, 60.

21 Duck, J.D. (1993) 'Managing change: the art of balancing', *Harvard Business Review*, December, 109.

Chapter 6 Player management

1 It is interesting that while performance management is such an important issue in sport, not much has been written about it from a *management* perspective. A useful guide is Day, R. (1994) *Management Strategies in Athletic Training*, Human Kinetics, Champaign, Ill.

Chapter 7 Financial management

1 Straughn, G. & Chickadel, C. (1994) *Building a Profitable Business*, Bob Adams Inc., Holbrook, Ma.
2 For more information on financial statements, see Hey-Cunningham, D. (1998) *Financial Statements Demystified*, 2nd edn, Allen & Unwin, Sydney.
3 Straughn, G. & Chickadel, C. (1994).
4 For more information on budgeting, see (for example) Bond, C.J. (1991) *Hands-on Financial Controls for Your Small Business*, Liberty Hall Press, Blue Ridge Summit, PA.

Chapter 8 Marketing management

1 The dramatic impact that marketing has had on sport is captured in Schaaf, P. (1995) *Sports Marketing: It's Not Just a Game Anymore*, Prometheus Books, Amherst.
2 This point is made clear in Pitts, B. & Stotlar, D. (1996) *Fundamentals of Sport Marketing*, Fitness Information Technology, Morgantown.
3 Martin, J. (1995) *The Great Transition: Using the Seven Disciplines of Enterprise Engineering to Align People, Technology and Strategy*, Amacon, New York, pp. 154–55.
4 Blanchard, K. & Bowes, S. (1993) *Raving Fans*, Williams Morrows, New York.
5 Martin, J. (1995), pp. 154–55.
6 Martin, J. (1995), p. 153.
7 Fowler, Floyd J. Jr. (1984) *Survey Research Methods*, Sage Publications, Beverley Hills, Ca, pp. 99–101.
8 Krueger, R.A. (1994) *Focus Groups*, Sage Publications, Thousand Oaks, Ca.
9 Minichiello, V., Aroni, R., Timewell, E., & Alexander, L. (1995) *In-depth Interviewing: Principles, Techniques, Analysis*, Longman Australia, Melbourne.
10 Strauss, A. & Corbin, J. (1990) *Basics of Qualitative Research: Grounded Theory, Procedures, and Techniques*, Sage, Newbury Park.
11 Sarantakos, S. (1993) *Social Research*, Macmillan Education Australia, Melbourne.
12 Strauss, A. (1987) *Qualitative Analysis for Social Scientists*, Cambridge University Press, Cambridge.
13 Miles, M. & Huberman, M. (1994) *Qualitative Data Analysis*, 2nd edn, Sage, London.
14 A neat application of this model to the leisure industry is given in Leadley, P. (1992) *Leisure Marketing*, Longman, Harlow, pp. 61–66.
15 Shani, D. (1997) 'A framework for implementing relationship marketing in the sport industry', *Sport Marketing Quarterly*, 6(2), 9–15.
16 Mullins, J., Hardy, S. & Sutton, W. (1993) *Sport Marketing*, Human Kinetics, Champaign, Ill.
17 Victorian Football League (1985) *VFL Football: Establishing the Basis for Future Success*, VFL, Melbourne.
18 Covick, O. (1986) 'Sporting equality in professional team sports leagues and market controls: what is the relationship?', *Sporting Traditions*, 2(2).
19 Covick, O. (1986).
20 Victorian Football League (1985).
21 Covick, O. (1986).
22 See Mullins et. al. (1993) *Sport Marketing*, p. 121, where they talk about a 'bundle of benefits'.

23 See also, for example, Brookes, C.M. (1994) *Sports Marketing: Competitive Business Strategies for Sport*, Prentice Hall, Englewood Cliffs, pp. 86–89.
24 For more on these, see Rossiter, J.R. & Percy, L. (1987) *Advertising and Promotion Management*, McGraw-Hill, New York.
25 Birkett, J. (1990) *Sports Sponsorship*, Jones Printing Service, Victoria.
26 Geldard, E. & Sinclair, L. (1996) *The Sponsorship Manual*, Sponsorship Unit, Olinda, Victoria.

Chapter 9 Facility management

1 For more detail on feasibility studies for facilities, see Daly, J. (1995) *Recreation and Sport Planning and Design: A Guidelines Manual*, Department of Recreation, Sport and Racing, South Australia.
2 Mathews J. (1993) *Health and Safety at Work: A Trade Union Safety Representative's Handbook*, 2nd edn, Pluto Press, Sydney.
3 For information on State and Federal Government policy and codes concerning sport and recreation facilities, refer to: Commonwealth of Australia (1989) *Australian Sports Commission Act 1989*, Government Printer, Canberra.
Department of Environment and Planning (1990) *Guidelines for the Administration of Section 94, Environment Planning and Assessment Act*, New South Wales.
Department of Local Government (1990) *Local Government Planning and Environment Act*, Queensland.
Department of Sport and Recreation (1990) *Community Recreation—Municipal Recreation Planning Guide*, Victoria.
Government of Queensland (1988) *Recreation Areas Management Act 1988*, Government Printer, Brisbane.
Government of Queensland (1990) *Local Government Act 1990*, Government Printer, Brisbane.
Government of New South Wales (1979) *Environment Planning and Assessment Act 1979*, Government Printer, Sydney.
Government of South Australia (1993) *Development Act 1993*, Government Printer, Adelaide.
Government of Tasmania (1962) *Local Government Act 1962*, Government Printer, Hobart.
Government of Tasmania (1977) *Tourism and Recreation Act 1977*, Government Printer, Hobart.
Government of Victoria (1972) *Sport and Recreation Act 1972*, Government Printer, Melbourne.
Government of Victoria (1987) *Planning and Environment Act 1987*, Government Printer, Melbourne.
Government of Western Australia (1928) *Planning and Development Act 1928*, Government Printer, Perth.
Northern Territory Government (1987) *Northern Territory of Australia Planning Act 1987*, Darwin.
4 See Torkildsen, G. (1992) *Leisure and Recreation Management*, 3rd edn, E & FN Spon, London, pp. 319–28.
5 For a comprehensive examination of North American facility management, and some good general principles, see Farmer, P., Mulrooney, A. & Ammon, R., (1996) *Sport Facility Planning and Management*, Fitness Information Technology, Morgantown.

Chapter 10 Human resource management

1 Stone, R. (1995) *Human Resource Management*, John Wiley & Sons, Brisbane, p. 4.
2 Outstanding corporate leaders characteristically 'consolidate the talents of their workers to achieve world competitive results'—see Sarros, J. & Butchatsky, O. (1996) *Leadership: Australia's Top CEOs: Finding Out What Makes Them the Best*, HarperBusiness, Sydney, p. 6.
3 A good example of how this approach operates in Britain is given in Critten, P. (1994) *Human Resource Management in the Leisure Industry*, Longman, Harlow.
4 See, for example, Gardner, M. & Palmer, G. (1992) *Employment Relations: Industrial Relations and Human Resource Management in Australia*, Macmillan, Melbourne, pp. 206–13.
5 For a succinct summary of the evolution of HRM in Australia, see Nankervis, A., Compton, R. & McCarthy, T. (1996) *Strategic Human Resource Management*, 2nd edn, Thomas Nelson Australia, Melbourne.
6 For further details, see Nankervis, Compton & McCarthy, pp. 142–44.
7 See Cherry, N. (1993) 'Performance management: the challenge of the 1990s', in Gardner, M. (ed.) *Human Resource Management and Industrial Relations in the Public Sector*, Centre for Australian Public Sector Management, Brisbane, pp. 97–106.
8 See, for instance, Marquardt, M. (1996) *Building the Learning Organisation*, McGraw-Hill, New York.
9 A useful guide to competency-based training is contained in O'Neill, G. & Kramer, R. (1995) *Australian Human Resource Management*, Pitman Publishing, Melbourne, pp. 87–122.

Chapter 11 Legal management

1 See, for example, Fewell, M. (ed.) (1995) *Sports Law: A Practical Guide*, LBC Information Services, Sydney; Healey, D. (1996) *Sport and the Law*, 2nd edn, University of New South Wales Press, Sydney; Kelly, M. (1987) *Sport and the Law*, The Law Book Company, Sydney; McGregor-Lowndes, M., Fletcher, K. & Sievers, A. (eds) (1996) *Legal Issues for Non-profit Associations*, LBC, Sydney.
2 In 1990, lawyers with a professional interest in sport formed the Australian and New Zealand Sports Law Association. Anyone can now join for a small fee. The *ANZLA Newsletter* is published four times a year.
3 See Healey, D. (1986) *Sport and the Law*, pp. 40–41.
4 For further details on this incorporation process, see McGregor-Lowndes, *Legal Issues*, pp. 1–12.
5 An excellent introduction to sports safety is Frosdick, S. & Walley, L. (1997) *Sport and Safety Management*, Butterworth-Heineman, Oxford. A succinct introduction to risk management in sport is contained in Miller, L. (1997) *Sport Business Management*, Aspen Publishers, Gaithersburg, pp. 257–74.
6 For some good examples, see Healey, D. *Sport and the Law*, pp. 75–79.
7 For further discussion on this matter, see Fewell, M. (ed.) *Sports Law*, pp. 21–23.

Chapter 12 Structure management

1 See Martin, J. (1994) *The Great Transition*, Amacon, New York, pp. 393–406.
2 Most management textbooks have a chapter on the essentials of organisation

structure. A succinct summary can be obtained from Greenberg, J. & Barron, R. (1995) *Behaviour in Organisations*, 5th edn, Prentice Hall, Englewood Cliffs, pp. 575–604. For a good description of the ways in which structure has changed over time, see Bolman, L. & Deal, T. (1997) *Reframing Organisations: Artistry, Choice and Leadership*, 2nd edn, Jossey-Bass, San Francisco.

3 A number of useful North American cases are given in Bridges, F. & Roquemore, L., (1996) *Management for Athletic/Sport Administration: Theory & Practice*, 2nd edn, ESM Books, Decatur, pp. 198–204.

4 See, for example, Slack, T. (1997) *Understanding Sport Organisations: The Application of Organisation Theory*, Human Kinetics, Champaign, Ill, pp. 41–63.

5 A detailed summary of these elements is given in Robbins, S., Bergman, R. & Stagg, I. (1997) *Management*, Prentice Hall Australia, Sydney, pp. 321–43.

6 Peters, T. (1992) *Liberation Management*, Pan Books, London, p. 149.

7 Pinchot, G. & Pinchot, E., (1993) *The End of Bureaucracy and the Rise of the Intelligent Organisation*, Beret Koeller, San Francisco, pp. 193–209.

8 Osborne, D. & Gaebler, T. (1992) *Reinventing Government: How the Entrepreneurial Spirit is Transforming the Public Sector*, Addison-Wesley, Reading, pp. 25–48.

9 For an outstanding analysis of the Nike phenomenon, see Strasser, J.B. & Becklund, L. (1993) *Swoosh: The Unauthorised Story of Nike*, HarperCollins, New York.

10 Morgan, G. (1993) *Imaginization: The Art of Creative Management*, Sage, London, pp. 63–89.

Chapter 13 Event management

1 A good general reference is American Sport Education Program (1996) *Event Management for Sport Directors*, Human Kinetics, Champaign, Ill.

2 Catherwood, D.W. & Van Kirk, R.L. (1992) *The Complete Guide to Special Event Management*, John Wiley & Sons, New York.

3 For a detailed review of event planning, see Graham, S., Goldblatt, J. & Delby, L. (1995) *The Ultimate Guide to Special Event Management and Marketing*, Irwin Professional Publishing, Chicago. For a European perspective on event planning, see Watt, D. (1998) *Sport Management and Administration*, E. & F.N. SPON, London, pp. 173–92.

4 See Robbins, S., Bergman, R. & Stagg, I. (1997) *Management*, Prentice Hall Australia, Sydney, pp. 293–98, for a clear local account of these issues.

Index

Tables in **bold**; figures in *italics*